INTRODUCTION

"There is nothing secret that will not be revealed, and there is nothing hidden that will not come out'.

The Gospel of Mark (ch. 4: 22)

I stand by the waters of a vast ocean. Its vast waves lapping at my feet, shimmering in different shades. Everything is vast, inexplicable and majestic. I could stand there forever, contemplating and trying to penetrate the mysteries of nature. But I am only a speck of dust among the sands of the coast, and I undertake the impossible task of describing the phenomenon of Vanga-as vast and mysterious as the ocean waves. I'm an inept swimmer. And I have to dive into the deepest waters and get incredible wonders, clear them of mysticism and superstition. And then describe to people... can I? I don't know. And Vanga herself does not inspire me at all.

Such a book cannot be written now. How to describe the invisible, how to embrace the universal, how to explain the illogical, how to believe in the immaterial — " she told me back in 1979.

I don't know.

And yet I dare to realize this dream. Nature may have given us imperfect senses, but it has also given us dreams and a great curiosity about everything around us. This is what will lead me on a thorny path, where dangers lurk at every step. I have only a fragile pen in my hands and a decidedly insufficient knowledge of the world. But my love and admiration for the person and phenomenon of Vanga, her love for humanity, her desire to breathe calmness and faith, courage and hope into everyone will help me achieve this goal.

Is it worth putting such a heavy burden on your fragile shoulders? Is worth. Clairvoyants, prophets and soothsayers have existed at all times of human history, but information about them has reached us only in the form of myths and legends. And Vanga is our contemporary. And works wonders before our eyes. With amazing accuracy, it penetrates into the past-far and near, into the present and future, touches the hidden corners of the soul, heals mental and physical pain, reaches unknown worlds, informing about the incredible miracles that are happening there, prophesies to individuals, entire peoples, cities, states, the whole planet, communicates with nature. For her, there is no concept of "inanimate nature", and everything around her is perceived as a single whole, which lives and develops according to laws and rules that we do not understand.

So will posterity forgive us if we ignore the fact that at the end of the XX century there lived among us a woman who for many years showed us his phenomenal abilities, and we again left to future generations only

1

myths and legends about this unusual phenomenon. And just because you can't understand it or explain it yet?

Is the reference to the fact that the human horizon is limited, and we are lost in the face of all the extraordinary: we prefer to just brush it off, instead of paying due attention, exploring and studying?

It is impossible to make such a fatal mistake, because to reject the inexplicable means to slow down progress, to hinder development, to abandon the future.

And it is from the future science that we have the right to expect an answer to the question of what is the phenomenon of Vanga, and I believe that it will give a worthy answer to this challenge of nature. My confidence is reinforced by Vanga herself, who often says:

"The time of miracles will come, and science will make major discoveries in the field of the immaterial. Scientists will reveal a lot about the future of our planet and about space. And the data about this will be gathered in the old sacred books.

With their help, many ancient secrets will finally be solved.

It is to this future that all the efforts of the blind woman are directed, for she serves good, love, beauty, universal harmony:

"The time will come when the wheat will be separated from the chaff, for the future belongs to good people, and they will live in a world so beautiful that we cannot imagine it now. The time will come for the inspired work, love and brotherhood of all people on earth'.

Vanga's incredible gift first of all amazes, then awakens admiration and, finally, educates, because it can not but cause the desire to become more human, kinder, more sympathetic to the pain of others, and her life-simple, natural and full of work — makes you look at life from a different angle and rethink much of the past.

I encountered many difficulties while writing this book. How, for example, to describe the words available in our dictionary, strange and incredible predictions of Vanga or her unusual state? Special terms are needed, so I left Vanga's explanations as she pronounced them-with her concepts and explanations.

And some of the cases described by Vanga seemed to me so fantastic, beyond the limits of reason, that I did not dare to include them in the book. I left their solution to scientists and specialists.

And finally, memory. It is not to our credit that we started recording Vanga's phenomenal manifestations quite late. And now, when we decided to put together everything that we heard and saw — we, her family-it turned out that we can not remember everything she said, but only individual episodes, cases, words. A lot of things that would help to create a clearer and more full-blooded image of Vanga fall out.

Even 20 years ago, Dr. Georgi Lozanov, then director of the Institute of Suggestology, realized the importance of information about her unusual activities and, using his authority and knowledge in the field of parapsychology, discovered and introduced Vanga to the world, putting the study of her phenomenon on a scientific basis. Together with a group of scientists who studied the gift of clairvoyance, he conducted a survey of thousands of visitors, described more than 7,000 cases of amazing accuracy, recorded hundreds of sessions on a tape recorder, even made a film from a scientific point of view. At the same time, he told foreign journalists that Wang's predictions go far beyond the random. Very conditionally, we can say that the degree of guessing is 80%, and since this indicator is very high, the phenomenon must be investigated and carefully studied.

It was very difficult to compose the text. I had to describe thousands of cases, predictions and divinations. Moreover, what is said about something applies to many other things, the simplest words carry an important semantic load, and they need to be interpreted. The book is far from perfect, but all attempts to change anything — on the advice of friends or specialists-did not give the desired result. It seems that the book has taken on a life of its own and resisted any, even weak encroachment.

The greatest advantage of the book is its authenticity. I tried to keep everything Vanga said in its purest form. She tried to describe very carefully and accurately everything that I, my mother, and family members saw and heard. Nothing Vanga said was paraphrased or changed. At the same time, I was well aware of the degree of responsibility for each line I wrote, often saw skeptical smiles, and often gave up at the thought that people would not understand what I wrote and wrote. Will Vanga's high-minded messages reach their hearts, will they believe her?... But all doubts vanished as soon as she remembered her own words: "He who has ears, let him hear; he who has mind and understanding, let him reflect'…

In addition, I did not allow myself to express my own opinion or comment anywhere. I grant this right to anyone who reads the following lines.

THE PHENOMENON

Any honest attempt to get into the future is sure to interest many, but people are sick to death of all this scientific fuss. So let's explain less what's what, and just tell more…

John Wyndham

We, Vanga's nephews, her sister's children, often came to see her aunt, even when we were very young. We didn't find her oddities strange, or her behavior at all. Only sometimes we could not understand why my aunt suddenly turned pale, why she suddenly became ill, and incomprehensible words came out of her mouth, and her voice sounded unnaturally loud, even menacing, striking our imagination with a huge inner strength. If at such moments any of the neighbors were near, we heard: "Hush, hush, she's prophesying." Aunt Vanga is a prophet? In the child's imagination, this word usually merges with a vague image of an ancient sage, a silver-bearded old man with a Bible in his hands, next to whom stands, with his eyes fixed on the face of the prophet, a young man who later, after the death of the old man, will become a prophet himself. So we saw each other.

I remember the day I turned 16 years old. I remember it precisely because soon after a modest dinner in our house in Petrich, Vanga suddenly began to speak to me. And it was not her at all, and I heard the voice of a completely different person. The words I heard at the time had nothing to do with a completely ordinary table conversation, when you talk about everything a little, but in fact about nothing. That's when Vanga was broadcasting, now I know it for sure. "You are always, every second in our sight." Then she told me everything I'd been doing all day. How did she know about all those small events that even in my memory, if not for Vanga, would not have lasted until the next day? I was numb. And then I asked my aunt why she said all this? Vanga was surprised: "I didn't tell you anything." But when I repeated what I had just heard from her lips, she said softly:: "It is not me, then others who are always near me. Some I call "small forces" for myself, it was they who told you about your day through me, and there are also "big forces". When they begin to speak in me, or rather, through me, I lose a lot of energy, I feel bad, I am depressed for a long time. Baby, do you want to see them?» I was so shocked by everything I heard that I even screamed: "No! And after a while, when I had calmed down, I asked Vang, " What real things can I see?» She replied: "Nothing special, just glowing dots in the air, they look like fireflies that fly over dahlias on a warm evening."

Then, as the years passed, I tried to explain this phenomenon. At various times, when Vanga was in a good mood, I asked her questions, which she usually answered. Fortunately, my notes were preserved. I picked them up, processed them, and got a kind of questionnaire that gives an idea of Vanga's abilities. Naturally, I asked questions in a different form, but their meaning is absolutely accurate. I must warn you that Vanga, like all people who are focused on the inner depth of their lives, is laconic. Therefore, almost always the questions are much longer than the answers.

Question: Tell me, Aunt, do you see the specific faces of those people with whom you communicate, do you imagine any general pictures, the situation?

Answer: Yes, I see it clearly.

Question: Does it matter to you when an action takes place-in the present, past, or future?

The answer: Such trifles are of no importance to me. Both the past and the future are drawn equally clearly in my mind's eye.

Question: What you see, Aunt, is given to you as information about a person or as a person himself?

The answer: Just as accurately as in a living life: both as information about a person, and as this particular person himself.

Question: Does each person have his own "code", a personal cipher, knowing which, it is possible to unravel the" life line " of a person, his fate?

There was no answer.

Question: How exactly does the future of a particular person manifest itself — are only the main, main events highlighted, or do you see the whole life as a whole, in a series of events? In a word, like in the movies or something else?

Answer: I see the life of a person, as if filmed on film.

Question: Do you read minds?

Answer: Yes.

Q: And at a distance?

Answer: Distance doesn't matter.

Question: Is it possible to read the thoughts of people who know other languages, but do not know Bulgarian? (Vanga herself does not know any other languages.)

Answer: There are no language barriers. Usually a voice is heard, the language is always Bulgarian.

Question: Can you "call" the information you are interested in from a certain, pre-named, period of time?

Answer: Yes.

Question: If you listen to the radio, does the information you receive cause visual images?

Answer: No, it doesn't.

Question: Does the depth of your insights depend on the seriousness of the question posed and on the strength of the personality of the person who addressed you?

Answer: Yes, it is important.

Question: Does the depth of your insight depend on the state of health, not only yours, but also on the nervous state of the questioner?

Answer: It does not depend.

Question: If it so happens that you see with the inner vision given to you from above a near misfortune or even the death of a person who has come to you, can you do anything to avoid the misfortune?

Answer: No, neither I nor anyone else can do anything.

Question: And if troubles, even catastrophic ones, threaten not just one person, but a group of people, an entire city, a state, is it possible to prepare something in advance?

The answer: It's useless.

Question: Does the fate of a person depend on his inner, moral strength, physical abilities? Is it possible to influence fate?

Answer: You can't. Everyone will go their own way, and only their own way.

Question: How do you determine what sorrows a visitor has come to you with?

The answer: I hear a voice speaking about this person, his image appears before me, and the cause of suffering becomes clear.

Question: Do you feel that your gift of clairvoyance is programmed from above?

Answer: Yes. Higher powers.

Question: What are these forces that have affected you so much?

There was no response.

Question: How is the "signal" of these transcendent forces usually perceived?

Answer: The voice is most often heard.

Question: Do you see the one or those whom you call "higher powers"?

As clearly as a man sees his reflection in calm water.

Question: Do they consist of "glowing dots that twinkle like fireflies over dahlias"?

: I would say yes.

Question: Can these forces materialize, acquire human flesh, for example?

Answer: No, they can't.

Question: If you, Aunt, want to get in touch with them, will you succeed? Or should they be the only ones taking the initiative?

Answer: Most often, contact occurs at their request. But I can also summon these forces — they are everywhere and everywhere, close by.

Question: Is it possible to specify some smaller details at the request of the person who asks the questions? Will you get an answer by asking these kinds of clarifying questions?

Answer: The answer is sound, but very vague. And in general, it is quite difficult.

Question: The essence of a person, what is it-a symbiosis of several of his bodies, as if fused together? Perhaps we should talk about the unity of such different hypostases as the physical shell, spirit, soul?

Answer: Yes, you can. Fair judgment.

Question: How do you see the deceased person you are being asked about — as a certain image, as a certain concept of a person, or in some other way?

Answer: A clearly visible image of the deceased appears and his voice is heard.

Question: So, is the deceased person able to answer questions?

The answer: He both asks questions and can answer questions put to him.

Question: Is the personality preserved after physical death and burial?

Answer: Yes.

Question: How do you, Aunt, perceive the fact of a person's death-only as the cessation of the physical existence of his body?

Answer: Yes, only as the physical death of the human body.

Question: Does the "rebirth" of a person occur after physical death and what is it expressed in?

Vanga did not answer.

Question: Which kind of connection is stronger — related, by blood, or spiritual?

Answer: The spiritual connection is stronger.

Question: All people on the planet are one family, because all people think: they constitute a community of intelligence at a certain stage of evolution. Does there exist, parallel to the human, human mind, another more perfect, higher one?

Answer: Yes.

Question: Tell me, Aunt, what is the origin of this supermind? It permeates only near-Earth space or the entire Cosmos, did it come to us as a legacy from ancient, extinct civilizations, or was it sent down by a messenger from our future? Where does it come from and where is it "located"?

The answer: This mind begins and ends in the Cosmos, it is eternal and infinite, it is subject to everything.

Question: Were there large, highly organized civilizations on Earth before?

Answer: Yes.

Question: How many were there when their time was up?

There was no response.

Question: Dear aunt, do you think that our modern human civilization can be perceived, let's say, as a child's age-the age of the whole and the one, the mind, in the existence of which you are so firmly convinced?

Answer: Yes, maybe this is the right comparison.

Question: Is there still a mind in the universe that has reached the same stage of development as the mind of our civilization?

No answer.

Question: Tell me, Aunt, will there ever be a meeting with representatives of other civilizations?

Question: Do those alien ships that are so primitively called "flying saucers" really visit Earth?

Answer: Yes, it is.

Question: Where do they come from?

Answer: With the planet, which in the language of its inhabitants called Vamfim. So, in any case, I hear this unusual word-Vamfim. This planet is the third from Earth.

Question: Is it possible at the request of earthlings to contact the inhabitants of the mysterious planet? By technical means, or perhaps by telepathic means?

Answer: Earthlings are powerless here. Contact is carried out, in accordance with their desire, by our guests.

I repeat: I deliberately refrain from commenting. My questions were, of course, not random at all, they are related to specific events, I asked them to Vanga only when, as it seemed to me, she was most predisposed to listen carefully to me. Specific events will be discussed below, please be patient. Now I will return to my preface. Although, maybe this is not a preface at all, but just a kind of explanatory text. It is possible that I will continue to give some explanations or clarifications.

Vanga is a deeply religious person, she believes in God, in his existence. But when asked by journalist K. K. (I still have a tape recording of the conversation), who interviewed her back in 1983, when asked if she had seen Jesus Christ, Vanga replied: "Yes, I have. But it is not at all the same as it is depicted on the icons. Christ is a huge ball of fire that is impossible to look at, so bright is he. Only similar in appearance to a man, know that there is a lie hidden here."

I believe that the most amazing quality of her supernatural gift is the ease with which Vanga is able to move through time and space: from the distant past to the most uncertain, somewhere out there, in the depths of time, faintly shimmering future. Not her physical self, of course, but her spiritual self. (This is exactly where words are missing, either I alone or the human language in general is sorely lacking).

... Near the village of Prepechene, between the towns of Sandanski and Petrici, lies the Rupite Valley, widely known in Bulgaria for its warm mineral springs. From the west it seems to be blocked by a small mountain, thick as sheep's wool, covered with bushes and small forest. The mountain is called the Casing. At its foot once flowed a deep river Struma, now the channel is filled with water only during floods and heavy rains. In the heat, the river dries up completely, and its sandy bed glistens under the sun with clean glass. Wang has a small house there, where she spends her days in peace and quiet among the undisturbed nature of man. It also accepts visitors.

Every year, on October 15, when Peter's Day is listed on the church calendar, Vanga gathers guests. Neighbors, friends, and acquaintances sit at a modest meal. The meal is quiet, without libations and solemn speeches. So, does Vanga celebrate Peter's Day? Not at all. The reason for a modest feast is different — no one can guess. I'll read my notes, dated 1985. Here is what Vanga said: "On the same day, a thousand years ago, there was a strong eruption of a volcano. Lava flows flooded a large and rich city, thousands of people died in the fire. And the people who lived here were tall and stately, very beautiful, dressed in white clothes that shone with a metallic luster. The city had theaters and libraries, and its citizens valued enlightenment more than other goods, deeply revered wisdom, and felt themselves on an equal footing even with tsars. A blue river ran through the city, its waters flowing over a bed of golden sand. In this river, newborns were baptized, and the children grew up healthy, gradually turning into young people, strong in body and healthy in spirit... The main city gate was decorated with golden-winged griffins-the patrons of the city. Nearby were three large churches: St. Petka, St. Theotokos, and St. Panteleimon. Earth's red-hot abysses are still breathing, their breath is warmed by mineral water. Listen, you will certainly hear the sighs of long-dead people. And so I dare to ask you, my guests: while we are alive, let us remember with quiet prayer all those who died so suddenly, in the color and grandeur of a joyful earthly life. Should they have died? And isn't there a deep prescient meaning hidden here?

"The Rupite Valley attracts Vanga very much," says her sister Lubka, " and I can't understand what exactly? If there was trouble here a long time ago, what's it got to do with us? A long-standing misfortune should not affect us. Although no, it does: both I and many others feel here as if in a depressed state of mind. And Vanga hears voices that are not heard far from these places, they excite her-voices that sounded a thousand years ago. And it also reminds us that the house was built on the site of an ancient, pre-ancient sanctuary, which means that it is in a good place.

My brother Dimitar is also ready to put in a word when it comes to my aunt. He speaks, and his face changes from a simple one, which does not stand out in any way among the same faces of our neighbors, to an important one: Dimitar puts on a "professorial air". A little more, and it will start "broadcasting". However, he interprets quite sensibly.

— I'm neither a historian nor an archaeologist, and yet I like to dig through old books. He even created his own versions about the origin of some historical monuments. I can honestly say that I am glad if my modest assumptions are confirmed by archaeological excavations.

I have read that there were indeed ancient shrines in the Rupite Valley. Not only archaeologists, but also ordinary residents find here a lot of fragments of religious objects. It seems to me that pottery, crafts, and architecture have reached a remarkably high level in the valley. It is not necessary to have a rich imagination to guess the steps of rich Thracian temples among the stone blocks, and if you do not spare your pants and climb on your knees among the rubble, you can find a Roman coin that has turned green with time. And not only Roman. The valley was bustling with life. Pilgrims from near and far came here to pray in bright, solemn temples, as well as to heal bodily ulcers in warm mineral springs.

Old people like to tell stories, heard in childhood, about how the ritual of healing with water took place. Even in the evening, each sufferer dug, as much as he could, a hole in the sand. By morning, warm mineral water was accumulating there. At sunrise, always at sunrise, when the first rays lit up the curly top of Mount Kozhukh, they scooped up water with a vessel hollowed out of a pumpkin-a crater-and poured themselves over. Again and again they scooped and poured. They looked at the soft morning sun and prayed to God, asking for their health and spiritual strength. We prayed mentally… According to the ritual, during the entire time of the "ablution at sunrise" — as it was called — it was necessary to remain completely silent. It was also believed that anyone who performed the ritual with sincere and deep faith, the treatment was beneficial. The effect was achieved quickly, and old ailments were cured.

— There is another belief, "my brother continues to" broadcast " — " and it has a very strong effect on my psyche, forcing me to embark on a maze of the most strange assumptions, to make guesses, one more incredible than the other. So, it is believed that in the city square there was a large statue of a horseman. The horseman is none other than Saint Constantine himself. The statue was removed from its pedestal when the janissaries came to this blessed land. Personally, I believe that it could also be a statue of the Thracian god Heros, since it was here that archaeologists found plates with his image. I understand that the question is largely purely scholastic, and one day science will give an accurate answer to it. The matter is different. I will talk about what is connected with my aunt Vanga. The oddity lies in the fact that her first insights are connected with the rider. They "met" at the well when Vanga came for water. The horseman warned her about the impending trials, about when to expect war, it was he who informed Vanga that she would become a clairvoyant — " to predict the fate of the living, to hear and understand the voice of the dead." Their first "meetings" took place a long time ago, 30 years ago, when Vanga settled in the valley. She is not going to move to another place.

We Bulgarians are generally not indifferent to the legends, the protagonist of which is the horseman. After all, scientists still do not know by whom and when the "portrait" was carved on the rock, the historical name of which is "Madara Horseman". Experts suggest that on that rock is depicted Khan Tervel or another warrior from the time of the first Bulgarian state. But I wonder if this is the same horseman who once stood in the middle of the square of the beautiful city, and then, hundreds and hundreds of years later, began to appear to our Vanga, usually only on the eve of some fateful events.

It seems to me that it was not by chance that my aunt chose the Rupite Valley: there are, I know, a lot of places nearby that are much more picturesque. Vanga says that he draws here the cosmic energy in full measure. The energy flow is "attracted" to the dried-up riverbed of the Struma, because there, in the depths of the earth, a great secret was buried, the solution of the mystery is the key to reading the ancient history of the Bulgarian people. What this energy was that attracted the pilgrims of the hoary times to the valley, and which still nourishes Vanga's prophetic gift, I do not undertake to judge. But I want to go up to the high platform and address our academicians and doctors of science from it: come here, friends, dig sand, crush stones, also delve into the essence of the cipher inscribed by the Almighty in the high sky-mysterious and eternal starry letters, strain your mind, fly on the wings of fantasy, fed by facts, and you will open — must open! "an ancient secret. Go, you will find fame, and not only among fellow scientists, world fame.

This is the reasoning of my brother Dimitar, and I confess that it is not always boring to delve into the meaning of his oral crosswords.

* * *

We often asked Vanga: why do you live here, there are so many places nearby that are much more fertile? Move closer to the clear spring water, to the dewy bushes in which the voices of robins and thrushes are so sweet in the morning. Why, Aunt, are you attached to this dreary desert? And what did we hear most often in response? Almost always the same, mysterious and incomprehensible to ordinary mortals:

— I have to stay here for a certain amount of time. I feel good here, while I feel good: energy flows through me from the earth and from space on an invisible bridge, I easily absorb it, breathe it like a life-giving balm. In my mind's eye, I see the infernal flames that once, in time immemorial, burned this land. All things were consumed and melted down by fire, and all things that were unclean before were cleansed of filth. The secret of purification by fire is hidden by the mountains, they are not far away, I feel their presence.

Is it only you, Aunt, who can feel the bridge over which the energy flows, or can others "step" on it?

"Me and the birds. Are your ears closed to the noise of the wings of countless flocks of birds, do you not hear the sad voices of birds flying away in autumn and their joyful cries, their trumpet songs in spring? Places like this mountainous terrain attract energy, and birds are able to capture it, they are charged with it. They fly from one "place" to another, not knowing tired. (Conversation in the summer of 1988)

Somewhat earlier, I noted that Vanga is not very talkative. But she has a special peaceful mood, and then you need to listen carefully to her: he who has ears, let him hear. Vanga continues.

— I'm left here!" This is where the confused and hopeless should come, and this is where they strive, like birds finding a landmark. The one who longs for deliverance finds a way. And I can only read the writings of his soul, without listening to the language, which is so talkative, so able to mix everything up and mix it up, that a hundred minds will not know the truth. And another thing: I must not only read yesterday and today, but also give the right direction to tomorrow. But I'm so tired! (Summer 1988)

We move away from Vanga, who has thrown her face up to the sky and closed in on herself, not a muscle twitching, not a hair moving. In concentration, it is as if petrified, and awe fills our stupid human hearts. Where is she now? What if her soul had flown away for a while to talk to God himself? Or maybe her soul, like a girl in the sunny streams of a warm river, is bathed in powerful energy flows that unknown, unknown, flow from space to the earth, from the earth, like steam, rise to the sky? Who knows… She knows the birds, too.

Well, we, the nephews, can not understand anything, but the opinion of our mother:

— We've been together for so many years! Since the day of my birth, I can say that I have not moved away from her, and yet I am in complete ignorance-where did my sister get such abilities? What are these abilities? I don't know. As soon as people do not call our Vanga: and clairvoyant, and fortune teller, and healer, and oracle. For me, she is a mysterious soothsayer, who sees the past, the future and, of course, the present equally clearly. I have long refused explanations, not looking at them, knowing that nothing I find, not trying to peek into the lab of her soul, although just to look no need, Vanga whole is wide open, but not those eyes to look at it. No, not the ones on our foreheads, but quite different ones. That's how I think and think.

Well, my mother is a village woman, busy with everyday everyday chores around the house, she has no time and no need to try to penetrate into the inner world of her sister. Well, was she the only one looking through the wide-open door, seeing nothing? How many learned people came to Vanga to, as they say, throw up their hands, make big eyes and go home without understanding anything! "Allow me, because here is a miracle, undoubtedly a miracle," said the Soviet scientist Mikhailov. — I don't believe she could have heard the voice of my mother, who died 10 years ago. However, only my mother knew what Vanga had told me. So, miracles happen?" The

Soviet doctor Z. M. modestly asked Vanga to tell about the folk healers of antiquity, about their methods of treatment. Z. M. is a serious, well-read specialist, and when the soothsayer began to tell her the names of doctors (and only such specialists as Z. M. know them), the methods of their work, the doctor was unspeakably surprised: "You might think that Paracelsus is her personal friend."

Vanga told the famous Bulgarian historian in detail, as if reading a fascinating book, about the main events of the XII century, about the wars that swept through the Bulgarian land at that time, about the heroes of great victories and those who left the battlefield ingloriously. The historian, a great connoisseur of that era, did not doubt any of the facts given. In addition, he heard and learned a lot about that time for the first time. So much for the authorities of the old schools, so much for the knowledge preserved by the works of the ancients-far from all, on the contrary, the charters covered with the dust of centuries have brought us just a little.

Here is another interesting example of how Vanga imagines God, and I would say-the absolute: in her deep conviction, God reminds her of a certain unsleeping eye. "No one hides in the house, no one hides in the shade of a tree, no good or bad deed goes unnoticed. And do not think that you are free to do what you want, in your actions no one is free, and everything is predetermined. You can only experience feelings: joy from a good deed, bitterness and remorse from a bad one." That's what Vanga thinks.

She is indifferent to our earthly vanity, everything earthly seems to her petty, uninteresting. People know that she is a completely unselfish person, but people are people, there is probably no country from which she would not receive a gift, only she does not need gifts at all. So it happens in life that a little boy in faraway Korea grows up like a blade of grass on the road, not receiving gifts from his poor parents even on his birthday, and an Arab sheikh, the owner of oil storerooms, rich as Croesus, accepts the next offerings with a bored expression on his face.

There is no justice in the world, and Vanga knows it. Is that why she is indifferent to fame and gifts? Yes, I know, for her, the Korean beggar boy and the Arab millionaire sheikh are equal (as if she had risen above all human things, shaky and loose, short-lived and only seemingly extended in time). Moreover, it is not the indifference of insensitivity, but a certain hypersensitivity. Developing the metaphor, I will say this: Vanga sees that the poor boy is strong in spirit and body, rises to the heights of human joy and earthly glory, and the rich man will give all his gold to be cured of a malignant disease, and will achieve nothing. The scale is wavering, and only faith in the ultimate justice of any decision of fate is a sure support for a person in his fleeting earthly life... I want now to transfer to paper my bright, childlike memory of the rainbow.

So, after the rain that dampened the reddish July dust in the valley of Rulite, a rainbow rose in the sky. It was very close, shone with incredibly beautiful pure colors and, most incredible of all, it seemed to me a wonderful bridge spanning our little river. She called to the unknown and full of wonders of the country that stretches across the river, behind the mountain Kozhukh: rather on the road — not far to go. Under the power of childhood dreams, I was sitting quietly on the porch of Vanga's house and suddenly I heard her voice:

"Take a chair, baby, and give me your hand, let's go out on the lawn, I want to walk under the rainbow." It's so low that we'll have to bend down. You can bow to a rainbow, can't you, baby?

She saw the rainbow through the eyes of her soul as clearly as she saw everything she told people.

I asked Vanga:

"Tell me, Aunt, what does a rainbow mean-a symbol of beauty, a bouquet of bright flowers that can only bloom in the sky?"

"The rainbow is just a reminder," she said. - Reminder of the flood. You have read that a punishment was sent down on people for their sins: it rained for forty days. Water flooded the earth, drowned living creatures, drowned, of course, and people. Noah remained alive and with him in the ark of " every creature in pairs." Noah on his ark, although he did not completely lose faith in salvation, despaired of fighting the waves, and then a rainbow rose in the sky. The snow-capped mountains glittered under the rainbow, and a dove flew from there with an olive twig in its beak. That was the signal: you are saved because you believed.

Aunt, but it's a biblical legend, nothing more. And what do you think of the rainbow?

— Oh, honey, I can't tell you anything else. A legend, you say? And where do the legends come from? Noah's Ark is right next to my hut. If I walk ten paces, I'll put my hand on his warm, mossy side. The sun-warmed wood is so pleasant to the touch!

She paused and went back to thinking about something so deeply hidden that I would never see it again. The rainbow called me, but I didn't run, probably won't call again.

I remember such a case. One morning there was a timid knock at the door of the cottage. I looked out of the window and saw a modestly dressed woman and those with whom the guest had come: a very tired, with a kind of drooping face, a monk and a bent old woman with him. Vanga came out to them. It was very early, the sun's rays barely illuminated Vanga's very calm, even a little like a mask, sightless face. In a flat voice, not loud, but very confident, she said, addressing the monk specifically.

— You didn't have to go that far.

— My mother is ill, and I only hope for you.

"Sick?" You are a monk, your mother is the church. You must live and work only for the church. You made a vow to the holy mother Church and died to the world.

The monk, who was quite young, was embarrassed and blushed. After a moment's silence, he continued in a very low, sinking voice:

"I have brought a relative with me. She is still young, but she wants to go to a monastery and become a nun, I do not know what to advise her.

"Let me see —" said Vanga, " your relative is not so young, she has a family.

"Yes," said the monk, " she has a family, a husband, and two daughters. The trouble is that my husband is completely at odds.

"Well, the mother will leave the children to their fate, and she will hide behind the church gates. I made it up. She can't hide anywhere, her tearful children's eyes will be seen everywhere, the tears of children will burn the apostate mother. Go away, you shouldn't have gone so far.

I think I mentioned in my rambling notes that Vanga can "read" a whole human life. From birth to death. And in the same way, she sees the threads that make up the fabric of every human act. To clarify my point, I will retell a small, but well-known story with thieves. That's how it was. In one of the old, somewhat dilapidated from the time the Church worked restorers, the cultural and well-educated young people. Who would have thought that they were planning an evil deed-to steal icons. And they did it so cleverly that no one would have thought of them, they were looking for thieves all over the area, and our restorers continued to renovate the wall frescoes and did not blow their moustaches. We were sure that everything was covered up. Only when all the searches ended in complete failure, decided to ask for help from Vanga. She immediately said who the thieves were, listed in detail everything they had stolen, smiled at the thought of human naivety, she unraveled the entire logical chain of crime and "entanglement of traces". The "cultured people" were shocked, confessed everything and bitterly repented of what they had done. For as long as I can remember, the court took into account their tearful plea for mercy.

And here is another story of a similar property. Our old friend, an elderly man who already had grandchildren-schoolchildren, decided that it was time to think about the near old age. He had no money, but he had a monisto of ten gold coins of old coinage. These necklaces, often made from simple cheap coins, and is still common in Bulgarian villages. So he decided that if he became infirm, he could — when the gold came in handy — hire someone to look after him and collect him on his last journey. And, out of harm's way, he hid Monisto in a bundle, and sewed the bundle in the pillow. It was a troublesome business to hide money, the old man could not cope with the task, the grandchildren peeked. Somewhere in a couple of days, our neighbor found a torn pillow in his room, and the gold coins-tyu-tyu, disappeared.

Who stole it?

A neighbor, the old man decided, and immediately went to court. The judge, fortunately, had no time that day, the old man went home, and on the way turned to Vanga.

— Right I've done that he decided to sue the thief? "What is it?" he asked.

— How do you know who the thief is?" Vanga replied. - Go home, under the shed near the barn you have a bag of oats for the donkey, there rummage well — you will find the lost. Don't ever offend people with suspicion again.

The next day, before the sun was up and the grass glistened with the dew that had fallen heavily during the night, the old man knocked on our door.

- Vanga, open up, there is no strength to wait!

Vanga opened it, and the old man fell at her feet.

"Thank you, I'll never forget, you saved me from sin and shame. After all, my neighbor and I have been friends all our lives, from an early age. The brat grandkids have done something they only learn at school.

For many years, we all lived as one big family in a squalid little house, in darkness and unusual crowding. I once asked Vanga if there would ever be an amazing day when we would move into a new, spacious and bright house. Vanga, as if waiting for my question, answered without hesitation:

— I see our old house broken, part of the roof, pieces of walls, frames without glass miraculously held on some pillars, because the foundation is destroyed. Then there will be a new house.

I didn't understand anything.

As the days passed. Every morning I hurried to work, returned late, tired, often in a bad mood due to the fact that I really have no place to rest. But one day, coming back from work, I saw a cloud of lime dust on the site of our house. The house collapsed!

The following happened. Next to us, workers were building a new building. When we were digging a pit for the foundation, our "ancient dwelling" moved into that pit — like a boy on a sled slides down a hill! Before my astonished eyes, the remains of the roof, walls and window frames without glass hung literally in the air. Fortunately, none of our people were injured.

"If I tell people what I know, they won't want to live," Vanga once said.

Family is sacred to her. If she is dissatisfied with each other wife, she does everything to explain to everyone the fatal quarrel, of the gap assures that any causes and their effects are disposable and must be eliminated for the good of the family as a whole organism. Because there is no life outside the family, but only an existence that is not inspired by higher goals, empty, worthless, unable to fill the meaning of everyday work, everyday life. No matter how much you draw water from the cheshma (spring) with a leaky mug, you will not get drunk, you will not quench your thirst... Vanga immediately sees the true culprit of the family drama and utters her decisive, often very heavy word for those present, not at all afraid that she may be offended. It does not" expose", as is customary in a secular court, but only makes an unpleasant verdict. It is given such a right, and if so, by whom? I don't know, I only know that she has no enemies, and there are no people who are offended by Vanga. At least, I haven't met or heard of them.

Another story from the category of detective stories, but fun. In her new home, here in Rupit, her dress was stolen. It was a beautiful velvet dress that suited her very well. Vanga, having discovered the loss, was not upset.

"Never mind, the poor woman who took it will be glad of the dress, and after that she will suffer with shame. Won't know how to return it. No need to lock the closet, the dress will be returned soon.

A week later, the dress was hanging on hangers in the closet. Vanga only smiled mysteriously.

And soon-here is bad luck! "another theft. Thieves turned everything upside down, looking for treasures, of course, since Vanga is a "sorceress", then she must have treasures. But, of course, they didn't find anything, they probably took some small change out of annoyance. I remember very well that we called the police. The policemen, not long breaking their multitudinous heads over possible variants of this boring case, directly asked Vanga:

- You yourself suspect whom?

- Why should I suspect, — she answered, - young people were hooligans. Nothing, they will bring it themselves and put it in its place.

Two days later, a whole "deputation" arrived; underage thieves and their parents. The older ones wept, the younger ones stood with their eyes downcast. As they say, they burned with shame. Vanga sat down on the porch, paused, and then read a little lecture to the fools who had been fooling around.

— No theft has ever been and will never remain a secret. You steal, and your conscience is a witness to the theft. People with a sensitive heart will see that your conscience is uneasy, they will suspect something is wrong, and your bad deed will gradually be revealed. You can run away from people's contempt,but you can't hide from yourself. Go on, don't let anything like this happen to you again. Never.

Did they hear my Vanga? Did you feel the truth of her words? Sorry, but I don't know.

Oh, Vanga, if only you could see! As good morning valley, Rupite, as weightless, almost ethereal muslin clouds to the pearly morning sky, as gently fanning red breast Robin welcoming new day draws blue of its light wing quick swallow... Morning is a feast for eyes that have not forgotten how to look.

But Vanga knows something else-contemplation, and I do not know what colors glow before her inner eyes when she sinks into her tormented soul. Suddenly her sightless eyes open wide like windows to the sun, and she looks, yes, she looks and sees the unknown, the beyond, the mysterious. A few minutes pass, the light goes out, Vanga's face, which has just been unusually inspired, seems to fade, again becomes like an artful mask.

It happens that we sit together on the porch, talking about all sorts of things, the thought jumps, without stopping, from object to object, and suddenly Vanga falls asleep. It happened once that I read her a book, a work of fiction, with characters, with a fascinating plot.

Vanga listened for a while, I got carried away and read with an expression, changing the intonation, highlighting the tone of the author's speech, the replicas of the characters. And then I noticed that my eloquence was being wasted: Vanga was asleep. Dumbfounded, I fell silent, but Vanga, without opening her eyes, said: "Read. I'm not sleeping. I wanted to see how people really lived at the time described in this historical novel" — "Well, how?" - I asked, not coming up with a more worthwhile question. "I'll make you sad: in the book, the main character is not true. I'm sorry, the book is well written, not only for you, many people like it, but it's not true. I was transported for some time to the years when the events described take place. "I'm sorry, but none of this is true." So said, repeated several times Vanga. I threw the book in the closet, thinking that I would never, ever be a writer. My readers, I think, have already realized that I then chose the right path. Well, and notes about the lived and seen to the forces to make everyone who wants. Isn't that right?

We, mere mortals, even the most intelligent and far-sighted of us, imagine the world around us in one plane, Vanga in a completely different one. Our world and hers revolve in different orbits, which is why, by the way, I do not undertake to reason, interpret, comment, but only take the liberty of documenting what I have learned as far as I can remember.

A quiet, warm evening, the smell of sweet tobacco is intoxicating to the near rain, yellow dahlias are burning, a ladybug is crawling on a geranium leaf, Vanga goes to the very edge of the flowerbed, bends down to the flowers. Her lips open, and she says something, as if she's talking quietly to a close friend.

"What are you talking about, Aunt?" And with whom?

— You don't see with whom — with flowers. Geranium just told me: "I'm the best cure for a nervous breakdown." She's funny, I've known that for a long time.

Let me ask the most intelligent of my fellow citizens, the sages of our dear planet Earth, let me ask: explain the mechanism of receiving and reproducing information, which is so skillfully launched into the work of Vanga? I know no one will answer me, I won't hear anything intelligible. And then I ask Vanga:

— Aunt, how do you see?

"You know, baby, everything happens by itself, and it's pretty simple. A man comes to me, and with him his life bursts into my life, with all the joys and passions, failures and pain. A window opens in my brain, through which I observe the life of my guest. It doesn't matter if he's talking, he's silent. It is better even if he is silent, because the pictures of his life that I see are accompanied by a detailed story, I hear words that are completely clearly not heard by you or anyone else.

— You need a lot of time to talk about life.

"Of course. But the main events are not so much.

"Aunt, I'm writing something down, look for interesting examples for me.

"What's the use of looking for them, that I'm hiding them?" You know all about it. Well, if you want, write down for example the story of the Chinese Song. There was a Chinese artist, her name was Sun. She studied in Sofia, where she married a Bulgarian. Back in 1971, she once looked in on me for a light. I said to her then: "You will return to your own people, you will become a famous and respectable person. I see your country, your native places, fields flooded with water, green rice sprouts, low houses, people work hard, but they are poor, they don't even have shoes, they have some wooden sandals with strings on their feet. And the country is beautiful with the beauty of tireless human labor." Do you understand me? And I also said to the Chinese woman: "Poor girl, your child is sick, he has paralysis, only one person can help him — you. You will be comforted, you will cope with this serious illness, you will overcome it, your child will recover." Then Sun went to China, began to study acupuncture and, having achieved amazing success, put many people on their feet, and cured her child. She visited us again in Bulgaria, but now I see her in her homeland. Now she is very famous in China, she is happy.

Among the many celebrities of the world, so to speak, of the class have been visiting Vanga and artists. Once I met Svyatoslav Roerich here. He was passing through Bulgaria — he was going from India, I think, to Amsterdam. He sat in silence opposite Vanga, and his aunt spoke in a smooth and calm voice, her usual voice, without intonation and even as if without emotion. She saw Roerich's study, saw a large ceramic vase with well — cultivated land, and in it a flower-a white, downright alabaster lily as a symbol of heavenly-pure beauty, Vanga said: "This is the greatest spiritual decoration of your home. The beautiful lily glitters for me like the silver of the eternal celestial snows of Tibet and the Himalayas. From there, from Tibet, the history of mankind began, there it is necessary to look for its roots, there-the explanation of many amazing and strange mysteries of the earthly life of man and people. Your father, "Vanga continued, turning to Roerich —" was not just an artist, but also an inspired prophet. All his paintings are epiphanies, predictions. They are encrypted, but an attentive and sensitive heart will tell the viewer the cipher, and the meaning of the canvases will become clear. You must continue your father's work with all diligence. It's meant to be."

I do not remember whether Roerich said anything or not, I only remember that he left us in deep thought: the shadows of clouds seemed to wander over his face.

Vanga is easily transferred to a completely different environment, "visits" countries about which she has not heard anything before, and speaks not in general, but specifically, as, for example, about the alabaster-pure lily — the favorite of Svyatoslav Roerich, about which he never told anyone. Why, the lily of Roerich! Here comes to us…

But all in order. A neighbor comes to us. On some trivial matter, mainly, of course, to chat with my aunt. He begins to brag to her about what a home-loving, diligent hostess she is, how everything at home is cleaned and decorated. Not at all, they say, at the neighbors, and they are sloppy, and dirty, and incompetent, they do not like their husbands or their children… In a word, a famous song. Vanga, apparently, was pretty tired of her, and she began to tell her neighbor: the curtain on the window was torn, her husband's dirty socks were lying in the middle of the room in a box with tools, the bed linen was washed, no better than a prisoner's. "You are no mistress and do not imagine any more, I do not like such people." The neighbor, shamed, quickly left. It is heard that now the order in her house.

Vanga is not worth anything, being in the present, talking with a visitor, suddenly look into the past for a second. So, she told one of our guests suddenly, out of the blue, that he had a man in the family named "Turk".

Our guest did not know this and smiled incredulously — is it not a fantasy? But he soon visited us again and told us that during the war his uncle had found his wife in the house of one of the neighbors and had stabbed her to death out of jealousy. From then on, he was called "the Turk".

In 1944, a peasant from the village of Kromidovo in the Sandan district learned that his son had been killed by the Germans near Novy Selo in Macedonia. When it became possible, the peasant went there in the hope of digging up the corpse and reburying it at home. Seven graves were opened, and the peasant did not identify his son. The wretch turned to Vanga. She said the grave they were looking for was on the bank of the river, near a big bush. When it was unearthed, documents and a photo fell out of the pocket of the dead man's jacket — it shows the son of a peasant from the village of Kromidovo.

The young man D. G. in the barber shop made a strong infection: a terrible eczema appeared on his face, boils poured out, he suffered greatly. The drugs didn't help. The unfortunate man came to Vanga. She did not listen to the story of the dirty barber shop, but immediately ordered to take some river mud and mix it in the same proportion with ordinary salt, put a compress of this mixture on her face at night. The patient did so, and a day later the sores began to dry up, and soon everything passed without a trace. Another patient, doctors could not make a diagnosis. Vanga said that he had visible adhesions in the diaphragm and advised him to go for treatment "on the water", in Germany, adding that he would return healthy. And so it turned out.

An officer who was going to the front, she warned: do not rush into the attack on horseback. The latter, in the heat of the first battle, forgot his advice, his horse was killed outright by a shrapnel, and the officer himself, severely wounded, miraculously survived.

In 1979, the famous Soviet artist Vyacheslav Tikhonov came to her. Vanga told her sister: "Let him wait outside for a while, I need to get a signal that I can already receive him." It was at this moment that Tikhonov crossed the threshold. Vanga got angry and asked in a dissatisfied tone: "Why didn't you fulfill the wish of your best friend Yuri Gagarin?" Tikhonov was silent in perplexity, and Vanga continued: "When Gagarin went on his last test flight, he came to say goodbye and said, smiling cheerfully: "I wanted to give you a gift, but there is no time for shopping, buy yourself an alarm clock, put it on the table — this will be a memory of me."

The artist, hearing what was said, almost lost consciousness, he was drunk with valerian. When he came to himself, he confirmed that everything was true: he forgot to buy an alarm clock because of the turmoil after the death of Gagarin.

Vanga then added: "Gagarin did not die, he was taken!" How, why, where exactly-does not say.

To the writer Julian Semyonov, Vanga said: "You have to work hard and supplement the film with a few more episodes (we were talking about the acclaimed film" Seventeen Moments of Spring " (a film about a Soviet intelligence officer during World War II). But take your time, you're still "barefoot" for the next series. First, go to Spain, where you will find a certain Vladimir, who will tell you a lot of interesting things. And your plan-to end the book with the death of the heroine — is implausible. In such a life, it should be different: leave the heroine's life, and the book will be true."

Vanga described in detail the entire situation of his house to a well-known engineer, then stopped at the marital status of this engineer, and a little later she noticed with a smile: "You have a lot of junk in your attic, some of it is stored in chests, and your dead grandfather's typewriter is also stored there." The astonished engineer actually remembered that his grandfather had an old typewriter, but where the typewriter was removed after his grandfather's death, the engineer did not know. Knew, it turns out, Vanga. To that engineer, she also suggested a significant error in the calculations, due to which the final result was incorrect. The engineer fixed the error, and was very pleased with the advice.

Many years ago, a famous painter came to Vanga. They talked for a long time. The artist, saying goodbye, gave Vanga his canvas " Christ with his disciples in the middle of a large field." The painting is still the only decoration of Vanga's house. She then said to the artist: "You have worked hard, but you are poor and have nothing. Try to keep your high spirit, vitality, faith in your vocation. Great difficulties await you. You will have a very big defeat in your life, and then you will go on the road all alone."

After a while, Vanga received uninvited guests, as it turned out, the parents of a young woman who married this artist against the will of her father and mother. Vanga, a stern and implacable judge, pronounced her sentence: "Yes, your daughter married an artist whom you hate without knowing why. He may be poor, but he is honest. You will not bring your daughter back, because she and her husband were united by love." And yet the parents, with all their strength, destroyed the family. So what? Two children were orphaned. Their father, broken and lonely, left both his home and his homeland. And the parents of this woman did not long celebrate their "victory" over the hated artist.

Their daughter was soon involved in a car accident and died. So, alas, Vanga's prediction came true.

There are many such stories. Their strength is that they are absolutely true.

So, one woman, a resident of Montreal, traveled around the world in the hope of finding a wise healer who would help her overcome an acute mental crisis. The criminals killed her husband and kidnapped her only child. The killer was caught, but the child disappeared. However, some time later, the police informed the heartbroken mother that her child was found at the bottom of the lake. And then, in desperation, this woman went around the world to look for a healer and found herself on the threshold of Vanga's little house. That was in the summer of 1987.

"Indeed, you have suffered great grief," Vanga told her, " but tell me without reserve — you did not give birth to the child, did you?"

"No," said the woman, " my husband and I adopted the boy from the orphanage.

— Then listen, - continued Vanga, - the boy is alive, he was taken away from Australia, now he lives in a big city, goes to school. His new "parents" do everything to make the boy forget you, your home, homeland. Soon you will receive news of your son, and in April next year — detailed information about him. You will have many more trials, at the end of which you will meet.

The further continuation of this sad story is as follows: the murderers of the woman's husband were tried, one of them confessed that the child had really been kidnapped, that he was alive and was in a rich and noble family. It remains to wait for the denouement — the future meeting of mother and son.

Vanga predicted to a poor and sick art teacher from Petrich that in his old age he would be rich and widely known. A few years later, the teacher won in sportloto (this is plaing lotery) first 20 thousand leva, then another 10 thousand. He was able to seriously do what he loved-painting, achieved some success. The public became interested in his paintings, and there were also buyers.

"You just don't see," Vanga says, " a tall, beautiful woman in blue — and — white clothes standing next to me. The one who has come to me already by his presence evokes in my mind various pictures from his life, and the one who is always next to me, tells me the right words, I hear them and pass them on to all of you.

Does Vanga read minds? Yes, she often tells her visitors what they thought just now, or an hour ago, or even earlier. Reads minds and at a distance. The thoughts of foreigners, whose language Vanga, of course, does not know, reads with the same ease as the thoughts of a Bulgarian. There is no language barrier. She hears a voice speaking in Bulgarian, no matter who is next to a Chinese or an Englishman.

She tells me, and I hurry to write down what I heard in a thick notebook.

— Recently I was visited by a Romanian whose son drowned in the Danube. The unfortunate man was sure that his son was pushed into the water by an evil boy, and this thought did not give rest. And I looked at how it all happened, and I told him. His son could not swim, got entangled in the river seaweed, got scared, began to flounder and drowned. No one is to blame for the misfortune. I could see the place where the accident had happened, and I could describe it in detail.

Among the questions that Vanga is asked by a variety of her guests, many are often repeated. So, for example, people who come from different countries often ask her: if she foresees something fatal in the fate of a person, then perhaps she can prevent a tragic outcome. "No," Vanga always answers, " it's not in my power. No one will overcome fate. A person's life is strictly predetermined."

Once a young man came to Vanga, they talked quietly and peacefully and were already saying goodbye, when Vanga, as if remembering something important, said: "I'm waiting for you on May 15. Don't let anything stop you from visiting me on May 15. However, you can't."

And it so happened that on May 15, this young man was invited by his friend to help with the construction of the house.

It was awkward to refuse, he decided to go to Vanga on May 17. And it turned out that on the fateful day, the 15th, he was hit by a train, the driver could not brake, the brakes failed. Vanga tensely waited at home for the visit of this guy, saw everything that happened in her mind's eye, tried to help somehow, but could not.

In my notes, I refer not only to the stories of Vanga, but also to my mother Lubka. Here's a funny story my mother once told me.

— My father-in-law, a teacher, a self-taught artist and a home-grown violinist, decided to "create" (as he put it) a portrait of Vanga, who agreed to pose for him. During the long sessions, she sat in silence and only once or twice repeated to my father-in-law: "Uncle Boris, whatever happens, do not sell the extension to the house and your violin."

My father-in-law was very puzzled by this advice, since he was just thinking of selling the violin and devoting his entire free time to painting. And here's what happened 10 years later. Our house in Sandanski was as old as the world, a ramshackle structure that collapsed one day. My father-in-law was sitting in the middle of the room at this sad moment, playing his violin thoughtfully. He miraculously survived, escaped with only a slight fright. In this sudden collapse, the outbuilding was not damaged, and we moved into it while we were building a new home.

Among the visitors to Vanga was one Bulgarian A. X., who had long ago emigrated to Austria. He lived there quite well, found a rich bride, married and became rich himself. He said all this in silence to Vanga, who was listening to him, and then added:"Everything is fine with me, but I miss my homeland, I'm completely exhausted." And he came to Bulgaria for the annual autumn harvest festival. Vanga told him that, according to legend, at the beginning of this holiday, a sacrificial lamb should be slaughtered and a ceremonial dish — kurban should be prepared. "The lamb," Vanga instructed her guest, " must be bought and slaughtered by you, otherwise misfortune will happen."

I do not know how it all turned out, but the "Austrian" Bulgarian did not buy lamb, did not prepare an ancient dish. The holiday seemed to be a success without the ancient rites, but the guest from Austria suddenly died and was buried in Bulgaria, forever united with the land of his homeland, for which he so longed.

Vanga once said in the circle of her family: "I am present in all the hot spots of the planet, I see military clashes, I witness terrible bloodshed, I foresee natural disasters and disasters. You sleep at night, and I turn over the pages of human existence and experience the tragedies of many, many people."

I listen to my mother's story and transfer it to paper:

— Many years ago, namely on November 1, 1950, several women neighbors decided to go together to the Rila Monastery. My mother-in-law was with them, and Vanga also went, she really wanted to defend the solemn service in the church on the occasion of St. Ivan's Day. The service was very beautiful and very long. Closer to its end, Vanga began to worry about something very much: she turned her head, listened intently to something. A little later, she began to persuade the pilgrims who were closer to her to go somewhere immediately, but not to stay here. But who will go without listening to the end of the solemn prayer service, who will suddenly leave the holy place in such a hurry? In short, Vanga got on the bus alone, and returned home alone.

And over the valley of the river Rila, reflected in the glittering domes of the church, a black storm cloud slowly swelled up. It filled the whole sky, thunder rumbled, lightning struck an old mossy tree, and it began. It's the end of the world! Streams of water, waterfalls fell from the heavens to the earth. Rila overflowed with water, it rolled stones, dragged whole trees with roots, flooded roads, many villages, demolished houses. My relatives were so frightened that they did not have time to put their belongings away from harm, and they were carried away by the current, as the cow licked her tongue.

My mother-in-law somehow got home, wet and cold, very frightened by everything she saw. After this story, she fell ill and was ill for a long time.

...Like a long ribbon, human life is before Vanga's mind's eye, all before her — from the day of birth to death. Of course, she herself does not know why it happens that a complete stranger comes to her and, as it were, hands her a certain scroll, on which she alone can see the writing, whether it is a long or short story about his fate. Moreover, it does not depend on the will of Vanga herself, nor on the will of her guest: whether to hand this ribbon, this scroll or not to hand it to the soothsayer. Formula (if we can talk about the formula here) This is: I came and brought my biography. And to the point. So, can it be true that from the very first day a person's life is strictly predetermined, his fate is" programmed"? But by whom? And why does the mysterious "programmer" so generously, easily reveal his super-secret secrets to a blind woman, a blind clairvoyant? (What a strange and surprising combination: blind — clairvoyant).

They bring a young girl to Vanga once, who feels very badly: she can't open her eyes, poor thing, her eyelids seem to close of their own accord. Vanga, without asking anything, passes his sentence: immediately go to Sofia, look for the best doctors, although nothing can be done, the girl will soon die.

The sobbing parents leave with their unhappy daughter, and Vanga sits with her hands on the ground. And I think: what a misfortune, what a bitter fate, to know the near fatal outcome and not be able to help. I know there are those who envy Vanga, they say, she has world fame, everywhere and everywhere they know Vanga ... Oh, the burden of this fame is heavy, sometimes unbearably heavy. Here she is sitting in front of me, her hands hanging helplessly to the ground, and heavily silent, her vital forces have left her-my poor Aunt Vanga…

I write down my mother's story, I don't remember whether she said it or not, just in case I remind you: my mother is completely incapable of fantasizing, exaggerating, she reminds me a little of a gramophone: the same melody is always on the same record. So, she says:

— I remember very well the visit of a very important Sofian to Vanga. The metropolitan guest did not come alone, with him two women. He carried himself with great dignity, spoke as if he were giving orders, his shoes shone blackly, and his cheeks were clean-shaven. I don't know why, but I wanted to ask him how old he was. He was so self-confident that you couldn't tell if he was young or old. Although it was very awkward, I asked: "Excuse me, how old can you be?" And suddenly this important gentleman laughed merrily and answered: "I am a very old stump, as an officer I participated in the First World War. By some miracle, I came back from hell alive, and since then, I have been diligently, with all my might, taking care of myself, only of myself. I will continue to do the same. This is the secret of my eternal youth." Vanga was present at our conversation and was silent, but at the last words of the officer, she stamped her foot and said with annoyance: "Uh, that's enough for you, up to here, and that's enough!» We did not understand Vanga's words, and soon the Sofian left, taking his ladies with him. Three days later, one of them reported that their master had died suddenly.

"That's enough for now," Vanga said, she said so, but who told her? Who!

In my notes there is a curious testimony of our other relatives. My sister Anna, a doctor by profession, recalls:

— From an early age, I lived in the" field of attraction " of Vanga, not only me, of course, all our relatives and friends. I remember well that the doctors flatly refused to recognize Vanga's extraordinary gift. There was a lot of talk about my poor aunt: that she was a charlatan, and a clever speculator, who had a whole staff of spies who collected preliminary data about her "clientele", and she herself could only assume a mysterious air of divination, and also that she was a fortune-teller, that she was engaged in black magic and God knows what else. When I was a kid, the neighborhood kids used to tease me that I was a fortune teller's niece.

But Vanga ignored all these nonsense, and there was nothing to reproach us and the most picky people: they lived poorly, did not have festive clothes. Vanga never took "fees" from anyone, so they probably talked about her out of simple human envy. So, unfortunately, it often happens, and yesterday was, and tomorrow will be.

Years passed, and strangers came almost every day to my aunt. She didn't say no to anyone. And then came the day when the official medicine in the person of Dr. Georgi Lozanov came to our modest home. A sweet and sensitive, very attentive person, Georgi Lozanov became almost a native person for us. He collected and accumulated facts. He and his closest collaborators put the research on a scientific basis, looking for (and not finding) scientific definitions of the"Vanga phenomenon". Then there was this, now widely known definition — "the phenomenon of Vanga".

I myself, as a doctor, was quite skeptical about everything I saw. Classical medicine taught us that it is quite possible to know a person, to reveal all the secrets of his psyche. It was not even theoretically possible that something unknowable could remain in the depths of the human psyche. And here I am, very proud of my profession as a doctor," dark "Vanga easily knocked off the "solid materialistic position". Knowing that she doesn't know anything about medicine, I'll never understand how she makes an unmistakable diagnosis. Okay, diagnosis. And how did she foresee fate? After all, her predictions come true with literally fatal accuracy.

And I came to the following conclusion: it is impossible for us, educated and intelligent, to be conceited, to be very proud of the knowledge we have received. We do not even know what "knowledge" is, nor are we able to determine the scale of "knowledge" in relation to "ignorance". "I know that I know nothing" - what a profound aphorism!

We Bulgarians should be glad that in our small, modest country there lived an amazing woman-Vanga. God has been very generous to us. Of course, Vanga's phenomenal abilities are being studied and will continue to attract the attention of scientists of various professions for a very long time. Who knows, maybe the most talented, the most attentive of them will open a window into the mysterious blind world of our clairvoyant Vanga.

So says Anna, a doctor and a close person.

Well, for those who have already flipped through these pages, I think it will be interesting to get to know Vanga better. I have heard many times and I am convinced that the biography of an extraordinary person is more interesting than the most exciting novel. However, it is not for me to judge. I repeat, my task is very modest: to transfer to paper only what I know quite reliably.

"I DON'T LIVE FOR MYSELF — FOR PEOPLE"

Vanga's house in Petrich attracts many visitors. What brings them here, what draws them from far away, from neighboring places? One wants a wise woman to help him unravel the tight knot of family troubles, another is looking for a cure for an incurable disease, the third is driven by ordinary human curiosity to see Vanga with his own eyes, to personally make sure that everything he has heard is not an invention of idle minds. As if you can just look at a person once and decide if they have a wonderful gift or not. But the road to Petrich is not reserved for people, and they go to Vanga's house, if anyone counted, they could easily count up to a hundred people a day...

Petrichans have long been accustomed to the fact that Vanga's house is always crowded with people, there is always a diverse queue, and they do not pay any attention to visitors. I think that few of our citizens think about what an amazing person their old neighbor, who has lived here since 1942, is. And to Vanga used petricone, and to visitors, and nothing special even in this very habit. One famous writer, I think, F. M. Dostoevsky, said that man is a being who gets used to everything. So, if we ask the townspeople who their famous Vanga is-a sorceress, clairvoyant or, for example, a healer, we will hear a simple and clear answer: a neighbor, a fellow countryman. That's all. But is that all?

Vanga was born on January 31, 1911 in the Yugoslav city of Strumica, in the family of a small landowner. From her father, who was physically strong and hard-worked in a meager field, she inherited a great endurance in physical labor, and in addition, a crystal honesty, a love of justice and an aversion to deceit and deceit. From her mother, too, she inherited a good legacy — she adopted from her a cheerful disposition, a love of cleanliness in feelings and cleanliness of the house, this special cleanliness is the only cult of Vanga.

The girl was born prematurely, seven months old, was very weak, ears pressed to her head, fingers on her hands and feet fused. No one could tell if she would survive. The baby lay wrapped in a swaddling cloth and a warm sheepskin, squeaking faintly. And since it was the custom in the Strumitz region not to give a name to a child if there was little hope that he would live (child mortality was very high), the girl remained nameless for some time. Also interesting is the folk custom of that time-the choice of the child's name. My grandmother used to go out and ask the first woman she met for a name. So did the grandmother of this tiny girl. She went outside and heard from a passing woman: "You ask what to call the girl? Call her Andromache."

In those years, many people in Strumica and the surrounding villages had Greek names, but my grandmother did not like this sonorous name, she remained standing at the door of the house and soon saw another woman. "What should I call the baby? "What is it?" she asked. — There is no name more euphonious than Vangelia - "bearer of the good news". A wonderful Greek name, let it be your granddaughter Vangelia."

The grandmother, and after her all the others, took this name, and it remained for the newborn: Vangelia, Vanga... Did her parents know who was lying wrapped in a warm lamb fleece? Unlikely.

Pande Surchev, Vanga's father, saw his vocation, the meaning of his whole life in the work of a farmer. Yes, here's the trouble: - it is rare for a peasant to have a simple happiness — to grow bread peacefully. A peasant is in the field today, and tomorrow on the battlefield, as has been the custom for centuries. Pande went to the partisan detachment, many of them then fought for the freedom of their land from Turkish enslavement. The partisans were called Chetniks, and the Turks hated and feared them. Panda was unlucky on the battlefield, in one of the battles he was captured and was sent to life imprisonment in the prison "Iedi Kule".

The prisoners had no hope of salvation, and it was only as a result of the Young Turkish Revolution of 1908, when a constitutional monarchy was proclaimed, that he, like many of his friends in misfortune, saw the light of freedom. Pande Surchev returned home.

Only I didn't find anyone alive at home. His parents died while he was fighting and sitting in a dark cell "Iedi Kule", his brother left his native places unknown where… What was there to do? And then he heard that the city community in Strumica was distributing houses and land plots abandoned by the Turks. I decided to look for shares in Strumica.

They gave him a room in an old house on the edge of town. Everything here was kept somehow: both houses and yards; and the unkempt land gave birth badly. However, the sweet air of freedom intoxicated all the inhabitants of this backwater: though hungry, but fun. Peasants, small artisans, merchants of small and medium income-all of them are used to get up early at dawn, work excitedly, live together. When the brass bell on the belfry of the Church of the Fifteen Holy Martyrs began to ring, Serbs, Bulgarians, Gypsies, and even the numerous family of the Turk Gul Bab, who did not want to leave his home and go to Turkey, automatically baptized their foreheads. They joked that he didn't leave because the roses weren't allowed in. Indeed, in Gul-bab's garden, roses bloomed from spring to autumn, spreading a wonderful fragrance throughout the surrounding area.

The new landlord began to live with their neighbors in peace and harmony. He was of a good disposition, and such people are loved everywhere. For some time he lived in bobyl, but soon he met a sweet, thin, like a reed, a girl, agile and cheerful: her name was Paraskeva.

They liked each other, made out for a while like a bride and groom, and then they began to call the guests: an honest feast and for the wedding. The young people were happy. In 1911, as I have already said, Vangelia was born.

Parents left a weak child, the girl began to gain strength, but grief happened — three years later, during the second birth, Paraskeva died. Swirled Panda, longed, nowhere to find a place, and then the war came.

The First World War knocked on the windows of peaceful homes. They also mobilized Pande and took him to serve in the Bulgarian army. The girl was taken to her family by a neighbor, a very kind and fair Turkish woman named Asanitsa. As one day passed three heavy thunderous years of war, from Vangelia's father there was not a single word. The neighbors thought that the girl was an orphan, but one day her father came home, incredibly thin, skin and bones, but unharmed. The girl was crying with joy.

Father and daughter began to live in the same old room, and hard times began. Vanga was already 7 years old. Thin, blue-eyed, brown-haired, very quick, the girl did not resemble the pathetic starvation, as she appeared in the light of God. The father quickly realized that the child lacks both parental affection and parental strictness. We should get married, but who needs a widower, without a good home, with a small child in his arms?

By the end of the war in Strumica, power passed to the Serbian mayor. Many Bulgarian soldiers and officers who returned home from the terrible war were forced to leave their native land. And Pande wanted to leave, because the townspeople were now forced to speak and write in Serbian. Only where will you go with the child? Panda remained, to the delight of the neighborhood children, and Vanga remained — the most cheerful and sociable girl in the yard.

Vanga loved that every object in the house had its own, and only its own safe place. And the most unexpected. One day, my father decided to go fishing and asked a neighbor to wait just a second while he took the rods. Seconds were not enough, he looked for them all over the house, disappeared-like a carp in the water pulled. Vanga watched with pleasure all this fuss and only then said that " the fishing rods caught on the hat." My father looked up: the fishing rods were lying comfortably on nails driven into the wall, near the ceiling. In the same way, the next time he searched for bast shoes for a long time, many times in his unsuccessful search he walked around the overturned old, forgotten cauldron, not realizing that the bast shoes were lying there.

Considering that one can not cope with the child and the household, Pande decided to marry a second time. He still had little hope of success, as he was poor, widowed, and with a child, but to his own delight he quickly found a mistress.

At that time of troubles, the Serbian authorities often issued ridiculous orders. One of them, quite medieval in nature, read: all women who are in any way connected with Bulgarian officers or soldiers, together with their families, must immediately leave Strumica. One of the most beautiful girls in the city, the bride of a Bulgarian officer, her name was Tanka, was just preparing for the wedding. And here's a ridiculous and absurd order for you! In order not to be shamed and evicted from Strumica, Tanka's parents quickly and secretly married her to a Panda. The poor girl felt deeply unhappy, although she met a good and hard-working man in the person of her husband. In the people say, it will be tolerated — it will be loved. So it turned out this time: Pande loved his wife, and she became a caring hostess and a kind mother for the girl.

The days of prosperity and mutual understanding began to flow. Pande was a good farmer and a strong owner, little by little his land allotment increased and soon reached 10 hectares. Pande even hired laborers in the spring and autumn to sow and harvest the crops in time, and people began to respectfully address him as "chorbaji Pande" (Lord Pande).

But, alas, the prosperity was temporary. A storm broke out again over the Strumice region. The Serbian leadership has set itself another ridiculous goal — to turn as many local residents as possible into Serbs. There was a very "diligent" leader for this wild action, a certain Popchevsky, who struck literally everyone with his cruelty: a human life was no more precious to him than a copper penny.

The Serbian authorities gave him the "right" to dispose of people's lives at his discretion. And he decided first of all to free himself from those who sympathized with the Bulgarians, and, of course, from those who were Bulgarian by nationality. One of the first victims of the Serbian lackey was Vanga's father and his family. Pande was arrested, all the land was taken from them. And just now it was time for the harvest, when the people were taking the grain from the fields. The harvest was gone, the family impoverished-from that terrible year and for a long time.

When father returned from prison, severely beaten and maimed, his wife was suffering from childbirth, and a kind grandmother-midwife was busy with her. Tanka gave birth to a boy named Basil. The year of his birth is 1922. Father went to the shepherds in the neighbouring village Bosilovo and Dabila. A shepherd, a farmhand, and the last poor man, he remained so for the rest of his life.

All day he was lost in the pasture, and at home his wife was busy with two children — Vanga and Vasil, and, I must say, Vanga quickly helped her new mother with the housework. She was already 11 years old. Vanga nursed her brother, came up with such games that she could play herself.

And one day she came up with a new game that bothered her parents a little. In the yard, on the street, near the house in a secluded corner, she hid some object, most often a simple toy, then returned home, closed her eyes tightly, and began, like a blind woman, to grope for what was hidden. Persistently, again and again, she played "blind", and no threats and prohibitions of her father and stepmother could stop her.

In 1923, the family moved to Novo Selo, to his brother Panda-Kostadin. He became rich, married profitably, but did not have happiness: he had no children. When Kostadin realized how difficult the situation of his brother's family was, he decided to call him to his house so that the two of them could look after the cattle and so that his relatives would not starve in Strumice. Father and wife agreed.

A new life began. As the oldest, 12-year-old Vanga had a serious duty: every day to drive a donkey to the paddock behind the village, and from there to carry two cans of milk home on it.

One summer afternoon, she was returning to the village with her two cousins. The girls decided to go get drunk from the spring "Khan Cheshma". It was only a two — hundred-meter walk. How all this happened, no one understood. Suddenly there was a hurricane. The sky darkened, and a terrible wind arose, which broke the thick branches of the trees and carried them along with the dust over the ground. The girls were speechless with horror, the wind knocked them to the ground, and Vanga, like a blade of grass, was carried into an open field. How long this hurricane lasted, no one knows. But when the wind died down, the girls ran home crying without Vanga. Only an hour later it was barely found in a field, littered with branches, covered with sand. She was almost frantic with fear, and with a terrible pain that pricked her dust-covered eyes like needles, and she couldn't open them.

At home, they began to treat her, washed her eyes with clean water, but nothing helped. They turned to healers, to those who could spell diseases, made her compresses, gave her mineral and" holy " water, smeared with balms, but even this did not bring relief. The poor girl's eyes were filled with blood, and her eyelids were swollen. Desperate to help his daughter here in the village, the father decided to return to Strumica and look for a good doctor there. In fact, they stayed in this village very little, about three months, and it seemed that they came there only to make Vanga's eyes hurt. A terrible thought haunted Vanga's father.

The news of the poor girl quickly spread in the city, neighbors came to them, again offered decoctions of herbs, ointments, told stories about the miraculous effect of these herbs, but, of course, no one knew an effective remedy for such a disease.

Finally, a professional eye doctor was found. He examined Wang and said that the situation is very serious, as the inflammation is progressing, an urgent operation is needed to save his vision. This required a lot of money, you had to go to Belgrade. The family did everything to collect the necessary amount — about 500 leva for the current money. Sold literally all things, although what could be sold in a poor family? An old sewing machine left over from his first wife, the only sheep they had, and some of their meager belongings. Pande borrowed a little more money — as a result, he scraped together barely half of the required amount. And the time of the operation was approaching..

The day before the operation, Vanga was sent to Belgrade with one of the neighbors, who was richer and was going to visit his son. Despite the fact that Panda really wanted to be at this difficult moment next to his daughter, he decided not to go, so as not to spend money on the road, money was already not enough.

When a neighbor brought Wang to the hospital, it looked as if a rich relative had brought his poor relative and wanted to get rid of her as soon as possible. That was the impression Dr. Savich had when he was scheduled for surgery the next day. When he saw how much money the attendant was giving him, he was terribly angry at his stinginess, and sternly and peremptorily declared: "When you bring me the right amount, I will perform the operation!". Still, I fixed the girl's eyes a little.

After returning from Belgrade, Vanga, though weakly, but saw. The doctor warned her that to recover, she needed plenty of food, cleanliness and complete peace of mind. Of course, these tips remained only a good wish, because the life of the family flowed along the old channel — in need and poverty. In 1924, another child was born-a boy, who was named Tom, and the poor Pande again went to work in the villages to somehow feed his family of 5 people. His wife worked in the fields as best she could, while Vanga looked after her two brothers and kept house.

Poor food, poor living conditions, and most of all-unfair treatment affected: vision worsened. The curtain fell again, there was no question of another operation, and after a while she was completely blind. Already forever…

Despair gripped the girl. All night long Vanga cried and prayed to God that a miracle would happen and she would see, but the miracle did not happen. Many months passed, and she still could not come to terms with the fact that she had become a burden to the family and that she had become completely helpless, she did not know how to find a way out of this situation.

Neighbors advised her father to go to the city of Zemun, where there was a House for the Blind, and leave Vanga there. They said that the girl would not starve, that they were taking care of the poor children there. My father agreed.

In 1926, the family received news from the Home of the Blind that Wang was being accepted. She is already 15 years old. When she realized that she was leaving, that she would have to part with her brothers, her father, her stepmother, whom she had managed to sincerely love, with her native home, her heart almost broke with grief, the girl did not stop crying.

Came the day of farewell to the family home. Thin and weak, strangely quiet, she "watched" the coming spring morning, or rather, listened to the coming day. Now she could only hear the world. Sighted people can't even guess how many sounds surround them. Here is a light breeze squeezing through the bindweed fence and then gently stroking the geraniums and leucoi, running through the young grass as if on cat's paws, swinging On the highest branch of the plum tree. And the gentle, gentle sun, it creeps over her face, warms her cheeks, blind eyes… This picture is imprinted in the mind of Vanga for life.

In the House of the Blind in the city of Zemun, everything was new: although scary, but interesting.

The children were immediately dressed in strict student uniforms — brown pleated skirts and blouses with sailor collars. They wore comfortable shoes. For the first time in her life, Vanga had her brown hair cut. She was embarrassed and, to her surprise, happy. For a long time she furtively felt and stroked the new clothes and felt like a queen, because she had never dressed so wonderfully.

The regime in the House was strict. Before lunch, the students were engaged in serious business: they studied Louis Braille for the blind, passed all school disciplines, studied music. The new student had an unusually developed ear for music and quickly learned to play the piano. If the keys are not only made sounds, and was telling her about the house on strumicki green fields, blue sky above the New Village, the courtyard colored flowers, on the cheerful murmur of the streams of the river TracIni, about childhood, about family, about the clear sunshine and high stars. What a pity that the music lesson could not last all day!

After that, practical classes began. They, blind children, were taught to put their things in their places by touch, to set the table for dinner, to clean up the room. It is clear that this was not too difficult work for those who see, and blind girls had to learn to " see " with their hands — to develop extraordinary sensitivity and flexibility of the fingers. Vanga learned everything easily, and there was no teacher who was dissatisfied with her.

Three years passed unnoticed. Vanga had gone from a skinny, starved teenager to a slim, fit girl, her thin face radiating deep calm and contentment. And after some time, this beautiful face also lit up with some inner joy. Here, among the pupils of the House, there was one young man, his name was Dimitar, he was from the village of Giaoto in the Geveliysky district. Vanga, as soon as she heard his voice, immediately flushed with joy, her heart fluttered anxiously and joyfully in her chest. The young man also recognized her voice, and they were both incredibly happy when they were together. On one of the happiest days of Vanga's life, Dimitar confessed his love for her and proposed. His parents were rich and didn't mind helping them both.

For days Vanga tried to imagine what she would look like as a bride-in a long white dress with a veil as soft as the breath of an angel. She was so happy. The administration sent word to her father about Vangelia and Dimitar's decision to marry, and everyone waited for his blessing.

A LIFE WORTHY OF ADMIRATION

"Above all things have fervent love for one another, because love covers a multitude of sins'.

The Apostle Peter

Ah, that terrible year of 1928! Instead of the expected father's blessing for the marriage, Vanga received news from Strumice that struck her to death. The father wrote that the daughter should immediately return home to look after the children. Two years ago, Tanga gave birth to her third child, a girl, and two years later, after the birth of her fourth child, she died.

That's how Vanga said goodbye to her first love, to school, to the upcoming wedding and to a more or less happy life. The journey back home was hard and painful, and she knew very well that the three years spent in the House of the Blind in the city of Zemun would remain the best years of her life and would never happen again.

Since then, the life of a blind girl has been marked by endless poverty, many torments that not everyone who sees can bear. And the strange thing is: the young girl did not break down — her spiritual strength grew stronger, they helped her to resist all the tests.

At home, Vanga found terrible poverty. The children, small and small, were dirty, sick from constant malnutrition. Her brother Vasil was 6 years old. Toma is 4 years old, and the youngest, Lubka, is 2 years old. And blind Vanga was to be everything to them-mother, mistress of the house, and protector. As soon as Vanga returned, my father again went to the villages to look for work as a farmhand or shepherd.

It is known that life experiences a break in the first place the poor. The Chirpan earthquake of 1929 also made itself felt in the Strumice region. From a strong push, the squalid dwellings of the poor collapsed, the house where the Vanga family lived also collapsed. From the pile of remains, my father collected a hut, smeared it with clay, and we were to live in this hut. Inside, there was only one small room and a tiny hallway. Then they added a small kitchen, too, where they fenced off the hearth so that they could bake bread when the family had flour.

They moved in quickly, as there was almost nothing to move to the new home. Vanga, with her commitment to cleanliness and order, tried to create comfort here as well. In a prominent place in the room, they put a colored chest left over from her stepmother, covered the earthen floor with matting, and in the corner they put a bed, for which Vanga knitted a blanket from old threads - "for beauty", there was nothing else inside. A small courtyard was fenced off near the house and beautiful flowers were planted.

In this little house Vanga and Lubka lived together for many years, the brothers, although they were still small, went to the villages and worked as farmhands or shepherds to get at least some food for the family.

In the city and surrounding villages quickly learned that a blind girl can quickly and well knit, and began to bring her whole bales of yarn for knitting. Instead of money, they gave small things or old yarn. From rags, yarn, colored threads, Vanga sewed clothes for children, for herself she did not sew anything, because she almost did not leave the house. Everyone knew about their poverty, and if a woman died in the neighborhood, her clothes were given to Vanga.

And she learned to weave, taught Lubka to tie up the broken threads, and her little sister became her assistant: the two of them listened late into the night to the noise of the loom, how the metal needles moved incessantly, how the crows tapped. And at night, Vanga gave vent to her grief and fell asleep in tears.

I got up very early in the morning, because there was always enough to do in the family. Vanga generally did not like to sit without work and did not allow anyone to do nothing. I wanted everything to be clean and tidy. So, for example, on Monday he and Lubka washed clothes, on Tuesday they swept around the house, on Wednesday they repaired clothes. Lubka, although still very young, sewed. Vanga taught her to do other chores and was very demanding towards her younger sister. After feeling a new patch on an old dress and feeling that one of the seams had failed, she would tear it open and make Lubka sew it again. Often Lubka cried, because there were a lot of old things, it took all day to fuss with them, and she could not go out to play with the children. Vanga remained adamant: everything should be as it should be, know work. On Thursday they kneaded bread, on Friday they went out of town to dig up red clay, which they smeared all over the house inside and out, so that it became more beautiful. On Saturday, we went to collect nettles and sorrel for soup for lunch. On Sunday morning-church, and after lunch, women came from the surrounding villages to pick up their things, often gathered in their yard and neighbors, talk, share news. Vanga was very sociable, had a keen sense of humor, and women liked to talk to her.

In Strumica edge existed a curious custom. On the evening before St. George's Day (May 6), the girls lowered a special mark into a clay wine vessel-it was called delva-and the next day they "recognized" their happiness by it. The neighborhood girls used to put delva in Vanga's yard, under a big old bush of dark red roses. Quite often, perhaps out of compassion for the blind, Wang was chosen as the "oracle". The next morning, May 7, she took out the marks and told the girls their fate. These stories often turned out to be prophetic, but no one even thought that Vanga had the gift of foresight.

There was another holiday - the Day of the Forty Great Martyrs, when the girls were guessing: they put branches across the stream-made a " bridge "and believed that at night they would see in a dream the future chosen one who would go over the" bridge " from the other bank. In the morning, the girls hurried to Vanga, and she ... told them their own dreams, each girl her dream, her secret. It all seemed very strange, but no one even tried to find an explanation for the miracles.

However, a festive, cheerful mood did not often visit Vanga's house, and she rarely allowed herself to relax, because poverty was always chasing the family on the heels, and she had to work all day long. Often, very often, they went hungry. Usually their food was wild cabbage, cornbread, or highly diluted sour milk, but often this was not the case. They rarely had money, and Vanga tried to hide it for the darkest day. One day the house ran out of flour. My father went to a well-to-do farmer, a friend of his, and asked for some flour to borrow. He said that he had a bag of flour, which is prepared for sale, there is money-buy it. My father took the bag and went home — Vanga found the money, the next day the debt was returned. Real wheat flour — what a joy it is! Vanga immediately kneaded the bread, and, not yet cold, it was broken and eaten in large chunks. And after about half an hour, both sisters became ill, they began to feel sick, dizzy. My father looked at the flour and realized that it was half made up of ground weeds. So the holiday of "delicious bread" almost ended in great grief for the family. And that peasant, he says, has no shame, no conscience, I don't know anything about it.

If the children asked their father to buy them something, he promised: "As soon as I sell the cherries, I will buy them!"

One spring they planted a bed of tobacco. When the leaves grew, they were cut, dried and ruffled from morning to evening. The finished raw materials were handed over to the Tobacco Monopoly, and they were paid so little that they barely had enough money to buy pottery, the old one fell into complete disrepair.

In 1934, Lubka became a student. She studied well. Vanga was glad of her zeal, because, although to a small extent, she had touched science in the House of the Blind and knew what happiness it was — real study. She was always strict with the children, and they obeyed her and obeyed her in everything, but with school ... the brothers stubbornly refused to go to school. The eldest, Vasil, told her that even if he had time, he didn't want to go to school.

An Esperantist club was established in Strumice, where almost all children from poor families gathered. Both Vasil and Thome signed up, began to visit him regularly, and allegedly studied Esperanto. They often made their little sister Lubka carry some books around the city, pass them to different people. After a while, it became clear that the club illegally studied Marxism. Two sons of the former guerrilla Pande quite naturally found their way to a real school, where they learned the truth of life. It was their father's ideals, his beliefs, and life itself that set them on the right path.

And Vanga was still the boss of the house and did not allow herself to relax in front of the children or, God forbid, complain to anyone. She became a support not only for the children, but also for the father, who was bent in Krivoy Rog by worries about daily bread, so much so that he sometimes came to complete despair. Vanga instilled confidence in him, constantly repeating that better days will come, they will certainly come, soon…

For a long time, unable to make ends meet, my father dreamed of becoming (come to think of it!) a treasure hunter and one day find a lot of money. One day Vanga told him that she knew a place where many old coins were buried, and described the place to him. It was located not far from Strumitsa: an abandoned village on the bank of a small river, a sparse forest. Between the river and the forest was a sharp-toothed rock, and the money, according to Vanga, was buried under it. My father was at first unspeakably surprised, and then he laughed long and loudly. Vanga was sullenly silent.

My father was confused, and then remembered that such a place really exists. It was called the abandoned village of Rayants, a long time ago it was mowed down by the plague, and people did not return there anymore. It stood, long since deceased, on the banks of river Rascati. Indeed, there was a forest and a rock.

Her father asked Vanga how she knew this place, and she told him that she had seen the treasure in a dream. Then her father suggested that she go with him to the village, so that-you never know what miracles happen in life-to try her luck.

And so they went, not just the two of them, but the whole family. Lubka remembers that in these places Vanga was guided quite freely, as if she had gone there many times, and everything was exactly as she described. They walked along the bank of the river under the rock, and my father decided that he would come here later with a shovel to dig up the treasure. Yes, after it happened that he fell and broke his arm, he could not dig any more-the wealth passed by. Later, the river was blocked, a reservoir was built, and if money was buried there, it remained forever under water to wait for treasure hunters of future centuries.

And shortly after this incident, a sheep disappeared from the herd that the Panda was grazing. The father came home very angry, because he had no money to pay the owner for the sheep. Wang reassured him, saying that a sheep stole one person from the village Consentono. She described his appearance in detail. The father was amazed, even he did not know such a person, and even more so could not know him Vanga, who did not go further than the yard, and they did not have any acquaintances in that village at all. Surprised to an extreme degree and rather disturbed, he began to question his daughter in more detail, and she replied that she had dreamed all this. She often sadly repeated that she dreamed of various unpleasant events, which then usually come true. This was probably the initial stage of her clairvoyance. The father went to the village indicated by Vanga and actually found a sheep in the flock of the person indicated by her.

At the end of each year, the community compiled lists of the poorest citizens in Strumica and gave them small monetary benefits. On New Year's Eve, Vanga and Lubka waited for a long time in the hallway of the Community House for this money. And the officials were still fidgeting, although some of them, passing by the two sisters, sincerely pitied them: Vanga stood for hours barefoot on the icy cement floor, and her feet were blue from the cold. Lubka was wearing wooden-soled shoes on her bare feet. Looking at them, so miserable and shivering, an aunt said: "If you have nothing to put on, you should stay at home, warm!»

In their house, rarely used heat. If there was enough time, the sisters went to the country, to the pine forest, and there they collected cones. This fuel was enough for a very short time, the room was dank cold, it seemed to meet all the drafts that only exist in the world.

This forced tempering for some time saved from colds. But in 1939, Vanga fell ill with pleurisy. About eight months she was between life and death, terribly thin, became light as a feather. In sunny weather, Lubka would put it in a trough and take it outside. Sometimes the doctor looked in, but could not advise anything, and once he told Lubka that his sister would soon die — the situation was hopeless.

The news quickly spread through the neighborhood, and the neighbors called the priest to perform the ritual of the last communion. The next day, when the workers of the Tobacco Monopoly were receiving their meager salaries, one of them, standing at the entrance with a hat, announced that he was collecting money for the funeral of a blind beggar girl.

Two days later, Lubka went to the well for water — it was quite far from the house — and on her return, when she came to her gate, she dropped the buckets in surprise. Vanga, whose death was expected every minute, got out of bed, went out into the yard and diligently swept it. Certainly it was impossible to say that she is "terminally ill". She was only terribly thin and a little paler than usual, but the movements of her hands were strong and confident, like those of a perfectly healthy person. When she heard Lubka's voice, she said to her: "Come on, start working quickly. You need to sweep everywhere, clean up-soon a lot of people will come here! "

1939 passed under the sign of mass unrest. The government pursued an anti-people policy of rapprochement with Hitler's Germany, strikes broke out everywhere, people went to protest demonstrations. Rumors spread, one more incredible than the other. Mass arrests began.

Vanga's father was also arrested — someone reported that he had publicly stated that such a policy was disastrous for the people. In prison, he was mercilessly beaten, forced to give the names of"comrades in the anti-government struggle". But since there was no evidence of such a "struggle", the poor fellow was released. Somehow recovering from the beating, 53-year-old Pande again went to the villages, to work.

In early 1940, Lubka fell ill with meningitis. She was taken to the hospital in the town of Steen, but they refused to accept her because there were not enough free beds. And only when the doctor realized that the girl would probably die at home without proper medical care, he agreed to put her in the hospital corridor. About two weeks Lubka struggled with a serious illness, it was written in her destiny to recover, and she recovered, got back on her feet. When I returned to Strumica, I saw Vanga, skinny as a skeleton. While Lubka was in the hospital, no one crossed the threshold of their house, and there was no one to even bring water. But Vanga endured and did not complain. She was very happy to see her sister alive and well.

However, the former health returned slowly. Doctors prescribed good care and healthy food, or at least a can of raw sheep's milk every day.

Her father decided in whatever was to get milk and was hired as a shepherd in the village Hamzali, which took and their children. Now there was enough milk, and Lubka gradually grew stronger.

Every day Lubka and Vanga went to get water, the well was located far beyond the village, in a field. While Lubka drew water, Vanga sat on a rock and sat silently, motionless, not paying attention to anything. Lubka once even got scared, it seemed to her that her sister had lost consciousness and was about to die. Numb with fear, she stood next to her sister until Vanga came out of oblivion. "Don't be scared," she said, " it's nothing, it's just that I was talking to someone. It was a horseman who wanted to water his horse. I told him not to be angry with you for not giving up your seat to him because you couldn't see him. The horseman answered me: "I am not angry, I can wait, and you pick now that grass with small white flowers, it is called "star grass" and helps to cure many diseases."

Lubka looked around and only now noticed the grass that grew near the well in abundance. Its flowers really looked like stars. The grass had a thin, leafless stalk, and soft white flowers stretched up to the sun. Lubka still does not know the name of this plant, because she has never seen anything like it in other places, but even in that region no one knew a plant with this name — "star grass". But then, when she heard what her sister said, she was even more afraid, because she did not see anyone in the field. What rider was Vanga talking about? Who could she really talk to without opening her mouth?..

It seems that their fate was to be ill in this difficult year of 1940. After the daughters, the father fell ill, ulcers appeared on the skin, blood poisoning began. Vanga and Lubka took care of him all summer, and even a temporary improvement seemed to come, the daughters thought that the Panda could recover. When Lubka asked Vanga about this, she replied: "Don't get your hopes up, little sister, I know my father is going to die soon. And we will remain complete orphans, without help and support."

In September, the father's condition worsened greatly, and both sons came to him to take shifts on duty near the patient. Now, after so many years of separation, the whole family was finally together. I want to clarify: to starve together. Every morning, the brothers went out to the shopping area to "intercept" any work. Vasil waited in front of the community House for someone to hire him as a porter, and Tom spent all day washing the offal in the slaughterhouse so that he could get something to carry home. Often they both came back empty-handed, and times were hard.

One day, when there was not a crumb of bread left in the house, my father remembered one of his friends and sent Tom and Lubka to ask him for some money to borrow. "They don't give money just like that," said their "friend", Hristo Tudzharov, who by that time had become quite rich. — Come to my field tomorrow and pick up the remaining cotton on the ground. I'll pay you."

Early the next morning, the Pande children went to the field and spent the whole day picking cotton. It was in a cold October. The wind was blowing hard, and their hands were blue and cracked from the cold. When in the evening they brought the owner the collected cotton, he threw 2 levs at Toma's feet-for three people — and added that Lubka was small, she was not entitled to money. The landlord slammed the door because it was snowing outside.

On the way home, the younger ones wept with resentment, their tears dripping on the small cake they had bought for their sick father.

At the beginning of November, the father felt the approach of death, he gathered the children at his bedside: "Children," old Pande told them, " I am dying. You remain alive and will live to see the day when our land will once again become the land of Bulgaria. I wish I could wait for this bright day. I have one big request for you: when the Bulgarians come, call some Bulgarian soldier, let him stick a bayonet in the ground over my grave, and I will understand that Bulgaria has come!»

On November 8, 1940, at the age of 54, my father died. The dead man, washed and dressed in all clean clothes, lay on the matting, and even the priest did not come to celebrate his funeral. The children did not know how to bury him, because even this sad rite needed money, and they, as always, as much as in the holes in the pockets of a beggar.

A neighbor, a servant of the Catholic Church, had mercy on the orphans, he told the priest about the death of Pande, and it was decided to bury the poor man for free.

The father is dead. And after some time, the Bulgarian troops came to Strumitsa. Then the boys called the soldier to his father's grave. It was Boris Yanev from the village of Belyushets in the Sandansky district, who stuck his bayonet into the grave mound and said: "Sleep well, honest Bulgarian." But that was later.

Days of hopelessness flowed by, and only Vanga's boundless patience, her strong character helped other children not to fall into despair. Although she was the hardest of all, she kept up well and set an example of firmness to the other children. The orphans believed that better days would come to them. Soon the brothers again went to other villages.

Vanga and Lubka were left alone for a long time.

BEGINNING

"There comes a time in the spiritual life of every man when he comes to the conviction that he must make peace with his assigned lot, that no matter what good things the universe may abound in, he will not find his daily bread unless he diligently cultivates the piece of land assigned to him'.

Henry Thoreau

A new terrible storm was brewing over the world. Everywhere there was talk of an impending war. From the shops, from the bazaar, products began to disappear. Who is richer, stocked up on food for the future. Neighbors often gathered in Vanga's small courtyard. Until nightfall, their anxious voices could be heard. Vanga often repeated that it was necessary to raise money and donate it to the Church of the Fifteen Holy Martyrs. "In a year's time there will be war," Vanga warned — " only the generosity of the inhabitants will save the city from destruction." The neighbors, as usual, were greedy and believed that the general uneasy mood was a reason for her warnings. Vanga persistently repeated that she had seen in a dream the terrible events of the coming war, that it would begin very soon, in 1941, in April.

Maybe her neighbors believed her, but what was the point, what could they change in the future fatal events?...

The whole year 1940 passed in anxiety and uncertainty. And at the beginning of 1941...

"He was tall, fair-haired, and divinely handsome. His ancient warrior armor shone in the moonlight. A horse with a waving white tail was digging the ground with its hooves. The rider stopped in the courtyard, dismounted and entered a dark room. It gave off such a light that the house was as bright as day. Turning to Wang, the guest said in a deep voice, " Soon everything will turn upside down in this world, many people will die. You'll stay here and talk about the living and the dead. Don't be afraid! I will be there for you, I will always help you."

Vanga asked her sister: "Lubka, have you seen the rider, he just rode away from our yard?»

"What rider? Her sister asked. — Do you know what time it is?"

"I don't know, (maybe I did, but it was a very strange rider, and a strange dream. Just listen to what I have seen»...

Vanga's anxiety was transmitted to Lubka, and both could not sleep until morning.

On April 6, 1941, as Vanga had predicted a year earlier, German troops crossed the Yugoslav border. Early in the morning, all the residents of Strumice left their homes and hid: some in cellars and barns, some in the woods, not far from the city. Only Vanga and Lubka stayed at home.

In the afternoon, glass rattled in the windows, and the rumble of heavy cars could be heard from the street. German tanks entered the city. The sisters heard someone else's speech and the patter of boots — the Germans were walking around the yards, looking for cattle, poultry, robbing. Their door swung open, and a soldier appeared on the threshold. The sisters stood in the middle of the room, livid with fear. The soldier looked around the poor little room, the empty courtyard, and left: there was nothing to take from this house.

After a day or two, the neighbors began to return. Many people reached out to Vanga's house to learn about the fate of the two sisters, people stood near the threshold, hesitating, not daring to enter. Those who came later gathered in the courtyard. Vanga could not be read. Within a few hours, she had changed beyond recognition.

Vanga stood in the corner of the room, in front of a lighted lamp, and spoke in a loud, strong, confident voice. A great inner tension was evident in every word, in every movement. The blind eyes remained blank, but the face was so changed and spiritualized that it seemed to radiate a bright light. From her lips came a strange voice that spoke with surprising accuracy of names, localities, events. By that time, almost all the men in the town had been conscripted or taken to forced labor in Germany, and she talked about each of them, whether they were alive, when they would return, what would happen to them. The sight was so startling that many felt the urge to fall to their knees as if they were facing a saint. So what? Those to whom she had predicted a speedy return had indeed returned at the exact time she had named.

Vanga's fame as a clairvoyant quickly spread throughout the city. Crowds of people began to flock to her house.

Here is one of her first predictions.

The wife of the neighbor Milan Partenova sat in the courtyard of Vanga and cried, as there was no news from her husband for a long time. She bitterly mourned her four children, as she thought they were orphaned. Vanga looked at her and said: "Don't cry, but rather attend to dinner and prepare your husband's clothes, because Milan will come home late in the evening, in only his underwear. I can see him. He's hiding in a ravine near the city."

The woman thought that Vanga said so, feeling sorry for her, but went home. I cooked dinner, got my husband's clothes, waited and waited, and fell asleep without waiting. Toward midnight, someone tapped softly on the window, and when she looked out, she almost fainted. In the courtyard stood her Milan, really in his underwear, in which he escaped from captivity. He was so hungry that he ate everything in a row, without making out, only surprised that his wife was waiting for him, knew that he would come: "No one could know this, I did not know myself whether I would dare to return. I was afraid of an ambush, " Milan kept saying.

At the beginning of the war, Vanga said the neighbor lady, mother of Christ Parkanova that her son is alive but not coming back soon. The bride of Christo did not believe such a vague prediction and married another. A year later, Hristo returned alive and well and was the first to see his former bride. She fainted with astonishment. The children ran to announce the news to the mother of Christ, whose heart nearly exploded with joy.

These two cases were discussed very widely not only in the city, but also in the surrounding villages, which, in fact, was the reason for people's pilgrimage to Vanga's house. Everyone wanted to know about their loved ones, and Vanga told everyone. And after a while, the predicted came true.

For her, the most difficult everyday problems were no secret, she answered everyone.

Vanga became famous as a skilled healer of various diseases, treated mainly with medicinal herbs. Interestingly, with her knowledge, she confused even the most experienced homeopaths, offering patients the simplest remedies or the most ordinary herbs that, according to doctors, did not have healing properties. And yet, her medications were producing startling and rapid results. So, for example, she cured one woman suffering from a mental disorder, telling her relatives to pick grass that grew in abundance in the water of the nearest river, and water the patient with an infusion of river grass. The woman has become calmer, now she is already 80 years old, she enjoys life, nurses her grandchildren.

Vanga told the peasants who visited her with absolute accuracy what was troubling them, advised them how to help their grief.

To a peasant who stole a pig from a poor widow, Vanga publicly told the whole ugly story. The man went away in shame, and the next day the widow found the piglet at the door of her house.

Of course, such striking cases have been widely discussed in Strumica. To the deep respect with which the neighbors now treated Vanga, a sincere reverence began to mingle. In a short time, she gained undisputed authority in the entire district. People consulted her on a variety of issues, and she helped everyone, easily resolving even the most long-standing complicated disputes.

Gradually, the legend of Vanga was born.

Some people were afraid of her prophecies, attributed to her incredible mystical properties, accused of witchcraft. Others, fascinated by her subtle insights, exaggerated everything she said, calling it " biblical miracles." And all unanimously recognized that Vanga enjoys the love and respect of people, many of whom have found in her their protection and support.

Great respect accompanies her until her death. Vanga was constantly invited to become the godmother of a newborn, then to attend a wedding, and not in one Petrich district, but literally all over the country. She was also invited to various family holidays. People believe that inviting Vanga to their home, especially her presence in the house, brings well-being and mutual understanding in the family.

"On the eighth of April, 1942," says Lubka, " Grandma Tina, our old friend, came to us and said that today we would be visited by an important guest. She explained only that in 1918 he lived in her apartment. She went out and returned a short time later with a small man with blue eyes, a neatly trimmed mustache, and dressed in a gray uniform and breeches. He asked Vanga, will she be able to give it a little time. Grandma Tina whispered to me: "Look at him with all your eyes, because this is the Bulgarian Tsar Boris." I was surprised, and it never occurred to me that our hut could be visited by the king. And Vanga, standing in her usual place in the corner of the room, before the guest had time to ask anything, spoke in a stern voice: "Your kingdom is growing, it is spreading wide, but be ready soon to fit your possessions in a nutshell. She repeated, " Be ready." — After a pause, she added: — Remember the date-August 28!"

The king, without asking anything, left very confused. He died on August 28, 1943.

After his death, three women from Sofia came to us in Strumica. With them was another woman from Petrich. They explained that they were relatives of the king, and asked Vanga to tell them what awaits the royal family. She replied: "When you return, tie a red ribbon over the king's bed." "Can't we, "one of them asked,"tie a pink or white ribbon? ""No," Vanga replied, " just a red one." The women left and never came back. And on September 9, 1944, the Red Banner of Victory flew over the former royal palace.

EVERYONE HAS THE RIGHT TO BE HAPPY

"... The wisdom that comes from above is first pure, then peaceful, modest, obedient, full of mercy and good fruits, impartial and not hypocritical'.

The Epistle of James, ch. 3 (17)

In 1942, the Yugoslav-Bulgarian border was opened, and people from Petrich and further afield began to come to Vanga. Everyone wanted to hear about themselves, their own and their family's future. Patients also came in the hope that Vanga would be able to cure them.

Once she was visited by several soldiers of the 14th Quartermaster Regiment of the Bulgarian Army. Among them was one dark-skinned 23-year-old soldier by the name of Dimitar Gusarov from the village Cringila. He, it turns out, wanted to personally talk with Vanga, to know the future, which did not promise him anything good. The villains killed and robbed his brother, a merchant, near the village of Sklava. Three children, whose mother was ill with tuberculosis, were orphaned.

Dimitar hovered in the courtyard, not daring to enter. Suddenly Vanga came out of the house and called his name: "I know why you came. You want to know the names of your brother's murderers, maybe I'll tell you, but you have to promise me that you won't take revenge. You will stay alive and become a witness to their crimes in court."

Vanga did not allow anyone to take revenge. She firmly believes that a person should strive to do only good, since evil deeds, including revenge, never go unpunished. And the punishment is always very cruel, and if it does not strike the avenger himself, it will certainly become a curse for his offspring. I often asked her why it was so unfair, and she always answered: "To make it hurt more!"

I can't understand, and I refuse to interpret it.

I remember another case. A few years ago, a peasant came to Vanga. He had 13 children in his family, but all died young, the last, the thirteenth, died at the age of twelve. Doctors believed that the mother, without knowing it, infected the children with tuberculosis in the womb, but Vanga had another explanation. Vanga reminded her guest that as a young man, he was foolishly embarrassed by the late pregnancy of his already elderly mother. And once he even cruelly offended her. Sorry, of course, but too late: both she and the child died. So it happened a long time ago that a person managed to forget, but not "forgot" Vanga, she immediately understood why nature is so ruthless to the offspring of this unfortunate. Vanga not only reminded him of what happened many years ago, but also told him a number of details that no one knew, and then added: "You should know that your wife is not the cause of your trouble. One must always be kind so as not to suffer for a lifetime."

But back to the meeting with the young soldier. Then in Strumice, in 1942, Dimitar Gutzerov was so impressed by what Vanga said that he did not remember leaving her house. Dimitar could not understand how she knew his name, how she guessed what was tormenting his soul. Then he came to see Vanga several more times, and they talked for a long time in a small room.

In mid-April, Vanga told her sister that Dimitar was courting her, and soon they would go to live in Petrich.

At that time, the brothers were not with them. Vasil served as a soldier in Dupnitsa, and Tom was hijacked to work in Germany.

On the morning of April 22, the painted carriage stopped in front of Vanga's house. Excited, Dimitar jumped to the ground. The carriage was filled with fragrant herbs and flowers, decorated with bright colorful rugs. The news quickly spread throughout the area, and neighbors began to come from everywhere, just acquaintances, to say goodbye to Vanga. Some even reproached her for leaving her native land. Vanga did not listen to them, because she was saying goodbye not to her relatives, but to heavy memories, poverty and a joyless orphan life. Their future was not entirely clear either, but they hoped that the young family would have happy days ahead.

The bride's dowry was purely symbolic: Vanga threw a red woolen shawl tied by herself over her shoulders, and as a reminder of her parents ' home, she took a copper pot and a copper can. That was all her luggage. Lubka sat down next to them and looked back at their miserable little house for the last time…

There was a big rusty lock on the gate, and no one knew when it would be unlocked.

The carriage swayed gently toward Petrich, and the three future relatives were silent, reliving their farewell to Strumitsa.

We arrived in Petrich in the evening of the same day, stopped at 10 Opolchenskaya Street. We came out in front of a rickety little house, which could not even be called residential. The loose roof could collapse at any moment. In front of the house was a large, untidy yard. From the windows of neighboring houses, dozens of eyes watched them curiously: the fame of Vanga the soothsayer reached this city. Some people went out into the street, some aunt began to wonder loudly: how can a blind woman be a hostess and, in general, what kind of worker is she… But Wang did not pay those words any attention.

They entered a dark, long, and dirty corridor. There was a small room on each side. One of them later became a bedroom, and in the other Vanga received her many visitors.

"There was another room at the back, added later," recalls Lubka, " in which the flooring was made of planks, a mattress was laid on it, and woolen bags filled with corn straw served as pillows. On this "bed" slept Baba Magdalena, the 70-year-old mother of her future husband, three children of her murdered son, and two more children from another son, and their tuberculosis mother. Dirt and poverty are depressing."

That's how Vanga exchanged one life filled with poverty and deprivation for another, no less poor and difficult.

On the tenth of May 1942, Vanga married Dimitar and began to manage her new home. It was very difficult for the young woman. Grandmother Magdalena, with the frankness of ordinary people, did not approve of her son's choice, and at the first moment of meeting said: "Is this really your fate?" She probably hoped that her son would bring a strong, healthy country girl into the house, who would take care of all the cares of the house, since Grandmother Magdalena was no longer able to do it.

Vanga silently swallowed the insult and very soon showed what she was capable of. She was not afraid of evil reproaches, nor poverty, nor any difficulties at all, because she had not only a strong character, but also a considerable experience of fighting for life, an experience acquired, one might say, from birth.

Day and night, together with Lubka, they washed, cleaned, painted, repaired, and soon the house shone clean. In those war years, it was simply impossible to create at least some comfort, but Vanga with her inherent ingenuity created amazing things out of nothing. A trait that is very typical of the style of Vanga, who always tries to make everything around her "beautiful and pleasant to look at".

Vanga has banned inhabitants of the surrounding villages to trade in their yard, they cleaned it, put things in order. Throughout the yard and the house, the firm hand of a skilled hostess was felt.

The family lived in the same way as other families of that wartime period, but it did not last long. Rumors about Vanga's visionary talent spread like ripples on water from a thrown stone, and again the human river flowed to Vanga's house. The husband was very dissatisfied with this development of events, he believed that after marriage, Vanga would stop his predictions and would only deal with the house and family affairs, following the example of all married women. Deeply respecting Vanga, he felt uneasy as he was not able to support the family himself. Vanga loved him very much and appreciated him both as a person and as a spouse, but she believed that her vocation — to serve people — is much stronger than family attachments, and even her personal life should be devoted to others. In addition, her amazing gift did not give her peace of mind, requiring constant self-expression.

A variety of people came and went to her: both civilians and military, and the sick, and the languishing — everyone's eyes shone with hope for help.

In those years, many Bulgarian youths fought against the Fascist yoke in partisan detachments. Their relatives and friends often came to Vanga in the hope of hearing something about the children. Partizan Assen Askarov and said to his mother: "Don't be afraid! Go to Vanga often, and she will tell you all about me."

Such visits did not remain a secret for the police.

Two policemen, Dimitar Chuchurov and Boris Lazarev, almost daily came to Vanga, threatened her, demanded to tell her what she was talking about with relatives of "enemies of the authorities". But Vanga was silent. Then the police came up with something else: they began to force her to work out the "labor service", from which blind Vanga had previously been released.

Meanwhile, the mobilization of reserve soldiers was announced. Dimitar was sent to the occupation corps in Greece. At parting, he told Vanga that if he returned alive and well, he would build her a new house in which she would forget about her misfortunes forever. Mitko had golden hands and a vocation as a builder, although he did not study anywhere. He fulfilled his promise only in 1947.

Seeing him off, Vanga said one thing:"Watch out for water."

Indeed, all those who survived and later returned home suffered for a long time from malaria and various kidney diseases, which they received in Greece, where they drank rotten marsh water for lack of clean water.

In 1942, to Vanga was frequently visited by a teacher from the town of Sveti Doctor Maria Gyurova. Vanga and Lubka quickly became friends with her. Maria grew four daughters and two sons, twins, who served in Bitola. Vanga used to say, " Aunt Maria, my sister Lubka is going to marry one of your twins." And so it turned out. Soon Lubka met Stoyan, the eldest of the brothers, they liked each other and soon got married. (I will add that we are talking about my parents.)

Both Maria and her husband Boris received a good and versatile education in their time. Boris, that is, my grandfather, played the violin well, studied painting and mathematics, and read the original French classics.

As a man of education and materialistic upbringing, he did not really believe Vanga's predictions, and one day, when she was visiting them at home, he decided to test her gift. He asked her: "Do you know what happened to the bones of my father, who was killed by the Turks at Mednik in 1912, and his bones were never found?" Vanga advised him to find in Melnik a certain Peter, who was a witness to the events and could tell in detail what really happened. The teacher was surprised and, continuing the experiment, after a while went to Melnik. I found the family of Peter, who had already died by that time. But his son told in detail about that battle-he knew from the stories of his late father.

It turned out that my great — grandfather — he was a priest and at the same time one of the most active fighters for the purity of the Bulgarian language, the Bulgarian school and the Bulgarian church, who devoted his whole life to fighting for this great cause-was arrested by the Turks as a like-minded Yane Sandanski and brutally killed. The hatred of the Turks for him was so great that they also desecrated the ashes of the priest: the bones were scattered under the trees, and instead of them they put horse bones in the coffin.

Having thus learned about the fate of his father, Boris Gaigurov believed in Vanga's gift and decided to ask her about the fate of two brothers who left the country in 1921. Vanga answered him: "Sero in the grave and Nikola alive. I see him, recently he was in a big city, in Russia, and there he studied-became a scientist. Only now he is not in the city, he is a prisoner in the camp. Don't worry, he'll be here in the spring. Wait for him, as soon as you see a gentleman in gray clothes, with two suitcases in his hands, and know that your brother has returned."

It seemed incredible. My grandfather could not believe that his missing brother had become a Soviet scientist, nor that he was in the camp. And at that time, he did not believe Vanga and decided that he would not be able to find out the truth, he would not be able to meet his brother.

Flying a certain number of days, and once in the early morning the tired traveler stopped in front of Boris Hagarova. He was wearing gray clothes, and there were two suitcases on the ground next to him. No one knew him. Boris didn't know him either. It was his brother Nikola. The younger brother returned to his homeland after a 22-year absence. Nikola confirmed everything Vanga had said about him.

After the death of Jane Sandanski, one of the groups of his party began to convince its supporters that it was necessary to act in alliance with the Communists, while the other was against it. Turmoil and armed clashes began.

Both brothers Boris Gyurova, like himself, were members of one of the factions. While still studying at the Faculty of Law of Sofia University, Scherjo became a communist and together with his brother Nikola organized the first communist group in the city of Sveti Vrach in 1919, he was elected secretary of the group. Both brothers were sentenced to death for their communist activities and fled the country to escape.

Nikola got to Odessa. After years of starvation, poverty and deprivation, he managed to get an education and became an electrical engineer. He built power plants in all Soviet republics. When World War II broke out and the Germans occupied part of Soviet territory, he was captured and sent to Germany.

He endured torture and deprivation, but managed to escape from the camp, hiding for a long time until he joined a group of Bulgarians working in Berlin. After a long ordeal, he managed to convince the Germans that he was a Bulgarian, received the necessary certificates and official documents from Bulgaria and Sveti Doctor and decided to immediately return to Bulgaria.

Nikola was as surprised as his brother at Vanga's predictions and the accuracy of his description of his life in the Soviet Union and then in Germany.

Since the described case is connected again with the stormy year of 1943 for our history, I present a letter of confession from R. B. for Vanga:

"Great streams of people have flowed before you since then, and much water has flowed away, and the vicissitudes of fate have touched me. I have seen many countries, met wonderful people, but I have never had a stronger experience than meeting you, and I have never met a stronger and more extraordinary person than you.

I came to you then, not believing in clairvoyance. It came after a terrible storm in my life, when on July 23, 1942, I had to become both a bride and a widow. Then I heard the most tender words of farewell and shots from the shooting range, which took away from me Anton and our friend Nikola Vaptsarov and four other beautiful comrades. [1]

You were known as the Strumitz medicine woman, although you lived in your modest room in Petrich and were not yet known to the world.

As long as I live, I will not forget with what skill and sympathy you reproduced the trial of the employees of the Central Committee of the BCP (Bulgarian Communist Party). How you transformed from the role of prosecutor to the chairman of the court, how you built the words of the defense and the defendants. What was especially amazing was that you spoke their language, in their style. With what deep compassion and anguish you treated the heroes of this drama-young, capable, loyal men!

I felt like a protector, an older sister, when you hugged me with the words: "Rositsa, Rositsa, how young you are, how early you turned black (in the sense of being widowed-ed.). And then she even described to me the model of the dress packed in the suitcase, saw under it and a bag of sweets that I bought for Anton's nephews — he always brought them something delicious when he came to Petrich (Popov comes from the Petrich region-approx. auth.) You, Vanga, talked to me for more than an hour, said that you will remember what you saw longer than me — the execution itself and the last moments of the convicts… And in the end, she began to raise from the dead and speak in the words of Anton, Peter Bogdanov. It was so amazing that words can't describe it!

(1) We are talking about the famous Bulgarian communist poet Nikola Vaptsarov and his comrades, who were sentenced to death by the fascist authorities in the trial of the Bulgarian Communist Party. After severe torture, six were shot. Among them was Anton Popov, with whom R. B. married a few minutes before the shooting. (author's note.)

And then she said: "Dimitar rises from the grave" I interrupted you for the first time and said: "I came to you, not believing in clairvoyance, but you talk to me for more than an hour, and about things that only I can know, but it seems that you are tired and confused, I have no relatives with the name Dimitar." However, you continued to insist, saying that there is, and very close. And suddenly she spoke in a completely different voice, not her own: "I... Dimitar Dimitar Daskala!" (teacher — approx. transl.) I was so insistent in my rightness, and what did it turn out to be? My mother's father's name was Dimitar and he really was a teacher, but he died when my mother was little, and my mother died when I was a child. She may have been thinking about her grandfather when I was there, but that information was lost somewhere in the depths of my memory, and you called it up from there. I just felt weak-where did you suddenly get this grandfather — from the grave or from the sky?

Since then, I've been talking about you everywhere, proving your superiority over everyone... because you predicted my future marriage then, even though I was sure that I would never marry. And you said: "You will marry a man who writes»…

In the spring of 1944, at the time of cherry ripening, Vanga's husband returned from Greece. Half of it is said to be left. From the rotten water they drank, from the attacks of malaria, his liver was greatly enlarged, he was constantly beaten by a severe chill. Mitko was so weak that he was unable to hold an axe in his hands. But it was necessary to fulfill the promise to Vanga in 1942, and in 1945 he began to build a new house. He did everything but the hardest work myself.

And now more and more people were gathering in the courtyard, all waiting for help from Vanga. She got up after dark, prepared food for the workers who helped Mitko build the house, kneaded and baked bread, and then received the suffering, instilled hope and faith in people.

Here is another testimony about Vanga's life and activities at that time. G. Ch. from Plovdiv tells about a meeting with Vanga in 1944:

"In May 1944, I was mobilized in Seres (Greece-ed.). We were assigned to move to Petrich by the end of September. My commander met a fellow soldier, a fellow student at a military school, and arranged a meeting. I went to this meeting together with the commander. We were sitting over a cup of coffee. The commander's comrade suddenly remembered: "You know, there is an interesting fortune-teller nearby, who long before September 9 predicted the seizure of power by the Communists, for which she was even arrested."

I was asked to find out where this woman lived, and in the early morning of one October day in 1944, we visited her. As soon as we entered her poor little room, Vanga fell into a trance and began to speak to my commander: "You are from the city of Ruse, your wife's name is

Maria, she is your second wife and a little deaf... Your house stands on the banks of the Danube, the son's name is Itsko"... etc. with all the details about the life and family of the colonel. I listened in amazement, because she was talking about things I had never heard before, even though the commander and I had known each other for a long time. At the end of the meeting, the colonel asked to say something about his brother, in whom he was very interested. Vanga instantly switched and began to read like a book: "Your brother, his name is so-and-so, is in the city of Bordeaux, in France, he lives very well, he has everything you need, there is even a boat, but he is very worried that leaving Bulgaria, did not say goodbye to you, you were against his departure."

From that day on, I became Vanga's friend and regular visitor. A lot of people really came to see her. They were people from different parts of the country. It was the time of the People's Court, and many wives and mothers came to learn something about their loved ones.

Grave grave, "she said to some with a pang in her heart, which meant that the man was no longer alive. Others: "Go, he will meet you." Or: "Go away, he will come after you!» And I know from my acquaintances who came to her with similar questions that all her soothing words were fully confirmed. Our meetings with Vanga lasted for about 50 days, but they left an indelible mark for life. Vanga is a superman, she is an oracle, God grant her long life!»

I also know of another case that dates back to the same time. One of the commanders of our army, who was among the first to enter Petrich, was given the task of eliminating all harmful elements in the city, including Vanga, because with her predictions she instilled superstition among the people, and the new system could not allow the existence of such harmful remnants of the past. While the commander was debating how to carry out the order, the following happened... A soldier on horseback was carrying a package of secret documents from one border post to another. From the sleepless work of establishing people's power in this region, everyone was terribly tired. Arriving at the outpost, the soldier found that somewhere along the way he had dropped a package of documents. The situation is hopeless! He was facing the death penalty. The guy was immediately arrested, and he was to be tried by a military tribunal. But the culprit asked for a day to search for the lost documents, and in order not to think that he intended to escape, he asked to be accompanied by an armed soldier. The commander refused, it was forbidden, but the guy so asked to give him one last chance that the commander agreed.

They came down from the mountains, and the soldier immediately went to Petrich to Vanga to ask her to help him. And she told him to go up into the mountains to the clearing where he had given the horse a break, and look carefully in the grass nearby. Exactly there. according to her, the package tied to the saddle fell, and still lies, unnoticed by anyone.

The soldiers immediately went to the indicated place, and found the loss. The commander asked how he managed to find the documents, and when he realized that Vanga had helped, he decided that she was a useful person and he saw no reason to "eliminate" her. (This incident was told by the commander himself).

One officer from Sofia came to Petrich several times with his wife, they were already recognized, many envied this "model family". But Vanga said: "Don't be in a hurry to be envious, the future will show whether they are worth envying at all." After the war, it turned out that the officer was an executioner. He was tried and sentenced to death.
Upon learning this, Vanga told her visitors ," Don't envy anyone until you see the end of their life."

Another case of those years. A woman from a Petrich village lost her three-year-old daughter in a noisy Sunday market. I searched everywhere for her, but to no avail. The inconsolable mother did not know what to do, she came to Vanga to ask about the fate of her daughter. Vanga said that the girl was stolen by gypsies in the bazaar. Now the search is futile, many years will pass until the happy day comes when the mother hears about her daughter and finds her.

Twenty-two years later, this woman was traveling to Blagoevgrad and accidentally, at the Kresna station, heard a conversation between two friends.

From it, I realized that there were several Gypsy families living in the nearest village. One of the young gypsies is different from all of them with her blond braids, blue eyes, and behavior. Something in her mother's heart trembled — she had waited so many years for Vanga's predictions to come true. The woman went to that village, quickly found a house and, before entering the hall, saw a Russian-haired gypsy woman. I thought that my heart would break with excitement, the young woman did not believe her story, she said. that she had lived with gypsies all her life, and her husband even wanted to drive out the impudent old woman. But his mother-in-law told him to be silent and told him the following: many years ago, this girl was given to her by gypsies who visited a fair in one of the Petrich villages, and they allegedly "begged" her from some completely poor peasant. The gypsy took the girl and adopted her.
Agitated, the old mother continued to tell her daughter about her childhood, and then something brightened in her memory. Her eyes watered, and she remembered that there was a deep well in the courtyard of her childhood and a huge boulder nearby.

Not doubting that she had found her long-lost daughter, her mother suggested that she go to her native village. And so they did. It was there that the "gypsy" remembered that she still had a brother, pointed out the yard itself, easily navigated the house. The whole village gathered, the meeting was so touching that people could not hold back their tears.

In may 1944, the younger brother of Vanga's Tome returned from Germany and stayed in Strumica. And on June 10, Vanga's older brother unexpectedly came to Petrich to say goodbye: he was on his way to Strumica, to a partisan detachment.

Then, at the end of the war, a partisan brigade was formed in the Strumitsky region, and many young people signed up for combat detachments. Secretly from Vanga with him decided to leave and Lubka. Vanga was saddened by her brother's decision-with tears in her eyes, she asked him not to leave. Her brother insisted, explained that he did not believe in predictions, and on the same day, together with Lubka, they went to Strumica and further to the partisans.

On October 8, 1944, Vasil, who had already become the commander of a group of sappers, was assigned to blow up a bridge near the village of Furka. Parts of the German army were retreating over this bridge. Vasil completed the task, blew up the bridge, but did not notice that he dropped his ID card in a hurry. Then he took refuge with one of his friends in the village, deciding to return to the squad at night. After a powerful explosion, the Germans, dismantling the remains of the bridge, found an identity card. A woodcutter, captured near the site of the explosion, recalled seeing this young man in the village. The Germans immediately arrested all its inhabitants and herded them into the church. Of course, Vasil was also arrested. The Germans explicitly stated that if the inhabitants did not name the partisan within an hour, the church would be blown up. Many people here knew Vasil by sight, knew that it was he who blew up the bridge, but they were silent. Realizing the hopelessness of his situation, Vasil stepped out of the crowd and said, " I did it." They dragged him out into the churchyard and began to torture him brutally in front of everyone: they poured molten lead into his ears, beat him, stabbed him with bayonets, and then shot him. The disfigured corpse was ordered not to be buried — as a warning to others.

Vasil died on October 8, he just turned 23 years old.

Interesting memories of P. R. from Sofia in 1945: In March 1945, I was mobilized in Sveti Vrach (now Sandanski). I had to serve at the station, "General Todorov" in the village Pripiceni. One Sunday afternoon, for the sake of boredom, I decided to take a walk on the "cuckoo" on the narrow-gauge railway to the town of Petrich. He entered the car and sat down next to a woman dressed in black. Then I began to think about where I would go in the city and what to see. When the conductor came up, my neighbor asked him if he could tell her how to find Vanga's house. I listened to their conversation and remembered what I had heard about this woman in a shoemaker's shop in Sofia. A friend of the shoemaker told a lot of interesting things about her. Here are a few of these stories. One day a peasant came to Vanga in a state of alarm-his horse had been taken away from him in the bazaar. Vanga said: "Don't worry. Go there on the next market day, and you will find him at the same tree where you tied him last time. A man from a neighboring village took him to take sacks of wool."

And I remember one more case. One day, a shirt disappeared from the rope where the laundry was drying. The owner of this shirt went to Vanga on another matter, but incidentally asked about the shirt. And she told him. "Is it worth worrying about this shirt when you have others? Whoever took it did it out of great need, he didn't have any. I know who it is, but I won't tell you. And if you see him in your shirt, you will pretend that you did not notice!"

These memories inflamed my curiosity, and I also decided to go to Vanga.

Following the conductor's directions, I found the street easily. He stopped in front of the time-blackened wooden fence. I entered the courtyard and saw a squat old house with an open terrace, on which an elderly woman sat with her bare feet crossed and combed her gray hair. Seeing me, she asked Wang to do I go and when I confirmed that to her, she said that today is a Sunday, Vanga sees no one. I said that I just wanted to see Vanga up close, because I had heard a lot of interesting things about her. She went to ask, then came out and showed me which door to enter. I knocked, opened the door, and found myself in a shaded room, carpeted, and modestly furnished. And since I am not in the habit of looking at details, I only remember that Vanga was reclining on a couch covered with a blanket, and her fair head was propped up with her palm. I knew she couldn't see, but I looked into her eyes to make sure. I greeted her and said that I had only come to pay my respects to her.

While I was saying these words, the door opened, and a woman in mourning, whom I knew from the train, entered. She asked Vanga to tell her about her missing son, as she did not know where to look for him. Vanga told her to come back tomorrow morning.

The woman came out, but as soon as the door was closed, as Vanga put his head down on the pillow and cowered, huddled in convulsions, pale and rough baritone began to scream, "Grave, a fresh grave, Oh, my feet are killing me!" And repeated it several times. I was scared. I feel that in the gloom of the room there is some other woman, obviously an acquaintance or relative of Vanga, who gives me a sign to be silent. I thought this scene was caused by a woman in mourning who had just come out. After a minute or two, Vanga sat up and tucked her legs under her. She paused and said to me: "You have a lot of brothers and sisters, wait, now I'll name them... Ivan, Nedelya, Rada, Stanka", etc. "There are nine of us," I confirmed. "I have a big worry today, but in vain." When I later wrote to my sister about this, she told me that her son was arrested at the time, but was released a few days later. Vanga said that I have two brothers at the front, and that one with stripes. I said I didn't have a brother with stripes. "Yes, yes, remember," Vanga insisted. I remembered that my younger brother had sent me a picture of him in the uniform of a corporal in the Danube Fleet. Then she began to describe our house. She said: "A big house with an iron fence. Only now there's no one in the house." I said that my wife had gone to visit my brother's wife in the country. "Wait, let me see where," Vanga interrupted. "Here's the big river. This is probably the Danube. Wait, I'll see exactly what place — " and began to sort through it. - Ru, Ru, Rus, Ruschuk (now Ruse-approx. "Yes," I said. "And I also see here your close friend, the tailor, who is this?» I say there are no tailors in the family. "There is, there is," said Vanga, " an elderly man with a big mustache, a bald crown and glasses. He sits under a tree with his legs crossed and sews." I suddenly realized it was my father. After he retired, he took tailored clothes from cloth, sewed them, trimmed them with braid. He made vests and trousers. And before that, he worked as a messenger in the forestry department. "You see, there is a tailor," said Vanga. And then she turned to the other woman and said, " They are very clear." Vanga continued: "Behind the father, a little to the side, there is a woman holding the boy's hand. "I don't know,"I say," but maybe it's my mother, who died in 1922, and my child, who died 5 years ago." "They are," Vanga confirmed. She asked me why I was wearing civilian clothes when I was in reserve. I explained that we did not have enough military uniforms, as they are needed for the front. "Yes," Vanga said. "Now the soldiers at the front are cheerful, they shave, wash their clothes, repair yoke, carts, generally rejoice and will soon go to Bulgaria. Like this. Well, do you want me to say something about you?» I said I didn't want to. I know that when I return to Sofia, only work awaits me. "And yet," Vanga insisted. I told her that I had a dream to build a house one day, like my colleagues. Vanga paused for a moment and said: "You will build, you will have two houses, you will be built twice!» Then he says, " Wait, I'll see what you do. Wow, you have a big workshop, lots of apprentices. I see kitchen stoves, watering cans, troughs, and either barbecues, or braziers»… I thought Vanga had told me about the two houses because I was rich, and I informed her that I was a co-operative tinker.

In 1952, I built a house. In 1975, we built it with the money of our sons and daughters-in-law. So it turned out that I really built twice and actually built two houses — the top floor for one of the sons.

When I said goodbye to Vanga, she told me that on arrival at the unit I was waiting for a letter, news. I decided that perhaps it was a dismissal order, and, very pleased, left.

When I returned to Prepechene, my comrades asked me where I had been, and I told them that I had been to Petrich with Vanga, and she told me that a letter was waiting for me. Indeed, I saw an envelope lying on my pillow. My friends asked me to tell them about the meeting, but I decided to read the letter first. However, they didn't leave me alone. They said I'd forget while I was reading. I agreed. I told them everything and left them to comment on our conversation with Vanga.

The letter was from my wife in Ruse. Carefully preparing me, she informed me of my brother's death. On May 14, after the armistice, 5-6 soldiers with a sergeant, combing the area near Graz in Austria, found a machine gun. The sergeant began to look for him, the machine gun suddenly fired and mortally wounded my brother Alexander in the heart. He was taken to the hospital, he lived for another 3-4 hours and died. The message read " died in an accident."

"Grave, a fresh grave," said Vanga. So these words were meant for me, because my brother died on Monday, and I was at Vanga's a few days later, on Sunday.

I began to cry. My friends read the letter and began to comfort me. The lieutenant came and, probably to distract me, asked me to tell him about my meeting with Vanga. Then he said he wanted me to take him to her tomorrow. But it so happened that the next morning two others came with him — Pavel and Mincio. This Mincho told us not to tell anyone where we were going, especially if there were strangers around. Because he assumed that Vanga had spies who would inform her.

We were at Vanga's gate very early to be first. It was very quiet everywhere. But when they opened the gate, they were surprised. The courtyard was full of people. We barely managed to get in. We decided that the case was hopeless, someone suggested that we go somewhere to eat and return later in the evening. Just as we were about to leave, the man in front, who had voluntarily assumed the role of steward, shouted: "Let Petko come in!" I shivered, because that was my name. I waited for someone else to respond, but there was no sound. They shouted my name a second and third time. Then I said that I was Petko, but that I had just come. "It doesn't matter, "said the steward,"since Vanga is calling you, come in!" "Yes, come in, how many of you are there! There's no time to waste!»— shouted the people. I was surprised and went to the door. The others came from behind. We sat on chairs against the wall in a small room. I'm next to Vanga, and the other three are opposite us. At some point, Vanga got up, turned pale and rushed to the middle of the room, began to moan, as if she was going to cry. She collapsed to the floor. He turned on his right side, curled up and a strange voice began to say the words that I heard the day before: "Grave, a fresh grave, my feet hurt!" We looked at each other fearfully. Then Vanga got up and backed away to the wall where I was sitting. She waved her arms as if pushing something away from her. When she reached the door of the room, she opened it and quickly left. A man, probably a relative, appeared from somewhere and quietly told us that she would probably rest for a while and come back. She's really back. Without sitting down, she asked who Petko was. I responded. And Vanga said: "Your brother (killed-approx. the author) is very stubborn. He insists that I tell you that you must not leave his child and must take care of it." I agreed. Then Vanga asked which of us was the officer. Lieutenant Urumov responded, and Vanga asked him why he was in civilian clothes. He replied ," So as not to stand out." Vanga: "And I look, where is the officer? Well. But here's the thing. Here before me is a person close to you, also an officer. Killed in March. Do you know who we're talking about?» The lieutenant confirmed it. Wang continued, " He has something very important to say to you, but I have no right to touch on political matters. But he says this: you know what party he was in. He suggests that you follow his example and go over to the side of his party: it's better for you. And more. He says that you should tell his wife to take off her mourning and get married as soon as possible, so that his daughter Malinka will get used to her new father. And to dress the girl in a white dress, buy her a watch so that he can see how it suits her. The lieutenant promised to write to the widow. Vanga changed the subject. To the lieutenant: "Before you came here, you served in another place. There were some tools, picks, shovels missing, and you never found them." The lieutenant confirmed what was said. Vanga: "Don't worry, there will be. When the waters of the Struma come down, their handles will appear out of the water." Vanga continued: "You had a scam with some suitcase. There was some lard in it, and the soldiers ate it without the master's permission. Don't scold them! They were hungry, and who would have stayed in such a famine. Well, you've had enough."

When we went outside, we couldn't help but exchange impressions about this and that, although everyone was surprised by what they saw and heard. I asked the lieutenant what party his friend was from. He replied that he was a communist, and that he was from the agricultural party, and that they argued a lot on political issues.

When Vanga asked, who's next, Paul volunteered. Vanga told him that he works in the office, and on one side she sees shelves with books. There are also books on the opposite wall, and a very beautiful woman is working opposite Pavel's desk. She's a widow and has two lovely daughters. "You're a bachelor, aren't you?» Pavel confirmed it. Said he was an official in the firm "Granainas" in the town of Elin Pelin. "Listen, Pavel, you're going to marry this woman. She likes you, but she's too shy to tell you how she feels. So you have to take the first step. And know that this woman will bring you happiness." Pavel blushed like a girl. Vanga said that he was going to be promoted, and he was very happy.

A few years later, I met Pavel in Sofia in a restaurant, on the site of which the Hemus Hotel is now built.

I asked him if what Vanga had told him had come true. He replied that he had indeed married this woman, that he had a wonderful family, and that he was already a director of the company.

The third person Vanga spoke to was Mincho. "And you don't see anything," said Vanga, " it's dark, you can't see anything. You don't believe it, that's why it's dark." Mincio said he was wondering if he was going to have a baby. "I will tell you as a person to a person," Vanga replied, " adopt a baby, and if you then have your own, it will be nice."

Mincho was the man who kept trying to tell us that Vanga was getting information from those who were eavesdropping at her request. Many years later, I asked him if he had listened to Vanga's words. He said he hadn't thought of it. At the same time, it was darker than a cloud."

In 1947, Vanga's husband finished building the house and fell seriously ill. He had not really recovered since his return from Greece, and the construction of the house had completely undermined his strength. Mitko suffered from severe stomach pains, and one of his friends advised him to drink a glass of raki daily to reduce the pain. Mitko began to drink a little and without noticing how addicted he was to wine, he became sullen and irritable, locked himself alone in the room, did not talk to anyone, only drank. Probably, he was experiencing some kind of internal, deeply personal drama, and he did not want to share it with anyone. Both the doctors and Vanga herself constantly advised Mitka to change his lifestyle, but he did not want to listen to anyone. Vanga walked around the house like a shadow, melting before her eyes from agony and anxiety, crying all night long. She knew that there was no salvation for her husband, she knew it for sure, but she kept it all to herself and prayed to God that a miracle would happen.

And people kept coming to Vanga, and she listened to them, gave advice, treated them. And no one suspected what a tragedy was being played out in her own home.

Mitko was "treated" in this way for twelve years, until he ended up in a hospital bed. The hospital was diagnosed with cirrhosis of the liver. Vanga was in despair. But she wanted to stay close to him. And she spent a long time at the bedside of her sick husband. When the attending physician hinted to Vanga that things were very bad, she replied: I know death is near. One day, the dying Mitko, feeling some relief, fell asleep.

On the floor, at his feet, Vanga also fell asleep. During the six months of her serious illness, Vanga was close to her husband, as if she wanted to give him a piece of her strength, her firmness. Or maybe it was one continuous farewell to a loved one with whom two decades have been lived.

It is not customary to talk about those difficult days in our family, I hardly learn something, quite a bit, from my mother.

"When Mitko was dying, Vanga knelt before his bed, tears streaming incessantly from her blind eyes. She was whispering softly. Whether she was praying to the Almighty to spare him, or saying goodbye to her husband, I do not know. Mitko died on April 1, 1962, at the age of 42. And when the great mystery of death had already been accomplished, Vanga stopped crying and fell asleep.

We did everything necessary, people started coming, and she was still asleep. I slept until the burial. Then she said: "I accompanied him to the place that was assigned to him."

The next morning I went out and told the unsuspecting people who had gathered at our door, as usual, that Vanga had buried her husband yesterday and was not in a condition to see anyone. But she protested: "Bring back the people. I'll take them all. They need me."

From that day on, we, Vanga's nephews — Krasimir, Anna and Dimitar, of course, and our mother — Lubka, witnessed her bitter, lonely, widowed life, her personal tragedy and at the same time her amazing tireless life in the name of people. It seems that this is how she was born: to be happy with the happiness that she gives to people.

I remember her in those days: under the black widow's kerchief, which she has not taken off since, her face was pale, as if frozen. Her whole being lives an inner life, tense, concentrated, detached from everything that surrounds her. And people are coming and going, they are becoming more and more, they seem to be rushing here from all over the world. With different problems, with different questions, scientists and completely illiterate, skeptics and believers, healthy and sick, they cross its threshold with fear or ridicule, with distrust or curiosity. And she doesn't say no to anyone.

I remember an old case. A young, intelligent woman came to visit my mother in Sandanski and asked her to help her get to Vanga, whom she trusted very much. The woman's child was seriously ill, but she was afraid to do anything without consulting Vanga. Here's what she said:

"In 1944, my father, a doctor and a committed materialist, decided to visit Vanga just out of curiosity. In Petrich, there were a lot of people in front of her house, everyone was waiting for their turn. Vanga appeared in the doorway and called my father, calling him by a diminutive name that was never used outside the family circle. In disbelief, the doctor came to her, and she told him much of his past. My father was married twice — she described his marriages correctly, gave details that even the doctor's wives did not know about. Then she talked about the future. She said he would die of cancer in fourteen years. She told me about me and her little brother. About me, she said that I would be very happy in my marriage, but my husband would soon die. I will remain a widow, with a small child in my arms. Then I will remarry, and this time unsuccessfully. About the fate of my brother, Vanga said that it would be very cruel: he would die from an accident at the age of 20.

My father was terribly upset by everything he heard, wanted to keep everything a secret, but could not stand it and shared it with his second wife. Then I learned the secret.

Time passed, and my father fell ill. He thought he had an ulcer. He had two operations — the second time only opened. He died of cancer in 1958, on a day aptly named Vanga.

I myself eventually got married, was very happy in the marriage, we had a child. But suddenly my husband fell ill and died. My second marriage was very unsuccessful and ended in divorce. And just before that, my brother, hurrying to the tram, slipped and fell right under the wheels. He was twenty years old. Everything that Vanga predicted to my father came true with amazing accuracy."

Or here is such a case. The child of our neighbors, a baby of ten months, had a temperature of 38 or even 39 degrees for three weeks. Doctors could not understand the cause of the disease, treated with all diligence, different medications, but to no avail. We brought the baby to Vanga, she ordered to bathe him in the infusion of forest herbs. After the first bath, the temperature dropped, after the second, the child calmed down completely and soon recovered.

A Russian ballerina who married a Bulgarian had motor disorders after a difficult birth. The doctors thought she couldn't dance anymore. The saddened actress did not know what to do. Someone had advised her to visit Vanga, so that she could be sure of her future, of what to hope for.

The meeting took place. And how happy the ballerina was when she heard this: don't grieve, you will soon recover, give birth to two more children and dance to the glory of Russian ballet. So it happened.

F. S., nurse:

"Many years ago, my mother went to Vanga to find medicine for her sister, who became deaf as a child. It happened like this. The owner of the house in which our family lived returned in the evening drunk, entered the parents ' room and hit the girl-touched some nerve. Vanga told the mother to show the girl to the ear doctor in Varna, and warned that the child would feel only a slight relief, but not completely cured. And so it happened. My mother was told to rest more, because she would die on her feet. And so it happened, the mother five years ago died suddenly from a stroke at the age of 54 years. I saw Vanga and my uncle, who died a long time ago, who was holding a glass in his hands. An uncle died while trying to prevent a head-on collision between two passenger trains. He couldn't jump out in time, and two locomotives flattened him like a flat cake. Indeed, it turned out that shortly before the collision, he drank red wine, and because of this, my grandfather (his father) could not get a pension for the deceased son for a long time-it was believed that the trouble occurred from the fact that he was drunk. And the fact that he saved the lives of so many people traveling in two trains was not taken into account."

V. G., writer:

"About seventeen years ago, one of my relatives was at Vanga's, they were talking about different things, but suddenly Vanga asked:" What is Vlado doing, the Old House?» Dora, the relative's name, called me later and said: "Look what nonsense Vanga says — what does Vlado, the Old House, do?»

After 17 years, I wrote a book of memories about my hometown of Bansko and called it "Purple Tulip". He gave the manuscript to the publishing house "Narodna Mladezh". The editor-in-chief was Evtim Evtimov. He said he didn't particularly like the name and suggested changing it. I replied that I had another title in store, "Memories from the Old House." "This is better," Evtim Evtimov said. And the book came out with that title. One night, in the middle of the night, the same Dora called me and said in an agitated voice that she could not sleep in peace. While reading the book, she suddenly remembered that Vanga had seen the book and even its title. For so many years to come. "

S. P., journalist:

The headman of our village told me this story (village Razlogko - of the author). Our neighbor's horses are missing. He came to Vanga, and she said: "The horses were stolen by gypsies and taken to a meadow in the mountains. They're connected. The gypsies are going to take them away and sell them." When they came to the specified place, they saw the hobbled horses grazing. They took them away, and the man was terribly happy, because he was responsible for the horses on the farm."

E.N., Ruse:

"Again, they took away horses — a couple and very good ones. Vanga told the victims: "The horses were taken over the Stara Planina ridge, and they are in one of the Gabrovo villages." Then she described in detail both the place and the village. Horses found. "

K. P., film actor:

"After shooting the film "Glow over Drava", I started editing the film. It was a joint production of several countries, in which large funds were invested. Colleagues were horrified to find that several films were missing. This could lead to a big scandal and trouble. They came to Vanga, and she said that the films were simply thrown away. She described a small abandoned house near the dump. Colleagues remembered that on the outskirts of Pancharevo, the Film Center really has such an old small building where damaged and rejected films are stored. We went there, dug for a long time, but finally found the films.

Kr. St. - heard from Seraphim Severnyak (writer):

"Vanga asked how many marriages he had. He replied: "Three." "No, not four?" asked Vanga. - Here I see your sister next to you, and she shows me four fingers." S. S. was very scared, because his sister died many years ago as a child. Even the people closest to him didn't know what Vanga had learned."

B. X.:

"The child of our neighbors has disappeared without a trace. They searched everywhere for several days, but to no avail. The parents came to Vanga, and she told them that on Saturday the child would be brought home alive and well by the authorities. People spread the news, and early on Saturday morning we all gathered at the entrance of the house to see the denouement. There were some pessimists among us who left, but those who remained were rewarded in full when a police car drove up to the house at lunchtime. There were exclamations of surprise. The boy got out of the car, accompanied by a policeman. The scene of the meeting was indescribable."

G.G.:

Many years ago, Vanga told me which Bulgarian language tickets I would get for the entrance exam. When I pulled out my ticket in front of the admissions office, my astonishment was so evident on my face that the examiner asked me what was wrong with me. I plucked up the courage to blurt out the whole truth. He laughed and said, " Well, what are we going to do? To change a ticket, once Vanga guessed it?"

G. P. from the village he turned for help to Vanga.

The sheep in his flock seemed to go berserk — for some unknown reason, they began to bite each other and refuse to feed. Vanga ordered to watch which of the sheep begins to bite, cut off some of its wool and bring it to Vanga. After he brought the wool, she ordered it to be chopped fine, mixed with the feed, and given to each of the sheep. The sheep calmed down.

A young pregnant woman cries and explains the reason. She is pregnant with her seventh child, and all the time before that, girls were born to her. If this time she gives birth to a girl, her husband will simply throw her out of the house. "Leave this problem to me —" said Vanga, " a boy will be born." Indeed, a boy was born two months later.

The boy was born with something wrong with his legs. He decided to get rid of the disease and had an operation. After the operation, it got even worse. Vanga's comment: "I shouldn't have had the operation. After all, this disease did not prevent you from walking. If God gives us horns, we will wear them."

The young man began to limp so badly because of the spikes on his feet that he turned to Vanga for help. Vanga: "Take an old copper plate, heat it in the stove, then soak a woolen handkerchief in gasoline. Put it on a heated plate, step on it with your foot. Hold it until the plate cools down. Repeat the procedure four times."

...After the death of her husband, who was a reliable support for Vanga on the difficult path of life, she alone could not cope with the many people standing in front of the gates of her house, begging for help, waiting for support. Once it turned out that the crowd almost crushed Vanga herself. After this incident, after talking with her sister, my mother, and also with my father Stoyan, she asked them to move to Petrich to be close to her and help if possible. We have just built a new house in Sandanski, but we decided to leave it and move to Petrich. That was in 1966.

Now consider it necessary to tell aunt what I heard from my father Stoyan Gaigurov.

— My family often talked about Vanga. My mother and father respected her deeply and often consulted her on various matters. The amazing thing is that she also predicted my fate without even seeing me when she was visiting us, I was in the army. Vanga predicted that I would marry her sister.

Vanga's constant presence in our lives was not so much the presence of a relative as of an amazing sorcerer. I will never be able to explain to myself how she was able to predict the fate of each of my three children when they were born. It had happened exactly as she had seen it.

So, my eldest daughter Vanga predicted that she would learn foreign languages, be interested in hieroglyphs. After finishing school, my daughter decided to enter the Faculty of Bulgarian Philology, but she was discouraged, and she entered the Faculty of Turkish Philology. So she had to learn a foreign language, and later hieroglyphs. My youngest daughter Vanga said, you will become a good doctor. And the girl enjoyed playing music, played the piano perfectly, dreamed of a musical career. I don't know how it happened, but after graduating from high school, Anna applied to the medical institute, graduated from it and became a good doctor who sincerely loves his profession. Vanga told my son Dimitar that he would become a technician. He became one.

A lot of people who are skeptical about Vanga's gift still believe that she has intermediaries who collect preliminary information about people who come to her. This, of course, is not only wrong, but also impossible, as thousands of people from all over the world flock to Vanga. In addition, Vanga predicts the fate of newborns and even unborn children, sees people and talks to them, despite the fact that they died 100, 200 and even more years ago, with people that even their loved ones no longer remember. Vanga knows what medicine or medicinal herb will help a seriously ill person when medicine is already powerless. How does she do all this?

That's the question that needs to be answered.

When Vanga realized that she definitely could not help the thousands of people waiting day and night at the gate of her house, she turned to the authorities for help. She was carefully listened to, decided to help And from October 3, 1967, Vanga, in her words, "entered the civil service." People were assigned to maintain order in her yard, responsible for her rest and tranquility. A special service has been established under the community council to keep records of all those who wish to visit Vanga. In short, Vanga received official recognition, and, as I said at the beginning, she herself became the object of scientific research at the Institute of Suggestology and Parapsychology, headed by Georgy Lozanov,

M. D., Ruse:

"In 1968, I visited Vanga twice. She came out of her room surprised, or rather shocked. Everything I wanted to know, she told me. Some tape recorders and equipment were working in the room. The chairman and secretary of the community council invited me to a medical examination and began to question me. There were about 30 people in white coats. They were doctors, psychologists, neurologists and other specialists.

A year later, I received two letters from the Institute of Suggestology with a request to fill out the questionnaires sent by them and answer questions about what Vanga said came true. I answered with pleasure, because everything she said came true absolutely."

Unfortunately, this serious work gradually stopped, and almost nothing of the numerous materials was published, at least with us. Many people would like to read something reliable about Vanga, but there is no literature, and if so, then everyone has the right to suspect the presence of some secret here, as if protected even by the Bulgarian government. In our country, and not only in our country, the most incredible rumors were spread about Vanga. They, in turn, further fueled interest in her phenomenal talent. This interest was the reason for the publication in the magazine" Pogled " in 1966 of a material about Vanga. The article was called "Parapsychology and Vanga". In it, in addition to an interview with Dr. Lozanov, a serious attempt was made to explain this phenomenon. At the same time, various materials about Vanga have already been published abroad and continue to be published. It can be said that it is known everywhere, as evidenced by the numerous mail: we receive letters and congratulations on holidays from almost all countries of the world.

Interestingly, back in 1970, a book about people of phenomenal abilities was published in the United States. In the first chapter, called "Vanga Dimitrova-the Bulgarian Oracle", based on descriptions of some facts from Vanga's life and interviews with visitors and specialists, the authors try to explain her abilities and pose a number of interesting problems. It's another question how plausible the descriptions are, but at the end of the chapter, which is about 30 pages long, I think it's fair to say that the book will probably be the most profound essay ever written about a living prophet.

I am a window for them

The most amazing manifestation of Vanga's clairvoyant gift, according to many experts, is her ability to "communicate" with the deceased relatives, friends and acquaintances of those who come to her. Vanga's ideas about death, about what happens to a person after it, are sharply different from the generally accepted ones. Here is one of Vanga's dialogues with director P. I. (recorded in 1983).

— I have already told you that after death, the body decomposes, disappears, like all living things after death. But a certain part of the body does not give in to decay, does not rot.

"I suppose you mean the human soul?"

— I don't know what to call it. I believe that what is not subject to corruption in a person develops and passes into a new, higher state, about which we do not know anything specifically. Something like this happens: you die illiterate, then you die a student, then a person with a higher education, then a scientist.

— So, then, a person is waiting for several deaths?

- There are several deaths, but the higher principle does not die. And this is the soul of man.

For Vanga, death is only a physical end, and the personality is preserved even after death.

One day, Vanga told a visitor about his late mother, and he asked Vanga if his presence had evoked the image of a dead woman in her. The clairvoyant replied: "No, they come by themselves. I am a window into this world for them." Sometimes her statements acquire the harmony of mathematical formulations. Well, for example, this: "When a person stands in front of me, all the deceased relatives gather around him. They ask me their own questions and are willing to answer mine. What I hear from them, I pass on to the living."

I would like to start this topic by telling you about a recent story, because even I, who was used to Vanga's sessions, was very impressed by it.

And the case is as follows. My parents, whose father is an engineer, had an only son. 16 year old schoolboy. From an early age, they used to take their son everywhere with them, and when he grew up, the trio became inseparable. When the boy turned into a young man, his father and mother were very reluctant to let him go, because they were always afraid that something might happen to him. Once the son asked permission from his father, then from his mother to go with friends to the dacha. Strangely, both parents, contrary to firm principles and without even asking what kind of friends they were, allowed their son to leave without a single objection or persuasion. He left and never came back. The young man was found electrocuted near an electric pole.

Heartbroken, heartbroken and blaming only themselves for sending their son to his death, the parents decided to go to Vanga. We advised them to take a potted flower with them, because the recent death could cause Vanga to have a severe mental state and even a seizure.

When her parents entered Vanga's room, she suddenly turned pale and cried out in a strange loud voice: "Here I am! And how is the engineer?" And then my father turned pale and felt sick. The fact is that the young man had a habit of returning home, instead of saying hello, to address his father with this joking question. Both confirmed that it was their son's voice. The voice continued: "Tomorrow be sure to go to Lyubcho (his friend-ed.) and give him gray socks. (The next day was the name day of Faith, Hope and Love-approx. of the author). Tell me, how is Lyudmila? I received flowers from Vanya, but there were also many tears. Don't cry so much, you pour so many tears on us and stain our clothes. Then there is nothing to clean it with. The sky is not blue as you see it, it is white, very white. And we're in white. I want you to order a piece of silver jewelry the next time you come, something like a necklace, take it with you, engrave the letters B. and K. on it. I'll come again. I will come to you again, but it will be at the ninth hour."

They did not understand the meaning of the last sentence, but the mother, who had recovered her speech earlier than the others, although she was dumbfounded and still did not believe in what was happening, found the strength to ask Vanga, who spoke in her son's voice, if she could describe him. Vanga said in a young man's voice: "I am here, I am the one you are asking about, and so that everyone will believe, I will tell you how you saw me off. I'm wearing dark gray pants and a gray sweater. Don't be surprised! When I left and asked you, you both let me go. I was called, and no one could stop me. My uncle is with me. author) and grandfather. After a short pause: "Well, all right, I'm allowed to stay and talk to you for as long as I can."

Vanga took a deep breath, brightened up and said, " Well, he's gone, he's gone up like a snow-white chiton." And then she said, " This is how all of us, believers and non-believers, will all fly in the same direction. It was your boy's last hour, he was called, and he left."

I write down the words of Vanga: "One day a young woman came to me, and I immediately asked her: "Remember when your dead mother had a scar on her left thigh?» The woman confirmed that there was a scar, and asked me how I knew. Where from… After all, everything is very simple. The dead woman herself stood before me. It was a young, cheerful, smiling, blue-eyed woman in a white handkerchief. I remember her holding up her colorful skirt and saying, " Ask if my daughter remembers that I have a scar on my leg from a bruise?» Then the deceased said to me:"Tell Magdalena, through your guest, not to come to the cemetery again, as it is difficult for her, she has no knee." Magdalena was the sister of my guest, and the guest confirmed that the sister has an artificial knee cup and it is difficult for her to walk."

I remember that there was a rather long pause after what was said, and then Vanga continued to speak, a lot and inspired: "I hear your mother's voice, she asks me to tell you the following. When the Turks wanted to set fire to our village of Galichnik, my father offered them a large ransom to save the village. And then we decided to build a church and cut down all the mulberries in the village, there were no other trees nearby. They moved tree trunks to the construction site secretly, at night. They built a church. And in front of it they made a three-horned cheshma (fountain)."

The astonished guest told Vanga that she had never heard such details, but when she was in Galichnik, she really did not see the traditional mulberries there, and in front of the church there was a three-horned fountain.

Vanga, meanwhile, continued to broadcast, speaking as if in the language of the deceased: "Recently, my son hit his head and is now very ill." "Yes," the visitor confirmed, " my brother had a blood clot in one of the brain vessels, he was operated on." Vanga continued, " Do another operation, but only for complacency. It won't do any good, your brother will die soon."

I will not repeat that it all turned out that way.

Another case. A woman came whose son, a soldier, was involved in an accident and died. Vanga asked:

"What was the young man's name?
- Marko, - she answered
— But he tells me his name was Mario."

"Yes," the woman said, " we called him Mario at home.

Through Vanga, the young man told who was responsible for the disaster, and added:

"Death itself warned me (through a premonition) on Friday, and on Tuesday I left.

The young man died on Tuesday.

The mother said that her son had lost his watch, and she promised to buy him a new one, but after his death, of course, she did not buy anything.

The young man also asked why he did not see his sister, and his mother replied that his sister graduated from the institute, lives and works in another city.

Five people from Sofia decided to go to Vanga, got in the car and arrived in Rulite. They waited for quite a long time, but Vanga wanted to accept only one of them. "Call Kirill," she said. Indeed, this man had a very good reason for visiting Vanga. His son went on an excursion to Vitosha (the mountain at the foot of which lies Sofia approx. transl.) and did not return. Vanga said only a few words: "At this moment, I see your son sitting on a rock and drawing something on a piece of paper.

I can't say any more. You'll get news of him in two days." The man, calmed and happy, left, because he thought that if Vanga sees him drawing, then he is alive and will soon return. He decided it was just another trick. And the father did receive news about his son two days later, but from the police that the young man was found dead at the foot of the cliff. He was discovered by an elderly man who saw him down in the gorge. He was sitting up, but he was crouched down in a strange way. I called out to the guy, but he didn't answer. And when I went down, I saw that it was a corpse. And next to him was a piece of paper on which he was drawn flying off a cliff.

The lines from the letters:

M. K., Sofia: "In 1970, my brother Vasil, 49, disappeared, and for twenty days we knew nothing about him. He worked as the chief accountant in the village council. My sister and daughter-in-law went to see Vanga. She described his appearance — the color of his shirt, his habit of looking at his watch, but at the moment the watch is not on his hand (he left it at home), that she sees him barefoot and somewhere high in the mountains. I described the area, but I couldn't say exactly where it was. Then we learned that my brother had died in a fall from the Black Rock on Rhyl. She saw his agony and said: "I see him barefoot, lying on the ground, but... not dead." When I told the investigator about this, he was surprised and said: "Yes, he was really barefoot, his shoes were on the side, and he really did not die immediately." But Vanga said goodbye to my daughter-in-law with the following words: "Go, my daughter-in-law, the authorities will tell you everything." Indeed, two days later a policeman came and told his daughter-in-law that he had been found. Isn't it a miracle!»

I. L., Sofia: "I will not, Vanga, recall all those words that were fully confirmed after meeting with you. But I will not forget the excitement that came over me when you called me out of the crowd, and by name. And when I stood before you, you said to me, " Behold, your dead father has appeared before you, and he has come from afar." Through you, my father told me about the amazing details of our family's life and its future. You said: "My father is not happy, he asks why his house was sold, which was built on the site given to him by Alexander Stamboliysky?» I just froze, because I had completely forgotten about this detail and didn't think it was that important. But nevertheless, I was sorry that I had upset my father, and I kept the excitement of that incredible meeting for the rest of my life."

Vanga says: "Soon, people will start meeting their deceased relatives on the streets." (1989).

Such an absolutely incredible ability of Vanga to communicate with the dead made a great impression on our famous literary critic Zdravko Petrov. In a Sofia magazine, back in 1975, he published a very interesting article entitled "The Prophetic Bulgarian Woman". I will give it with small abbreviations.

"Until the autumn of 1972, I attached very little importance to the fact that in the small town of Petrich, near the Greek border, there lives a prophetess who attracts the attention of many Bulgarians. From early morning until late at night, her yard is full of people. She knows about the fate of missing people, solves crimes, makes medical diagnoses, tells about the past. The most amazing thing about her gift is that she tells not only about the present and foreshadows the future. Her predictions are devoid of fatal consistency. Her own experience had taught her to be very careful in her predictions. In addition, not everything that is possible becomes a reality. The Hegelian term "split reality" can explain not only probability as a philosophical category, but also the phenomenon of Vanga. Some things she says with amazing accuracy.

During one of the sessions I attended, Vanga asked her "patient" to give her a watch, usually they come to her with sugar cubes. He was very surprised that she wanted to feel the watch. But Vanga told him the following: "I'm not holding your watch, I'm holding your brain."

Once by chance, I found myself in Petrich on vacation. I spent a few days there. My knowledge of this simple woman, who was endowed with the gift of divination, was thus somewhat expanded. I looked in on her, listened to her, and left. To be honest, I had no intention of being subjected to any of her "sessions". It seems that Vanga understood this state of mind in the first days of my stay in Petrich, because later she said to a friend of mine:"He came with a desire not to know anything about himself, and I told him everything." And she laughed her characteristic laugh.

But the most interesting part of the whole story begins now.

My friend, who introduced me to Vanga, had a car and offered to drive out of town after lunch. He offered not only to me, but also to Vanga and her sister. Together we drove to the village of Samoilovo, near which were the ruins of the fortress built by Tsar Samuel, an object of archaeological research and restoration. We drove in silence in the car. Having arrived, we decided to inspect the fortress and the excavations that had begun. Since Vanga could not enjoy the view of the ancient fortress with us, she stayed in the car with her sister. They were talking among themselves. I was taking a walk nearby. And suddenly, when I was 7-8 meters away from the car, Vanga spoke. I realized that her words were referring to me. She surprised me with the first sentence: "Your Father Peter is here." I froze like Hamlet contemplating the spirit of his father. What could I say? My father died fifteen years ago. Vanga began to talk about him in such detail that I was petrified with amazement. I cannot say anything about my feelings at that time, but those who saw me say that I was very excited and deadly pale. She repeated several times that my father was standing in front of her, although I still cannot imagine in what capacity and in what projection — in the past, present or future — she saw him. Nevertheless, Vanga even pointed at him with her hand. Obviously, she "got the information" (how?!) about some domestic event, long forgotten even by me. For Vanga, there is no concept of the present, past, or future. Time in its representation is one general homogeneous stream. At least that's the impression I got. So, she easily told me about my father's past life. She was "aware" that he, a lawyer by profession, had taught political economy and civil law at a Turkish gymnasium before the 1944 revolution.

Then Vanga started talking about my uncles. I named two of them. I told her about my third uncle, who died tragically. His death was surrounded by mystery. Vanga said that the reason for his murder was betrayal. I was also very surprised that she suddenly asked: "Who in your family name is Matvey?" I replied that that was the name of my grandfather. I was five years old when he was buried on a cold January day. It's been forty years since that day. That she knew my grandfather's name surprised me.

When I returned to Sofia and told my friends about everything, one of them asked me if I was thinking about my grandfather at that moment. I very rarely think of him even in Sofia, where there are several relatives with whom we could talk about him. Even my closest friends don't know his name. Vanga said he was a good man. That's how my relatives knew him.

Vanga talked about my relatives for a long time, about 10-15 minutes. She also told me about her niece, who made a mistake in the exams when entering the university. I even mentioned small everyday things, such as the fact that the steam heating in my apartment is faulty. Then she advised me to spend more time in the sun, as it is necessary for my health. I really don't like the sun very much, but she strongly advised me to walk more. She said: "Let the sun be your god." Then she said that I have two higher educations ("two heads", as she defined it), the audience added that I was on a specialization in Moscow.

Vanga said that he sees the warriors of Samuel. They passed in rows before her mind's eye. We know from history that they were blinded by order of Basil II. Vanga asked me who blinded them, what nationality he was. I was very confused: I had a blank in my memory, I completely forgot the history of this royal dynasty. Afterward, a friend of mine asked me how I could forget the pedigree of Basil II, knowing Byzantine history well. I guess I was just really confused by Vanga's ability to see such a distant past. Under different circumstances, Vanga asked me who the Byzantines were. She said that once, when she was in a church in the town of Melnik, she heard voices saying, " We are Byzantines."

She saw people dressed in brocade and the ruins of Roman baths underground. Several noble Byzantines were indeed forced to leave their homeland and settle in Melnik. She also talked about other historical figures.

I tried to understand her amazing ability to see past and future. There was a very interesting dialogue going on between us all the time.

Vanga started talking about death. We couldn't take our eyes off her still face. Obviously, she had visions. She told about some cases in which she felt the approach of death. She told me that she had seen the exact hour of her husband's death. Then she told how once, when she was cooking plums in the yard, death "rustled" over the trees. It was like a ballad. In the view of Wang's death is a beautiful woman with flowing hair. I had the feeling that this was a poet, not a soothsayer.

Death… This is a terrible and unwelcome guest, tearing the threads of our lives. But, according to Vanga, this is a projection of our " I " in some other dimensions that we do not understand.

... One day a young woman from Sofia came to Vanga. Vanga turned to her and asked:

"Where's your friend?"

The woman replied that he was dead, drowned a few years ago while swimming in the river.

Vanga described the young man, saying that she saw him as alive, that he was talking to her.

— I can see it in front of me. He is tall, dark, and has a mole on his cheek. I can hear his voice. The guy has a slight speech impediment.

The woman confirmed everything. Vanga continued,

"He said to me,' No one is responsible for my death. I fell into the water myself and broke my spine." He asks who got his watch and other things. He remembers many people, asks about friends and acquaintances. Advises his friend to get married soon and assures that the choice will be successful.

A Spanish scientist, professor told Wang about how kind and caring his dead mother was. But all her life she lived in poverty. Vanga interrupted him and said:

"Wait until I tell you what happened." On her deathbed your mother said: "I have nothing to leave you but an old family ring. You are alone, so let him help you and protect you in life."

The astonished professor confirmed that it was so. The Spaniard explained that once, when he was already a famous scientist, while resting on the banks of the river, the ring slipped off his finger and fell into the water. He looked for it, but never found it.

"What did you do, man?" You've lost touch with your mother! Vanga exclaimed.

The embarrassed scientist admitted that sometimes such a thought flashed through his mind, as failures began to haunt him at every turn since then, but as a materialist scientist, he drove such thoughts away.

A few years ago, during a flood, a husband and wife lost their only child. It was logical to assume that the child had drowned, but I didn't want to believe it. They came to Vanga to find out the truth. And Vanga — this case is told by herself-told them the following: "Don't cry, this is the fate of your child. He really is not among the living. But the body isn't where they were looking for it. He's down where the river turns. There are big trees, and the body is stuck in the roots. I see him as if he were alive. He gives me his hand, he calls me to show you the place. He wants to be buried."

After some time, relatives of this family came to Vanga and said that the child's corpse was found exactly in the place that she indicated. The body of the unfortunate child was removed and buried.

There are thousands of such cases, it is impossible to describe them all, and the topic, I must admit, is not very pleasant.

Vanga sees not only the "realm of the dead". She sees the destruction and rebirth of entire cities. For example, the city of Melnik.

"Here," says Vanga, " every blade of grass, every stone, every inch of earth is sacred. I come here with great pleasure and have the best rest. I am charged with strength, energy, inspiration. I sit down on a rock and just don't say anything. No one should disturb me. Everything that surrounds me speaks to me — stones, ruins, and shadows. The city tells me the story of centuries gone by. I see long-dead people, ruined temples, houses built thousands of years ago.

... Once we came here with my sister. Her six-month-old son was with her. It seemed to me that his soul said to me in the voice of Vanga: "Aunt, do you see Melnik? And you look like him."

I was very upset and cried bitterly: "Why like Melnik? What did Vanga mean? The ancient history of this city or its emptiness and abandonment? And why did I associate these words with the baby?"

I still don't know.

In the early 70s, Vanga had a strong desire to go to Melnik every day and it was there that he received many of his visitors. She believed that her gift in this town was more fully revealed, that she could tell people about very interesting things here. But this kind of activity for a small town is associated with a number of problems, and Vanga's desire was not satisfied. It is a pity, it remains unknown what revelations Vanga would surprise us all.

Another interesting case.

In 1983, director P. K. shared with Vanga his plans to make a film about Orpheus. Vanga said that he will not succeed, as the director's attitude to the legendary hero is completely wrong. She said literally the following (the conversation is recorded on tape):

"Orpheus' gift is not heavenly, but earthly. He listened to the earth and sang. The wild animals stood and listened to him, but did not understand. Orpheus-earth. He played and sang both to the willow leaf and to the willow itself. He was lying on the ground, and the earth itself was listening to him and singing to him. Orpheus sang with the earth. Wherever he went, he always played tunes. The birds sang to him, and he sang to them. It was good for him on earth and with earthly creatures. To the sounds of the sky, many times more beautiful, he remained deaf.

But tell me — "she said to the director —" will he be rich or poor?" How do you see him? I, for example, see him in torn clothes, with regrown nails. He sings all the time, the earth gives him all the voices. That is why he is so untidy and untidy, he is not from heaven. You can't make him look like that. That's what's bad.

It happens in different ways: sometimes I see old events and people who have passed away quite well, sometimes worse. I must say that I'm not always curious about it myself. I'm just sitting here alone thinking: "God, what was not in this world! I wish I could tell people! It would be nice, but the skill is not enough»...

With pleasure, Vanga talks... with flowers. She thinks of them as living beings, just like us, human beings. If only I could tell you how carefully she tended the flowers outside her cottage in Rupit! She always stops in front of each flower, caressing it. he waters it, whispers something to it. She says that the flowers tell her a lot of interesting things. Just a fairy tale, a beautiful fairy tale! But this is also true, it shows that it is true.

There are so many inexplicable things in her whole life... If you visit Vanga immediately after the death of a loved one, then she may become ill from contact with this recent death, there have been cases that she even lost consciousness. Immediately realizing who came to her, she usually says: "Why did you come without flowers? The information about the deceased that you unconsciously communicate by your mere presence is also known to flowers, but flowers are able to convey it more delicately than a person, thereby saving me from shocks." And at the same time, she does not like bouquets, says: "Flowers are most beautiful alive: in a meadow, in a flower bed, in a pot. The bouquet is like a crowd of people, where individuality is erased. After all, each flower has its own personality."

Her mother recalls how one day Vanga asked her to go out to the people gathered in their yard and call a woman. Vanga called her name and said that she works as a flower girl in Sofia. When asked how Vanga knew that a flower girl was waiting in the courtyard, the clairvoyant replied: "Yes, the cornflowers just told me. A woman wants to ask me what she should do with her completely bloated son. Call the poor woman, I'll tell her everything."

Vanga also had a long conversation about flowers with the Soviet writer Leonid Leonov when he came to Bulgaria in 1980. She said, in particular, that she envied his huge garden, full of wonderful, pure, like a child's eyes, flowers. Smiling conspiratorially at Leonid Maksimovich, she remarked:: "I know and you understand the language of flowers, it is true and beautiful." And then she reproached her master for giving a large philodendron, which used to stand at his house, to the Writers ' Union. I advised you to definitely find another one, as it is the philodendron that stimulates inspiration. He is the flower of artists and entertainers.

About flowers, plants and medicinal herbs, as I have already mentioned. Vanga also talked with Svyatoslav Roerich. To his question about the importance of medicinal herbs in medicine, Vanga replied: "There are two words can not do. This is a separate big topic. The world began with grass and will end with herbs. Everything that people leave on Earth will grow with the grass of oblivion. The herbs of each country are curative only for the people living in that country. So it is already defined. Everyone should only be treated with their own herbs."

THERAPEUTIC ACTIVITIES

"... Blessed are those who have not seen and believed'.

The Gospel of John, chapter 20 (29)

Human health, diagnosis and treatment of diseases have always and very seriously occupied Vanga. She believes that almost all diseases can be cured by herbs. Claims that Bulgaria. - a blessed country in this respect, as there are a lot of healing, truly precious herbs.

Vanga is convinced that the day is near when humanity will get rid of the terrible disease — cancer, that a cure for cancer will be found. She says: "the day will Come and cancer will be chained in iron chains". When asked to explain this strange-sounding prediction, Vanga said that the drug against cancer should contain a lot of iron, since iron is now not enough in human food and drinking water. She believes that in the near future, scientists will discover another drug that is necessary for the restoration of human strength and health. The drug will contain mainly horse, dog and turtle hormones. When asked why these animals, Vanga said: "The horse is strong, the dog is hardy, and the turtle lives long."

According to Vanga, medicinal herbs work especially well if a person is doused with their infusions, since the active substances are completely absorbed through the human skin.

Vanga never comes into conflict with official medicine and recognizes its success in various fields. The treatment offered by Vanga does not reject traditional medical methods, but only complements them. But Vanga believes that the abuse of medicines is dangerous, as they close the gate through which nature, through the action of medicinal herbs, can restore the balance in the patient's body disturbed by the disease.

It must be admitted that Vanga is keenly interested in all new discoveries in the field of medicine, and considers it right to return to acupuncture treatment. But here's what she said to one of the doctors who visited her, who was engaged in acupuncture:

- Treatment with needles is a strong remedy, but to achieve the most complete success, it is necessary to use non-metallic, but clay needles, as they did in ancient times. They need to be heated on a live fire, not by electricity, since there is already enough electricity in the human body, and you, dear, thus only increase its influence. Thinking that you are helping, in fact, you are interfering with the correct effect of needles on the body.

The doctor objected that such a technique would be a step back. Vanga did not agree and replied:

- Yes, everything is back to normal. Look closely around you and you will easily be convinced of this.

Is it possible to distinguish a certain number of tips from all her medical practice that are acceptable to everyone?

Yes, it is possible, although it should be emphasized that both herbs and treatment directions that Vanga advises different people with the same disease, of course, are different. Vanga firmly knows that every person is absolutely individual, and therefore needs individual treatment. I want to give some examples, confirmed by the patients themselves, as a result of Vanga's advice, their overall health improved. Many have completely recovered.

A patient with leukemia, who turned to her, Vanga advised to drink juice from the roots of mallow, and a child suffering from the same disease-to use juice from the flowers of mallow.

The patient with cirrhosis of the liver, she offered to drink milk, after mixing it with white wheat flour.

To the parents of a child who had badly bruised his head, which made him sleep poorly, she suggested a simple and effective remedy: to bathe the baby in the morning dew, which abundantly covers the grass with summer dawns. Then a wet diaper should be wrapped around the child. My parents did. Soon the father of the child personally came to Vanga to inform: the baby became better, he quickly recovers. Vanga literally worships this summer miracle-morning dew, believing that in the morning plants secrete a lot of healing substances, which is why it is so useful to wipe off the dew not only for the sick, but also for the healthy, for prevention.

The child, who had a high temperature for three months, was advised by Vanga to make a bath from an infusion of sour grapes. The mother did so — the fever subsided, the child quietly fell asleep.

A person suffering from eczema was told to pick a bouquet of forest flowers, moisten the affected areas with a strong hot infusion.

A woman suffering from scabies was advised to cook five glasses of barley, wipe the skin with a decoction.

The young man, who had kidney pain, was advised to drink tea from pumpkin seeds.

The worker, who was poisoned by harmful fumes in the shop, was advised to warm his feet in warm water every evening for a month.

A woman suffering from swollen legs was told to make a plaster of wax, olive oil and water and cover the sore spots with this plaster.

A child with epilepsy was ordered to bathe in an infusion of forest herbs. Such an infusion, in her opinion, is an excellent sedative.

The woman, who has been suffering from chest pain for 10 years, was told that she had inflammation of the lining of the lung, and was told to make hot poultices from bread dough mixed with homemade yeast, with the addition of vinegar, vegetable oil and sour wine.

For those who suffer from a debilitating cough, Vanga advises drinking flaxseed tea and not drinking cold water.

To prevent heart disease, he suggests that each person drink an infusion of hawthorn flowers four times a year for four days.

From rashes on the skin, bathing in an infusion of oak bark helps well.

Patients with asthma should regularly drink an infusion of mother-and-stepmother flowers.

The parents of a child with a sick bowel were told to keep it on a strict diet, sharply limiting the oil content in food.

In pre-infarction states, he advises drinking blackthorn tea in a row for four days, in the morning on an empty stomach.

A woman suffering from migraines due to severe nervous fatigue was told to drink a tablespoon of water with sugar every night before going to bed. And another patient, also with a strong nervous disorder, was advised to grate half a kilo of lemons, stir with honey, take one tablespoon in the morning and in the evening.

At the initial stage of diabetes, he advises drinking a decoction of blackberries, believing that this way you can stop the progression of the disease.

Vanga believes that stomach ulcers most often occur as a result of poor-quality food. It is impossible, in her opinion, to eat very hot food.

Asthma is the result of drinking cold liquids, especially harmful to drink cold water if a person is tired.

Metabolic disorders are usually associated with poor nutrition.

She explains mastitis in women with tight underwear and uncomfortable clothes.

Tumors occur, as a rule, as a result of a fall or other injury, they can appear quite a long time after the injury.

The kidneys get sick most often after a cold.

Infertility in women is the result of early sexual activity, fear of unwanted pregnancy, as well as frequent colds, uncomfortable underwear. Almost the same reasons explain the infertility of men.

In the first edition of the book, I described about 60 cases of patients cured by Vanga of various diseases. I received a lot of letters from people who read the book in manuscript, and they advised me to give more recipes, as the interest in this topic is very great. Listening to the advice of these people, I expand the chapter on Vanga's therapeutic activities, but at the same time I ask you to pay attention that these are not prescriptions, but only recommendations addressed to specific individuals.

I don't know if everyone can use them.

So:

Acne (teenage acne) — Before going to bed, a compress is applied to the face — a cotton cloth soaked in a decoction of lemon balm, soapberry and black elderberry.

Allergy — One tablespoon of wormwood is boiled in half a liter of water until half is left. Take one teaspoon, two to three times a day after meals.

Amenorrhea (scanty or absence of menstruation in women) - Cook the husk of two kilograms of onions in 3 liters of water until it becomes dark red Drink a decoction of one coffee cup on an empty stomach in the morning or in the evening.

Ambalac is a childhood disease in which the child drinks only water, the tummy is swollen, there are swollen glands on the abdomen (the size of a nut) - Mixed in equal parts tar, pork fat and a little wood ash. With this mixture, spread the baby's tummy, put it to bed, close it and let it sleep. Then bathe it in water in which sour apples, wild pears and a little anise (one tablespoon) were cooked. Let it lie in the water, and then spread with grape raki (Bulgarian fruit vodka).

Anemia (in children) - In early spring, when the leaves of the nut are blooming, do a few drenches with water in which the nut leaves boiled for 30 minutes.

Arthritic, rheumatic pains in bad weather — A hot poultice of boiled cherry leaves is placed on the knees.

Asthma (in children) - Dry 40 leaves of mother-and-stepmother and keep for some time in half a liter of raki (vodka). Apply a few leaves to the baby's chest until they run out.

Asthma - Drink tea from the flowers of the mother-and-stepmother, paying special attention to the nasopharynx.

Asthma — in a child) - 40 leaves of mother-and-stepmother insist in strong vodka for a day. On the first evening, attach 1 leaf to the child's chest, on the second evening, attach 1 leaf to the back, and so alternate until the leaves run out. The procedure should be done only in late autumn.

Asthma (in a child, the initial stage) - A cream is made from crushed aspirin and pork fat. It is applied to the baby's chest for ten days.

Asthma (in a child) - Dry the mother-and-stepmother's flowers. Then boil them and bathe in the broth of the child. After the bath, spread with honey and rub with vodka.

Asthma - 40 heads of onion seedlings are poured with boiling water until they soften. Simmer in half a liter of olive oil and then mash. This puree is taken in the morning and in the evening by one tablespoon.

Infertility (in women) - Take a handful of earth dug by a mole from a hole in the spring, pour boiling water in a suitable vessel. Squat over the steam for 15-20 minutes. The procedure is repeated several times.

Insomnia (in a child) - Take 1 kg of river sand, pour in a large amount of water and boil. When the water cools down, pour it on the child.

Insomnia (in children) - Wrap the child in a sheet that has absorbed the morning dew. Early in the morning, spread a sheet on the grass and it will absorb the droplets.

Insomnia — The patient sleeps on a pillow stuffed with forest hay.

Insomnia — The patient sleeps on a pillow stuffed with dried hops.

Insomnia — The patient should take a tablespoon of honey in the evening before going to bed.

Insomnia - Before going to bed, take one tablespoon of sugar, washed down with a glass of water.

Stomach pain (from unwashed foods) - Tea made from basil, chamomile or mint. One tablespoon of herbs boil for 3 minutes in 600 g. water. Drink three times a day for one coffee cup after meals, for children-one tablespoon.

Stomach pain — Chew one leaf of red clover every day. Swallow only the juice.

Pain in the legs-it is good to wash your feet in cold water, spread pork fat, put on warm cotton socks and sleep in them.

Pain in the hands (with arthritis) — 10 evenings in a row to do baths in cool water, in which the fern was cooked.

Arthritis pain — In half a liter of strong vodka, half a packet of mustard seed is boiled until half the liquid remains. Smear sore spots in the morning and evening. Make baths in a decoction of bird cherry.

Bronchitis (in a child) - Fry two eggs in melted lard and salt. When cool, apply to the baby's chest at night.

Bronchitis (in children) - Remove the middle from the head of the red onion and pour in one teaspoon of crystalline sugar. The child should eat one head a day.

Bronchitis (in a child) - Take a coffee spoon of castor oil once a day.

Bronchitis - 2-3 leaves of mother-and-stepmother cook in 0.5 liters of fresh milk. Add the melted lard on the tip of a knife. Drink one coffee cup in the evening.

Sick kidneys - Give the patient a decoction of pumpkin seeds. Grind two packets of flaxseed and add a little water, make a hot poultice, apply to the kidneys.

Sick kidneys - Once a week, the patient only eats boiled wheat and drinks water.

Sick kidneys - A large blackberry root is boiled in five liters of water until half is left. This is a decoction to drink three times 100 g. in the day.

Sick kidneys - Pour the pottery clay with apple cider vinegar and stir well. Spread this mixture on the canvas and apply it to the kidneys in the evening.

Chest pain (old) - According to Vanga, the pulmonary membrane is inflamed. The patient is recommended to make a hot poultice of bread dough with additives from alum: 100 g of wine vinegar, 100 g of sunflower oil and 100 g. dry wine. Apply to the sore spot.

Pain in the legs - Cook a bunch of clover in a capacious pot. When the water cools, strain and add one tablespoon of kerosene. Do foot baths 5-4 evenings in a row.

Sick gallbladder — The patient has two pears on an empty stomach. Drink compote of wild pears without sugar.

Pain in the gallbladder, accompanied by heaviness and nausea — (after eating fatty foods) - Drink the juice of half a lemon, adding half a teaspoon of baking soda to it.

"Burger's" disease (initial stage) - Red clay mixed with grape vinegar is applied to the canvas and applied to the sore spot.

Inflammation of the ovaries — The patient squats over a warm bath of water in which forest hay was cooked. The procedure is done every day until the inflammation passes.

Inflammation of the ovaries — Sit over steam with a decoction of fresh cabbage, poured with fresh milk.

Inflammation of the facial nerve - Heat a metal needle in hot coals and with a light touch (like injections) burn the skin of the face, first from the healthy side, then from the patient. Light burns on the skin quickly pass and leave no traces.

Headache (in a child) - Make a linen pillow out of immortelle. After sleeping, pour a decoction of immortelle over the child's head.

Headache (chronic) - In the evening, submerge the head in water and pour the body with water in which the thyme was cooked.

Headache - Wash your hair with a decoction of parsley.

Headache (and restless sleep) - In 2-3 liters of water, cook 1-2 leaves of agave, water the head and body several times in the evening.

Chest pain, teals, ulcers - 0.5 kg. rye flour mixed with 100 g. butter and a glass of milk. Put the dough on a cloth and apply it to the sore spot three nights in a row.

Pain in the body - A mixture of wax, ground wormwood and vodka is applied several times to the sore spot.

Back pain — Spread 1 m of white cloth with 100 grams of gun oil, make a patch and apply to the sore spot three evenings in a row.

Back pain — Spread honey on the back and rub it well.

Pain in the chest and right shoulder (According to Vanga, the pain appeared as a result of a fall several years ago) - Remove the rabbit skin, sprinkle with red pepper, smear with sunflower oil and apply to the back at night.

Low back pain (old) - The old Turkish tiles from the old house are crushed and sifted through a sieve. After that, mix with three whipped whites, a packet of ground frankincense and a glass of grape vodka. The mixture is applied to a linen cloth and tied around the lower back at night.

Lower back pain — Make a homemade patch from well-beaten two whites, one tablespoon of homemade soap and one packet of ground frankincense. Spread a piece of woolen cloth with the mixture and apply it to the lower back for 1-2 days, until the patch falls off by itself.

Sore gums - Rinse the patient's mouth with a decoction of wild thyme, to which one pinch of alum is added.

Water eczema (in children) - Fry in the oven until dark brown three walnuts in the shell. Once cool, grind half a teaspoon of fish oil with the shell. Pre-sanitized the sore spot to spread a few times.

High blood pressure - One tablespoon of dried blackthorn leaves to cook in 500 g. bring the water to a boil. Cool and drink in two doses only in the morning on an empty stomach.

High blood pressure - Take one spoonful of dried white mistletoe. Pour a glass of cold water and leave overnight. In the morning, on an empty stomach, drink the infusion.

High temperature - Cook the fruits of sour plums, apples and wild pears in an arbitrary amount of water (such as compote). Add one packet of anise. Do not filter the water. When it cools down, pour into a suitable bath for bathing, hold the child in the water for about 20 minutes. Then rinse with clean water, lightly wipe with vodka and put on. As soon as he sweats, change into clean clothes.

Sore throat - Tea from Bogorodskaya grass, chamomile and cherry.

Inflammation of the tendons on the hands — A sprout of gentian grass should be soaked overnight in 500 g. cold water, The next day to do water compresses on the hands.

Inflammation of the skin — One and a half tablespoons of dried lemon balm leaves to cook in 500 g. water until half is left. From the decoction, compresses are made on inflamed places.

Inflammation of the bronchi — 1 bay leaf to cook in 100 g. water until half of the liquid remains. Drink three times a day for one tablespoon.

Ear inflammation-Drink tea from the mother-and-stepmother, make baths from the broth of the mother-and-stepmother. Then rub the whole body with melted pork fat and vodka.

Inflammation of the vocal cords (wheezing) - Make a compress on the throat of ground wormwood, mother-and-stepmother and gentian.

Inflammation of scratches on the face - Apply moss from a stone that is doused with running water.

Inflammation of the throat - gargle 1-2 times a day with water and add a pinch of ammonia to 1 glass of water.

Inflammation of the tonsils is to Grind into a powder of dried roots of hellebore. A ribbon of dough is made, sprinkled with the powder of this herb. Tightly wrap around the throat-compress 2-3 times for half an hour to do for children, adults-at night.

Fungi on the nails of the hands - Cook strong coffee and make baths several times, without straining the grounds.

Fungi on the toes - Wash your feet well, make a foot bath of strong wine vinegar. Sleep in clean socks soaked in vinegar.

Fungi on the toes - Make baths of cold water, with the addition of 1 tablespoon of baking soda and 1 tablespoon of salt.

Fungi on the toes - Mix ground mint with salt and sprinkle between the fingers.

Fungi on the feet (unpleasant smell) — To do the foot bath in the decoction of cornflower.

Gas in the stomach - Drink tea from the mother-and-stepmother.

Nausea — drink a tea made from mustard seed.

Convulsions (in children) "Sleep on a pillow stuffed with forest hay.

Gastritis (acute) - 200 g of plantain leaves to cook in half a liter of strong grape vodka. Strain and drink one tablespoon in the morning on an empty stomach an hour before getting out of bed. Do not smoke while undergoing treatment.

Diabetes (initial form in children) - Collect the color of white mulberry, cook in water and pour the broth over the child.

Diabetes — Drink a decoction of the young tops of the blackberries.

Diabetes (in children at the beginning of the disease) - Cook 10 sour apples in five liters of water. After bathing the child pour this water.

Discopathy — Set up potatoes and apply to the sore spot at night, repeat until the pain passes.

"Lazy" rectum (delays processed food for a long time and does not throw it away) - Grind white chewing gum into a powder, stir it with olive oil and drink 2-3 times one tablespoon.

Multiple sclerosis - Copper therapy "pull" on the skin ,(like mustard plasters or "cans").

Children's skin rash - Cook nettle and elderberry in Equal parts. The child is completely doused with a decoction of herbs.

Children's cough - Cook one potato, one head of onion and one apple in a liter of water until half is left. Give the child to drink three times one teaspoon.

Hernia-Grind old tiles into powder and stir with two whites, add one spoonful of ground white frankincense and a glass of grape vodka. Spread the mixture on a piece of woolen cloth. Keep the patch on the lower back until it falls.

Eczema — After bathing, wipe the sore spots with a swab moistened with a mixture of one coffee cup of sunflower oil and grape vinegar.

Eczema - Cook a bouquet of forest flowers and pour a decoction over the patient.

Eczema - Smear the patient with a mixture of equal parts of engine oil and gasoline.

Eczema — (on the hands of washing powders) - Make hand baths by dissolving one teaspoon of baking soda in cold water. After that, immerse your hands in slightly warmed olive oil for ten minutes.

Eczema (in a child) - Bathe the child in a decoction of barley.

Eczema — Many of the varieties of this disease are treated in this way: smear the sore spots with a liquid extracted from elm cones in May.

Epilepsy — Bathe the child in a decoction of forest hay, use a pillow stuffed with forest hay to sleep.

Fastidious children in food — To collect still unripe, sour fruits. Cook in a large bowl until they turn into porridge. When the water cools down a little, without straining, immerse the child in it up to the neck. Let it lie in the water for half an hour. Then smear the body with lard and rub with grape vodka.

To strengthen the hair - After washing, water the hair with a decoction of walnut leaves and holly plantain.

To stimulate the metabolism — One tablespoon of dry Icelandic lichen to cook in 600 g. water until half the water is left. Drink three times a day after eating one coffee cup.

Diaper rash (in children and adults) — A piece of oak wood, eaten by worms, crushed and crushed almost to powder. After washing, powder the sore spot with this powder.

Constipation - Pour a baked apple with a solution of sugar (syrup) Eat the apple after it cools down a little.

Constipation - Take 2-3 times a day for one tablespoon of marmalade made from cooked black elderberry berries, without sugar. Instead, take one tablespoon of honey.

Mumps - Thickly prick the blue wrapping paper with a needle, smear it with a mixture of honey, vodka and incense powder. Stick it behind your ears. The disease passes in three days.

Shortness of breath — Mix 200 g. honey, olive oil and grape vodka. Drink three times a day for one glass.

Immune protection — Once a month to water yourself with water in which the Bogorodskaya grass was cooked.

Burn — The patient burned both legs at the hot exhaust pipe of the motorcycle. Vanga said that the fire is still "smouldering" in the legs. Recommended the following ointment: mix well six egg yolks and six teaspoons of butter until the mixture becomes like mayonnaise. Moisten the gauze with ointment and bandage your feet.

Bleeding (severe, prolonged in women) - Beat six egg whites well, add 0.5 teaspoons of citric acid and drink the mixture.

Cough -Cook mother-and-stepmother leaves and drink tea.

Cough (old in a smoker) - Boil the roots of the mallow grass in milk and drink one glass several times a day.

Cough (severe) - Four nuts, one tablespoon of elderberry flowers, one tablespoon of bee honey is boiled in half a liter of water. The patient should drink one tablespoon three times a day.

Cough (in a child) — One hundred grams of honey and 100 g. mix the butter with one packet of vanilla. Take three times a day, one teaspoon.

Cough (in adults) - A lump of white cherry resin with a walnut is cooked in one liter of water. Strain and add 200 g. honey and three seeds of cloves. Take one tablespoon in the morning and evening on an empty stomach.

Conjunctivitis — Crush fresh mallow leaves and make compresses on the sore spot three evenings in a row.

Hair loss (in a child) - Grate three clover roots the size of an olive and pour 10 g of pure alcohol or strong grape vodka. Insist for three days. Then moisten the cotton wool in the infusion and wipe the bald spots. 1-3 times a day.

Cramps - the patient to drink twice a day whey from the cheese by avoiding fatty foods.

Spikes on the heel - Cauterize the place where the spikes appear with hot mercury. And immediately take a hot shower.

Bleeding gums - Finely chop the green leaves of sorrel and apply a tampon to the gums.

Bleeding hemorrhoids - Blackthorn fruits should be kept in olive oil for 7 days in the sun. In the morning on an empty stomach, take 1 tablespoon, and after eating one cup of these berries.

Leukemia (in children) - Powder from dried ground mallow pods mixed with dried rennet of young lamb. Take with water twice a day for one teaspoon.

Leukemia — The patient to drink juice from the roots of the grass mallow.

Mastitis - Mix rye flour, butter and fresh milk. Make a small cake of soft dough and apply it to the sore spot. Keep it up all night. Do this several times.

Malaria - Wash a fresh chicken egg, put it in an enamel bowl, pour 200 g of wine vinegar, do not cover the bowl. When the shell is dissolved, shake the mixture well and drink on an empty stomach.

Uterine fibroids — The patient should drink one coffee cup of hemp seed decoction three times a day for 15 days.

Enuresis (in a small child) - On a piece of white woolen cloth, apply the following mixture: A tablespoon of grated homemade soap, two proteins, one teaspoon of crushed grains of chewing gum, in the same amount — white incense powder and a glass of grape vodka. Make a poultice on the lower back of the child on the first night, the next night - on the lower abdomen.

Cracked heels (with severe pain) — Instead of water to drink a tea made from grains of rye.

Metabolic disorders — Only in the morning to drink tincture of St. John's wort — one teaspoon pour a glass of boiling water.

Neuralgia (pain in one part of the head and facial nerve) - Drink anise tea three times a day, one cup before meals. In 600. water boil 3 teaspoons of anise for about 5 minutes.

A nervous breakdown - to drink a decoction of the geranium: cook 1 sheet of 200 g. water. Take one cup twice a day.

Nervous disorder (in a child) -To redeem the forest in the infusion of hay.

Nervous disorder — The patient to drink tea from oregano.

Nervous breakdown — The patient drinks a decoction of their young nettle shoots.

Nervous breakdown — The patient to drink a decoction of lemon balm.

Nervous patient - Mix in a jar of 500 g. sugar and 500 g. honey. Take one tablespoon twice a day.

Nervous stomach - In the morning on an empty stomach, drink a glass of water with the addition of a tablespoon of mastic (Bulgarian anise vodka). After 10-15 minutes, swallow a tablespoon of butter.

Bruised place - Attach pieces of sliced potatoes.

Rash - to drink tea from the seeds of the BlackBerry.

Rash (in a child who appeared suddenly, without any special reasons) - In a bottle, mix wine vinegar and sunflower oil in equal parts. Bathe the child and lubricate the affected area with cotton wool.

Rash on the skin - Dousing the body with a decoction of cornflowers is done.

Weight loss (acceleration of metabolism) - 3 times a day, one coffee cup before eating" coffee " from burnt oak bark.

Bloating - drink only forest tea and mineral water.

Swollen ankles - In 600 g. water cook for five minutes a tablespoon of mustard seed. Drink a coffee cup three times a day before meals.

Edema on the body - Pour ground frankincense on a cotton cloth, previously moistened with a decoction of mustard seed, smeared with honey.

Wounds from cutting objects - Quickly overgrow if smeared with olive oil, in which St. John's wort flowers were infused for 20 days. This olive oil is also suitable for the treatment of bleeding ulcers. Drink in the morning on an empty stomach for one tablespoon.

Elimination of scars from wounds - Lubricate with juice from crocus.

Pinched nerve after a fal - Make a patch of cotton cloth, cover it with a mixture of olive oil, melted wax and wax in equal parts. Apply a patch to the spine from the neck to the coccyx.

Cold of the throat - Feet of the feet should be smeared with an ointment of lard, dry ground wormwood and one teaspoon of baking soda. Put on clean cotton socks and sleep 1 night.

Cold (very bad) - Crumble 10 leaves of dry tobacco. Add honey and strong vodka. A hot poultice is made on the lower back for one night.

Pneumonia (unidentified) - Drink a decoction of flaxseed for a week. Do not drink cold water.

Abscess near the nail - Take one hot pepper, cut off the tail and pull out part of the seed. Fill the empty space with strong vodka. Put your finger in the pepper and tie it overnight, trying to keep the vodka inside.

Pyelonephritis (in a child) - Follow a diet, give corn bread to eat. Drink water from boiled corn.

Pneumonia — Patient's naked and wrapped in a sheet, lay on the hot sand.

Plexit — Apply a woolen cloth compress on the sore spot, on which a mixture of incense powder and apple cider vinegar is applied. Repeat several times. until the pain goes away.

With neuralgia - drink tea from melissa with geranium.

Cold (severe) - Make a patch of 10 leaves of dry crumbled tobacco, honey and strong vodka. Apply a patch on the lower back at night. Repeat if necessary.

Prostatitis - to Grind the coal from the burnt lime. Drink one cup instead of coffee for seven days in a row.

Overwork - Apply a patch of wax, olive oil and water to the lower back.

Dandruff - Boil a pan of water with a tablespoon of alum. After washing, rinse your head with this decoction.

Stretching the muscles on the arm - Submerge the arm up to the shoulder in water in which green elderberry was cooked with the addition of one tablespoon of baking soda.

Dilated veins - Put green nuts in a glass jar, pour olive oil to the top and keep in the sun for 40 days. The patient smears his feet until the mixture runs out.

Dilated veins - Pork lungs cut into pieces, "salt" with sulfur and put on the sore spot.

Weakened muscles (in a child) - 200 g. mix honey with 20 g. sulfur and using a mixture, make a good massage-preferably by an experienced masseur. Massage until the child sweats three times.

Small wounds on the skin (scratches) - Smear with an ointment of 1 teaspoon of lard, 1 teaspoon of honey and 1 teaspoon of baking soda.

Indigestion - drink mint tea.

A sinus infection is to Alternate every evening — in one nostril to put a piece of fresh butter the size of a kernel of corn.

Sarcoma (with bloating) - Apply game meat sprinkled with dry ammonia to swollen areas.

Strong cough — The patient should drink flaxseed tea for a week. Do not drink cold water.

Severe headache (after stress) - The patient should drink a glass of cold water in the evening before going to bed, after putting a tablespoon of sugar in his mouth.

Heartbeat (on a nervous basis) - Grate half a kilogram of lemons with the peel, add 200 g. honey and 40 g of ground apricot seeds. Take this mixture in the morning and evening for one tablespoon.

Itching on the body — The patient is doused with water from boiled barley.

Itching on the body — 50 g of combustible alcohol mix with 50 g. aspirin. In the morning and evening, smear the inflamed places.

Temperature (high in the child) - Pour a decoction of sour grapes.

Temperature (high in the child) - Collect forest hay in a mountain glade, cook in water and bathe the child in it.

Thrombophlebitis - Pork lungs "salt" with sulfur and tie three evenings in a row to the sick " place.

Bruised place - Well boil half a kilogram of white beans, knead into porridge and apply 1-2 times to the bruised place.

Frequent rash on the body — The patient should drink a strained decoction of rye.

Strengthening, cleansing baths - Alternate pouring broths-wormwood, chamomile, anise, cherry.

Hemorrhoids (external) - A decoction of white Dubrovnik, from which sedentary baths in a suitable basin are recommended.

Cirrhosis - Mother's milk mixed with white flour is used.

Boil — Make a small cake from the dough: rye flour, milk and fresh butter. Tie to the inflamed place for the night.

The deposition of salts (spikes) — Cut the onion head in half and put one drop of tar on each half. The halves are applied to the sore spot and tied for the night.

Salt deposition (on the lower back) — A piece of wool cloth soaked in apple cider vinegar and sprinkled with ground frankincense is applied to the lower back.

Salt deposition (in the hand) — The same treatment is recommended.

Salt deposition (on the heel) - A copper basin is heated, a piece of woolen cloth is placed on top of the bottom, the patient stands on it and stands until the basin cools down.

Ulcer (bleeding, duodenal ulcer) - The cream is made from one egg white, one teaspoon of powdered sugar and one tablespoon of olive oil. Take one tablespoon of cream on an empty stomach every morning for 10 days.

And so on.

Curious enough cases describes my brother Dimitar Gaigurov. Here I will give some of his notes. "Being around my aunt every day, I had the opportunity to look closely at her, of course, I was present at many of her sessions. I can't help but think of the shock I experienced at the beginning of May 1988.

Three days before, my aunt had been very silent, deep in herself, did not want to talk to anyone, and asked not to be disturbed. On the fourth day, she called me and told me to sit next to her. Then she spoke to me in a strange voice that sent shivers down my spine. She said literally the following: "I am the soul of Joan of Arc. I have come from far away and am going to Angola. Blood is flowing freely there now, and I must help establish peace there." After a short pause, Vanga continued in the same voice, " Don't blame this soul for anything. It's not yours. It's a draw. This is witnessed by your mother (our mother - Lubka), who carried it in the trough when she was on her deathbed. Then in an instant her soul flew away, and another soul took possession of her body. Your mother has recovered to continue her earthly life. But now her soul is not related to you, children, and can not recognize you." Another short pause, and Vanga continues. "Your mother should visit Notre-Dame de Paris, where she should spend the night in a prayer vigil — in this way you will discover great secrets about the world around you."

Vanga could not go to Paris and now, regarding her long   -standing desire, says: "When I wanted to, I was not allowed to visit Notre Dame and these words remained a secret." When the French woman asked if she was Joan of Arc, Vanga answered: "No, she's Jeanne d'Ark of his time, and I am Vanga of my time."

Then there was a long silence. Vanga slowly regained consciousness, the terrible pallor disappeared, her face was painted with a slight blush. But for a long time my aunt remained listless, even as if sleepy. I can't explain what kind of miracle happened before my eyes.

I also remember other strange cases concerning, first of all, her methods of treatment.

Late one night, my friend B. P. came from the village of Kolarovo. My friend suddenly lost his mind. He grabbed an axe and started attacking his loved ones. And so raged that the brothers were forced to tie him up. The friend changed unrecognizably. I woke my aunt and asked her what to do. She immediately said, " Buy a new clay jug, fill it with water from the nearest river, and pour it over the patient three times. Then throw the jug on the rocks to break into small pieces. Don't turn around at the sound of a broken jug."

Although it was very uncomfortable, we woke up the potter who lived next door to us. He was puzzled by the strange nocturnal visit, but gave us an earthenware jug.

The river in Petrich flows through the center of the city, and our house stands on its high bank. We went down to the river and did as my aunt had told us. I am grateful for the darkness and the lateness of the hour, as our" rite " by the river would have seemed very suspicious to anyone. But the most amazing thing is that my friend came to his senses, slept soundly all night, and woke up the next morning as a normal person. He didn't remember anything about his violent antics.

Or another such case.

A young man, an excavator operator, came to see Vanga. While working on draining the swamp, in the mud and stinking slime, he scratched his knee. The wound festered, the leg swelled and turned black, and the doctors said it would have to be amputated. But Vanga advised something else: to catch a frog, preferably exactly where the young man injured his leg, peel off the skin from it and apply the frog skin to the sore spot. The boy's parents did as my aunt told them. The pain immediately subsided, the guy fell asleep, slept soundly for two days. (During his illness, he had to take heavy doses of sleeping pills.) When he woke up and removed the bandage, there was a purulent abscess rod on it. A week later, the wound was completely healed, the leg was saved.

The treatment suggested by Vanga at that time surprised me very much, but later I read that there are substances in the skin of frogs that neutralize even snake venom. So, maybe there is nothing wrong with this "recipe", it's just that it is unknown to official medicine.

And here's how Vanga treated me. I suffered from pain in my left shoulder for a long time. The doctor diagnosed the deposition of salts. The treatment was painful and very long. Knowing how tired my aunt was from the daily visits of patients, I did not dare to go to her for a long time. Finally, when the pain became unbearable, I asked her to advise treatment. Vanga ordered to take two bags of incense, grind it into a powder and mix it with fifty grams of apple cider vinegar. Spread the mixture on a tight bandage and apply to the sore spot three nights in a row. I don't need to say that I immediately did as I was told. The pain was gone, and I'd forgotten about it.

My friend from Petrich suffered from the same disease, but Vanga advised him a completely different medicine. She ordered a woolen cloth to be soaked in gasoline, put on the sore spot, and pressed on top with a very hot copper plate. Conduct three sessions. And the pain was gone.

Our friend M. T. from Petrich had a wart on her hand, which really interfered with her. Once she tore it off. And then, about a week later, she had warts all over her body. Vanga advised the woman to pick a spur (such a grass), dry it, grind it into powder and sprinkle any wart. The woman did so — all the warts disappeared.

K. S. from Ruse had a child with asthma, and the doctors advised the family to go to live in Sandanski, which was very inconvenient for them. When they asked Vanga if the child could be cured, she ordered 40 dried mother-and-stepmother leaves and half a liter of raki to be brought. Vanga held both in her hands for a while, and then told the child's father to wet the leaves in raki and put them to the baby's chest. After several sessions, the attacks stopped and did not resume.

K. B. for many years suffered from internal intestinal bleeding, could not be cured. Vanga told him to find a white mistletoe (a parasitic plant) growing in a pine forest, crush the buds of the plant, soak it in a cup of water and drink this infusion in the morning. The treatment was very effective.

A. I. from Sandanski recovered from the initial form of diabetes by doing as Vanga advised him. He brought the healer about three kilograms of ripe beans, she held them in her hands for a while, and then told her to boil the pods and drink the decoction; one cup each morning on an empty stomach. The suffering ceased and did not resume.

My mother has collected a whole encyclopedia: cases of Vanga's cure of various diseases, as well as her advice. Here are some of them:

In the summer, go barefoot as often as possible, Vanga advises, so that the connection with the earth is not interrupted. Let the children run around naked and barefoot, let them mess around and play on the ground, this will protect them from diseases that lie in wait for children in winter. Children's food should be liquid. You can't let them eat dry.

In addition to swimming in the river, in the lake, in the pond, it is necessary to wash your feet at night with "natural" water (from the river, lake).

Sometimes Vanga satisfied all of us lessons in botany. I lead her through the glades in Rulit, and she, like a teacher, patiently explains to me what this or that plant is called and what it can give to a person.

I don't know how or what she "sees", but sometimes she even points her finger where you need to look.

"Do you know what kind of grass grows where you're standing?

" - Knotweed.

"Yes," Vanga continues — " it's a knotweed. It is useful to give it to children suffering from anemia. And there you see-a shamrock. This plant does not allow those who grow it at home to sleep peacefully, poor people are tormented by nightmares. The shamrock is especially poisonous at the time of flowering. Yes, I can't see them, but I can hear them talking to me. That plant over there, with flowers that look like bluebells, came from a country that is very restless right now, where riots are raging. I can smell celery, a wonderful cure for rheumatism. Pick a lot of it and make a salad for breakfast. You're about to step on a plant that's good for hard-to-heal wounds. So many things are told by flowers and herbs, but there are many of them, and I do not have time to remember.

I remember well that Vanga cured a doctor suffering from boils by telling him to drink a decoction of vetch seeds for twenty days.

She believes that against stomach diseases there is a very simple remedy that cures completely in three days. As soon as the disease manifests itself, it is necessary to drink the juice of one lemon with a spoonful of baking soda for three days in the morning on an empty stomach.

Vanga advised a young man with leukemia to drink a decoction of wheat, corn, oats, rye and millet. Some time passed, and the young man reported that he felt well and even gained five kilograms.

Another young man with seizures, thought to be epileptic, Vanga said that most likely he had a pinched nerve as a result of the fall. She advised me to take a piece of linen, soak it in a mixture of olive oil, melted wax, and wax, and apply a plaster all over the spine-from top to bottom. The seizures stopped.

Another person who had an unsuccessful operation on lymph nodes inflamed due to infection, Vanga said that he did not need a surgeon, but a dentist, because, in her opinion, the infection was caused by the inconvenience of the denture.

A woman with leg edema was offered the following treatment: in 1 bucket of cold water, dissolve a package of rock salt. Then take a handkerchief, soak it in this water and put it on the small of your back. As soon as the handkerchief is heated, wet it again in water. After these compresses, the swelling no longer appeared.

When we were little, my mother says, we often had malaria. Vanga treated us as follows: in a clean enamel bowl, she put a fresh chicken egg and poured 200 grams of wine vinegar, leaving the bowl in the yard, in the sun. By the next day, the eggshell was dissolving. Then Vanga stirred everything well and gave us to drink on an empty stomach. The disease was receding.

In case of fish poisoning, Vanga advises drinking a tablespoon of mastic (aniseed vodka) mixed in a cup of water as soon as possible. Once I was very poisoned myself. I felt very bad, I thought I was going to die. I vomited all night, and by morning I was unconscious. After learning about what had happened, Vanga told me to drink mastic with water. After five minutes, I felt better and soon recovered completely.

I do not know how medicinal herbs work on people, and I do not practice homeopathy, so I cut off my story about the herbal treatment that Vanga practices. And it would be possible to name thousands of cases that confirm the amazing abilities of Vanga. To describe them is the task of specialists, to describe and discover the rational grain in her medical practice.

Vanga says: "I do not recognize the treatment in which you need to drink 20-30 herbs at once. Sometimes people drink a whole bag of different plants, and the effect is negligible. I recommend only one herb or one remedy for a particular disease, so that a person knows what heals him and what cripples him. It is important to determine exactly which herb helps with which disease. I do not claim that I am a great connoisseur of herbs, as the herbs themselves tell me. Very often the name I pronounce is unfamiliar to me."

However, I have a different impression about her treatment. I do not know why this is happening. But even if the herbs and other remedies recommended by Vanga do not have healing properties, they still acquire healing power after she holds them in her hands. As if from this touch, various herbs acquire not only a powerful healing, but also a suggestive charge.

It happens that she recommends other methods of treatment. They are strange, illogical, and inexplicable. It was they who caused the fierce denial of Vanga's gift from the official medical science, which branded her as a sorceress and a clever speculator. I am hurt by such characteristics, because whatever Vanga's advice may have been during her nearly fifty years of practice, it has not harmed a single person. As an illustration of what has been said, I will give a few examples.

Women who give birth to dead children, she recommends that the next pregnancy bring her a new doll, diapers and a basin. She holds them in her hands for one or two minutes, and then tells them to do the following procedures. On the first evening, the woman should tie a diaper around her waist, and the next-wrap the doll in it. Alternate this three times. After the birth of a child, bathe it only in this basin. Usually, after such procedures, women give birth to live children and they develop normally.

One adult visitor who had nighttime urinary incontinence was told by Vanga to bring a pig's kidney. After holding it in her hands for a while, she suggested that he do the following procedure: tie the kidney to his belt, take two empty bottles from the house, fill them with water from the well in the yard. Then pour this water in the garden, away from the well, then untie the kidney and bury it far away, in some meadow. The man immediately recovered.

A child with the same disease was offered a similar treatment, but in a slightly different scenario: the child had to be taken to the forest and there told to urinate on a pig's kidney, and then bury it in the ground.

A woman with a nervous breakdown was told to bring a pillow filled with dry forest hay and a liter of water from the house. Then she advised to wash only the eyes with this water, and divide the hay into three parts and cook one of the parts in a large amount of water for three evenings and pour this water from the shoulders to the bottom.

For a child who was progressively losing his sight, she demanded to bring and held in her hands the following things: two eye-sized tortillas made of dough and baked, and a liter jar filled with water from their home. And then advised: these" eyes " from the dough should be held for one evening in the same water, then hung on a branch of a non-fruit tree-poplar, willow, etc., and wet the child's eyes with water. The progressive loss of vision stopped.

A visitor who could not get married was helped in the following way. She asked him to collect the water of the first spring rain in a vessel and bring it to her. Then go to a clean place-a mountain, a field, pour this water on yourself and leave without turning around.

A student of a technical school in electronics, frightened by the high demands at school and without much attraction to this specialty, while in a strong depression, received a nervous breakdown. Vanga told her parents to bring her the earth collected in the manger for the sheep and a new small mirror. I don't know what my parents did with these things later, but the guy who often brawled, after visiting Vanga calmed down and recovered.

Here is another conversation on this topic, which I recorded literally:

Vanga: This young woman standing in front of me is married, right?

"Yes," says the other older woman who accompanies her.

Vanga: You came to me because you have no children?

- Yes, - the visitor confirms.

Vanga: You picked up a bucket full of water when you were pregnant and the fetus wasn't fixed yet. In the third month, she had a miscarriage.

"Yes —" the visitor confirms.

Vanga: You will become a mother. But to do this, you need to sew a children's craft, on the one hand pink silk with lace, on the other hand-white. You will fill it with cotton wool and give it to the Church of St. Kozma and Demyan. You'll be a mother. Once you get pregnant again, don't lift anything heavy. "And to the older woman:' This girl is very beautiful, look at her white teeth. Tell me, has her left eye ever hurt? "

— Yes, - confirms the mother.

Vanga(to me): You should know what I see! I see everything that is in a person. Both outside and inside!

Another mother, whose child has urinary incontinence, Vanga ordered to catch a bee, kill it, press it into a piece of bread and let the child swallow it.

Another woman with psoriasis, Vanga advised:

"Take the wax and mustard. Take the wax to the church and put the mustard in your pillow.

As she carried the wax to the church, the woman felt relieved. Cured.

Vanga also had parents from Burgas, whose ten-year-old son was ill, but the doctors could not make a diagnosis; Vanga was silent for a while and then asked: "What do they want from this boy? "She pondered, twirled a piece of sugar in her hands and spoke:" I finally understand what they want. On the boy's birthday, bring the first fruit that will ripen in your garden." My parents brought me an apple. Vanga asked the boy to take one bite of the apple, and told him to give the rest to a sheep or other herbivorous animal to eat.

In a short time, the parents, together with the calmed down and recovered son, came to Vanga to express their gratitude.

A. N. from the village of Levunovo, Petricheskaya region, also had a sick child with an unspecified diagnosis. Vanga ordered to bring her a nail from the house and one bread baked by her wife. She held these objects in her hands for a while, and then asked them to break the bread over the child's head and let him eat one piece, and give the remaining bread to the pets to eat. The child recovered.

Regarding curses, Vanga states: "Fathers do not repent, so the curse sent by the father to the guilty son haunts to the seventh generation. Therefore, fathers, be careful! "

After the disaster, an eleven-year-old boy received a mental disorder, he was treated twice in psychiatry. Vanga says that this boy is restless because he is not baptized and "he does not have a guardian angel." The parents agreed to baptize their son on the condition that Vanga would become his godmother. She agreed and after a while the boy came to his senses, calmed down and became a student.

V. N. from Smolyan had no children for more than seven years and came to Vanga to ask if she would have a child. Vanga ordered to bring her a liter of water, one bracelet and a new dress. After holding a little in her hands, she said: "Wash yourself with water, wear the bracelet constantly, and when you wash the dress, wash it separately from other clothes. Less than a year later, Vanga received the news that the woman had given birth to a boy.

P. B. from Chirpan was working in the field when a terrible storm hit and in the evening the man was paralyzed in his right arm and right leg. His relatives brought him to Vanga literally in their arms. Vanga said: "On the same day of the week that the storm caught you, you will go to the same place and take the cup of earth. Instead of land, you'll leave the same amount of sugar. Bring me the land." Holding it in her hands, she told the man to pour the earth into the river. The man recovered.

I have recorded many such cases. Here are some more strange "recipes". The parents of the child, whose eyes hurt, asked to make two eyes out of wax to bring it to her.

The medicine for another child, who was very restless and cried incessantly, was the child's washed shirt and two hundred grams of water from the one in which he was bathed. After holding both in her hands for a while, Vanga ordered to put a shirt on the child, and pour water over the legs.

A woman in the sixth month of pregnancy, who was constantly sick, Vanga cured as follows. She asked the patient to wash the plates and dishes after dinner, rinse them again with clean water and bring this water to Vanga. Then she told the woman to drink some of this water, and she stopped throwing up.

The eleven-year-old boy stopped growing. Vanga helped him with the following advice. I asked my father to make a small ladder out of wooden planks with a number of steps equal to the age of my son and give this ladder to the Bachkovsky monastery.

One woman was very frightened and fell ill, because while working in the field, she saw a wolf. Vanga asked her to bring a new skirt and told her to wrap it around a piece of wood that had been burned by lightning. After holding her for a day, she told the woman to put on a skirt and wear it for three days, and put a piece of wood under the bed.

The child is addicted to eating earth on the street and anywhere. Worried parents turned to Vanga for help and she cured him, saying: weigh a lump of earth on the scales and then offer the child to eat from it. He licked his lips once or twice and never ate earth again.

And again about libra, but this time in connection with another child who had kleptomania. Vanga advised to weigh some object stolen by the child on a new scale and bring it to her. Placed later among the child's belongings, this object completely discouraged him from taking other people's things.

Another example of a child kleptomaniac, who stole the money. Vanga ordered him to take the stolen coin and bring it to her. After that, the coin was put back in the pocket of the child, who suddenly lost the desire to steal.

We are somehow more concerned with children's problems. Another mentally ill child was cured after Vanga, at her request, brought a new red skirt for the girl and a bottle of water filled from a well near the old church of the village. The child was washed with water, and the skirt was put on and told to wear it for several days.

For the child, who could hardly move, the cure was a pair of shoes bought for his birthday, which was then given to the church.

And here is a rather unusual case. The parents of the child, who had severe colitis, Vanga ordered to bring three willow branches. After holding the branches in her hands, she advised to bury them in the ground outside the village.

I once asked Vanga what a person should do to preserve such a priceless gift as health, are there any universal recipes here?

— How is it? " she asks. - Yes, very simple! I don't have any special advice or suggestions. Everyone knows what not to do.

Although I will not reveal anything new, I will repeat the textbook rules. First of all, you can not overeat. Products are now so spoiled by all sorts of chemicals that they can be poisoned. In addition, abundant food is burdensome for all human organs. Perhaps the Almighty would have given us two stomachs if He could have imagined that we would eat so much. If I were asked what to sow in the fields, I would say: as much rye as possible. People should eat more rye bread to stay healthy. Today, more than ever before, the importance of rye in the diet is great.

You should drink herbal tea more often. Reduce the fat content in food. Those who are healthy should gradually reduce the proportion of meat dishes, and it is better to give up meat altogether. At least once a week, you should eat boiled rye and drink clean water. That's what will give a person the strength to cope with various ailments.

Don't smoke. Tobacco is a slow, voluptuous killer. He acts with certainty and kills in cold blood.

Go to bed early — at 22 o'clock, and get up early — at 5-6 o'clock. It is during these hours that both the body and the brain rest best, nerves calm down, muscle tension weakens.

Raise the purity of the cult. Do not wash with very hot water, use best homemade soap.

Be careful! Soon there will be unfamiliar, unknown diseases (1981 recording). People will fall on the streets, get seriously ill for no apparent reason. Even those people who have never been ill will become seriously ill. But the general disaster can be prevented, everything is in your hands.

It is impossible to misuse of fertilizers and chemicals. Nature is already suffocating. The day will come when various wild and cultivated plants and animals will disappear from the face of the earth. Onions, garlic, and peppers will be the first to leave our gardens forever. Apiaries will be left without bees, the milk will become bitter.

MAN AND HIS MENTAL HEALTH

Herbal medicine is prominent in Vanga's practice, but she believes that neither herbs nor harmony with nature give the desired effect if a person does not strive to maintain their mental health at a high level. From her point of view, human life is an inseparable chain of interrelated processes and relationships, and the violation of one of the links can lead to a violation of harmony in nature. We ask her what she means by mental health and how to preserve it, and she invariably replies: "Every living being, the entire earth, and the entire universe are subject to a strictly defined cosmic rhythm and order. Violation of this order leads to mistakes, for which we all then pay a heavy price."

- Okay, but how do we move in this order?

- Without breaking the harmony.

— And how to live in tune with it?

- Striving to be kind.

What gives such confidence to the blind clairvoyant Vanga that kindness is the basis for preserving life in all its manifestations? Maybe this confidence is supported by her incredible gift to overcome time and space, to see the invisible, such that the most sighted person is not able to see? Or is it her personal philosophy of life, formed during the years of poor orphan life? It is difficult to answer this question, because Vanga's behavior in everyday life and her phenomenal prophecies are so intertwined that it is difficult to separate one from the other.

She is a person of exceptionally high morals, and perhaps that is how it should be. And how can you teach people to be kind and love each other without this, if you do not love them yourself, if you are not able to open your heart to everyone who seeks your help, if you do not understand that happiness consists in giving joy to other people, that it is impossible to live a full life if you do not sacrifice it for others.

Let us now see what Vanga's opinion is of those human qualities and deeds that distance him from the kindness so much desired by all.

Take the attitude towards children and their upbringing.

Vanga says: "Before you give birth to children, you should know that you will no longer belong to yourself, but to the child. You give a life for which you are fully responsible."

Here is a woman complaining to Vanga: "My daughter beats us, I just can't stand it anymore." Vanga: "You should have hit her when she was little. Your child is fed up with everything, you have humored her too much and now she is not all right with the psyche. So it turns out - it seems that you have a child, but in fact you do not."

"I'm an unhappy mother," cries another, " one son is a recidivist, it's not the first time he goes to prison, and the second is unhappy in his marriage. My daughter has a nervous illness." "Be patient," Vanga tells her, " your children will serve their sentences, and everything will be settled. Such is the human destiny - undiscovered as yet by none of us."

In other similar cases, Vanga concludes: "Leave people to suffer and fight for themselves, so that they can overcome everything themselves, otherwise nothing will help them. It is only when the disease takes hold that the drunkard begins to understand what he has done, but sometimes it is too late."

"Nothing good will come out of your son," Vanga says to the minister, " he lives on everything ready - made, does not make the slightest effort to do anything. He was four years old, and he already has an apartment and a car. A lousy upbringing. You can't build a house out of its bricks. Such a person will let everything go to the wind."

A couple of years later, we learn that this same son became a drug addict, so the evil seeds sown by his father gave ominous shoots.

"My daughter does not put me in anything," the former teacher complains, " she got married, gave birth, and the child is sick. What should I do?»

Vanga replies: "Well, I taught other people's children, but my own was left homeless, so I distanced myself. You have ceased to be close people. But nothing! She pays for her behavior by suffering with the child."

Or here's a picture. A young family with a child of about three years old. The child is in the mother's arms, constantly whimpering, asking for something. And the mother, in a commanding tone that brooks no argument, chases the father to the car and back, ordering him to bring this and that. With her sharp and unmistakable hearing, Vanga, who is sitting in the garden and hears the whimper of a child, catches the situation. She asks irritably whose child it is and tells them to bring their parents to her.

"You, Mother, do not take good care of the child, you do not bring him up properly. Mark my words — it will grow big and encroach on your life, almost to the point of murder. And you have quarreled with the whole world because of him, as if you were the only one with children! "

— So it is, Aunt Vanga, - the husband intervenes. — We have seven children in the family, I am the youngest, but my wife does not trust my mother, that is, my grandmother.

" Vanga asks.

— I am a researcher, and my wife is a kindergarten teacher.

- Oh, my God! Is this really the way to raise children? Vanga exclaims.

— Because of others and on their own nerves are not enough, - the mother justifies herself.

- Nothing like that," Vanga says angrily. — The thing is, you just don't know how to raise your own. Give it to your mother-in-law. She's raised seven children, maybe as many books as you haven't read, but she knows how to raise children in practice.

"Never!" -   her wife says through her teeth. — So that my child can mess around in the dust with the animals?

— Well, that's up to you, - says Vanga. — But please remember this meeting well. The day will come when you will bitterly regret that you did not listen to me, and then no one will be able to help you.

About such and similar cases, Vanga says. "The laws in our country need to be changed. When they try spoiled and arrogant children who have committed a crime, it is not them who should be put in prison, but their parents."

And more. "All children are the same. No matter what kind of mother-white or black, queen or beggar-she still enjoys the closest thing to her being — her own child. Mothers tremble when their children pass exams. And in life, everything is an exam, a test. I also refer to those who adopt and raise children, although I did not give birth to them, as loving women."

"Adopt a baby," Vanga says to the young woman — " because there are still unworthy mothers who voluntarily deprive themselves of the joy of motherhood. Nature pays with equal generosity both to the one who gave birth and to the one who raised. The greatness of the mother who adopted the child is no less than the greatness of the one who gave birth. Your merit will be even greater, for your heart is open to give happiness, and you are worthy to bear the name "mother".

A desperate father asks what happened to his daughter, an adult girl who has lost more than forty kilograms and is not feeling well. How to treat her? "I'm a miner,"a father replies, " I work underground." Vanga abruptly turns to him: "And you, man, have you ever shown your daughter your calluses?» The man was confused: "I work for her to be good, to learn!" Vanga "And instead of studying, she got involved with some religious sect, I can not say which one, stopped eating and now — I see — completely exhausted, to the point that she can not get out of bed without help. Ah, man, man! Education does not only mean giving money, but first of all it is necessary to demand from children, to educate diligence and instill responsibility. What did you make of the child? And your parental guilt is great. If you can, bring her to me, and I'll talk to her. I'll help her get back to normal.

Another worried mother literally flew to Vanga and said that her son was detained by the police and she, without going into details, immediately came here. "Don't lie," Vanga cut her off. "Don't deny it, because you know that your son and the boys cleared out the store. How many were there? Another one was detained with him. Why did you come to me? He stole it, and he'll get what he deserves. Left him unattended? "

About children left in the House of an infant, abandoned, often because of some kind of injury:

— It would be better for the state to search for such mothers who irresponsibly abandon their own children, and give them allowances for their maintenance. Why do other women have to be unhappy due to the fact that adopted an unhealthy child?

There is another topic that Vanga often likes to talk about. The theme of reckoning. Here are her words: "Let everyone know that nothing goes unpaid in this world. People commit crimes in the hope that no one will notice. Nothing like that! Everything is known, and there comes a time when the culprit will have to pay the bills!»

And again: "There is no sly person, even the most cunning, who would be able to outwit his own fate. He will cheat as much as God allows. And then let him not wait for leniency!»

Two women came to Vanga, who had been waiting for the reception for twenty days. The women were knitters, and while waiting for Vanga's reception, they sat on the ground near her house and knitted. When they came to her, she told them the story of their family in such detail that it is simply impossible to forget. I asked: "And who is this priest who stood next to you?" One of the women says: "Don't talk about him. We're here about a brother who was hit by a train." "But the thread of your suffering comes from this person," Vanga objected. "I know," the nurse said. "Why did you come to me then?" — asked Vanga and told the following story: "When your mother was young and very beautiful, one day she went to pray in a monastery. The young monk, seeing her, fell in love. Captured by her beauty, he abandoned the robe and married her. They had three children, and then their mother was paralyzed. She was bedridden for thirteen years. The father decided that this was a punishment for breaking a monastic vow and returned to the church again, praying in the monastery for forgiveness. Meanwhile, the mother died and the three children were abandoned to their fate. The son got drunk, one of the daughters went mad, the second married twice and twice remained a widow: her husbands died suddenly. One day, after another drink, her brother threw himself in front of a train, and a widowed sister was left all alone." And now she stood in front of Vanga and shed bitter tears, frightened in addition by the power of Vanga, who told her in detail their family tragedy. "This is what is called God's punishment. But don't cry, you have suffered a lot and you will be saved."

The father-villain committed a lot of crimes in his life, but never got caught, having lived to old age. But the children were punished for the wayward father. One went mad, the other became epileptic, and all together brought a lot of evil to their own father. So the executioner became a victim, being punished for the evil done to other people.

The adopted daughter came to Vanga to complain about her father, who disinherited his own children in favor of his second wife. In the new marriage, he had a sick child with a large hump, a girl. It was to this child that the father bequeathed all his inheritance, spoiling the girl while she was growing up. When the girl grew up, because she was rich, then the groom was found. Vanga agreed to be a witness at their wedding and participate in the wedding. But after the birth of the second child, the young woman died. Left in turn two orphans. "Eh boy," Vanga said to a widowed son-in-law at an early age — " your father-in-law abandoned his two children to give everything to your wife. And so fate decreed that her children were now left without a mother. This is payback for the tears of those abandoned children."

And Vanga's sister Lubka remembers such an incident that happened many years ago.

A father gave birth to three boys, one after the other, motionless from the waist down to the tips of their toes. And the man brought Vanga to find out why fate had so punished him? Vanga said: "Now you are paying for the crimes of your grandfather, who, for the sake of the opportunity to rob Muslims fleeing to Turkey after the Russian-Turkish War, killed and broke the legs of both adults and children. Now you are rich from that looted gold, but the curse of the slain is upon you. There is no cure for your children, so you will raise them and suffer as long as you live."

There are many such people who suffer for what their ancestors did.

Here's another story. A man came to Vanga and said: "I came to you to tell me… I have a fourth son, but if he is like the first three, I will go home and kill him." "How do you kill it? Vanga jumped up. "No, I'm not," the father replies — " my three sons are deaf and dumb, and the girls can hear, but they don't speak." "And all because," says Vanga, " you are very guilty, and you have offended an innocent person who loved you." "That's right —" the man said, and began to cry, and then he told me: "When I decided to get married, I invited a very good woman as a witness, but the day before the wedding, together with the bride, we decided that she would not fit — her family is poor, and without saying a word to her, we invited richer people. The next day, on our way to the church, we passed her house without saying a word to her, as if we hadn't noticed that she was dressed up and was meeting us with the whole family. Our neglect shocked her to such an extent that the woman, offended and humiliated in the eyes of others, could not stand it and uttered a terrible curse. She said: "God willing, and a boy will be born - let him be deaf and dumb, and if a girl is dumb as a swallow!" "Listen," Vanga said to him, " trust this child to me, I will baptize him, I will become your godfather, and he will not be deaf and dumb." And so it happened. Vangin's godson grew up normal, heard, talked, now he has his own family, a great master builder.

Divorce and broken families are the other side of human existence, which greatly upsets Vanga. She has no good feelings for people who get divorced, no matter how high-ranking they may be. I heard her say, "Sodom and Gomorrah will come down on you, you dishonest people, and fire and ashes will fall on your heads. It is hard and bitter for such a humanity!»

The young wife asks Vanga for advice on whether to divorce her, because she is disappointed in her husband. "No," Vanga tells her. — You shouldn't have gotten married if you didn't realize from the start that your husband wasn't your mother to wait on you." Now you'll have to wait on your husband. And even if you marry five times, until you understand this, your fate will be the same."

A young man brought a beautiful black-eyed girl to Vanga and said that they wanted to get married, but their parents were against it. "But you are not suitable for each other," Vanga told them, " you are just starting your career and you will make a big mistake if you get married." "But I love her," the young man replied, but Vanga repeated: "You're not right for each other." The young couple left disappointed and, despite Vang's warning, got married. But their seminal happiness lasted no more than a year, until the birth of the child. And then the feuds began. Several times they parted, then came together again, until they finally parted. A ten-year-old boy remained at the crossroads, tied only to his grandmother, who raised him.

"Today's husbands are no longer the same reliable support that wives can rely on," says Vanga. "They're like a sunflower." And how secure is his shadow, how solid is their nobility?»

One husband sent his wife to work abroad so that she could earn dollars, and when she returned, she immediately demanded a divorce. Vanga said to him, " Why did you come to me? Or don't you know that you don't give up your wife and your gun voluntarily? And you gave up your wife voluntarily. I was even glad that she would earn money. In vain now to pad the thresholds! She won't come back to you."

A foreign woman, overcome with nostalgia for her homeland, shared with Vanga that she feels very lonely and unhappy in Bulgaria. And she asked Vanga to advise her whether she should go back to her parents.

Vanga was silent for a while, and then as if cut off: "No, you married a Bulgarian and will live here. We have such a saying: "With my father and mother to the sea, and with my husband beyond the sea!" And you will have to drown-together! Listen to me! Soon you will calm down and solve your problems. And you will be grateful to me for not destroying the family."

One man brought his second wife into the house, and she robbed him and left him. Terribly upset, the abandoned husband asked Vanga what to do. Vanga told him: "Yes, do nothing, but only remember how you once left your ex - wife, who was innocent in front of you. Do you understand now how much you hurt her? And it was even harder for her, because two children were left without a father." The man said that these children gave him so much trouble that he could not stand it and left them. "Yes, but the reason is you, because you're a bad person. Now collect the stones you have scattered."

But a woman, with beautiful makeup and fashionably dressed, asks Vanga why she will not get married, and Vanga replies :" Well, look at how you are made up, men are afraid of you, because they can not see you natural. To them, you are something incomprehensible, because there is nothing natural left in you." "But that's the fashion now," the woman said. "Well, if you are like this," says Vanga, " then you will remain unmarried. People like you are only fit to be mistresses, not wives. O My God, what a girl! Even your parents got sick because of you. Go home and think carefully about what I've told you."

To another very cold and arrogant woman who told Vanga that she had traveled all over the world, she said, " And that's all you have. The day will come when you will be left alone like a finger."

Vanga is very hostile to those people who do not like to work, but prefer to spend the money obtained without much difficulty. Because, in her opinion, hard work is the greatest human virtue.

"Teach children to work from an early age. You set them a bad example, because you yourself have already forgotten how to work. They live on everything ready - made, you satisfy all their desires and discourage them from working, and then your children send you to a nursing home in "gratitude"."

One young man came to Vanga with some problem, and she immediately recognized that he had decided to be a "perpetual student", and even at the door she stopped him: "What are you doing, boy? Your father had no strength left. How long are you going to turn out his empty pockets? I see that you are not studying, but doing empty, useless things." "I have a girlfriend," the guy interrupted. "Yes, and not alone," Vanga continued. "You're wasting your time. You can't cut a whistle out of your branch! You're a bad person. How many exams, and did not pass any.

Don't make excuses for getting all the hard tickets. It won't work with me. You just don't prepare. Go away! I have nothing to talk about with you."

A visitor from Yugoslavia:

- One night, Vanga, I was sleeping in a field with a rock under my head. And I dreamed that money was buried under it.

Vanga asked him what he was doing in the field, and he said that he had a vineyard and he came to dig it.

— The harvest was bad this year. True, I did not dig the vineyard properly, but why so few grapes were born, I do not know.

"Man, man," said Vanga — " you haven't dug in, you haven't worked hard, and you're still waiting for the harvest and profit. And you look for the buried money all the same, so that you come yourself, without much effort, to get rich. You're just a bum, and I don't know what kind of help you want from me. Go away!" to

another visitor: "Are you finished?» "Philosophy". "Philosophy, you say? And what is your philosophy - from one woman to another? I don't think you'll make a philosopher. You have to work hard. And if you want to know more, get close to the church. There are many charitable, good and well-read people there, many books and knowledge."

Another visitor is writing a very serious book and asks Vanga if he can finish it. "What book are you writing, nothing about the sky? Do you know how high the thing you want to write about is? Huge spaces separate us, it is difficult to reach it."

An old woman many years ago, as a bride, received a wedding gift from her father — in-law-a monisto of twenty-four gold coins. I cherished it as a memory of my younger years. But one day, her already grown-up grandson asked her for this monisto, so that his bride could be photographed in it on their wedding day. A grandmother gave it to me and only saw it. The next morning, the grandson said that they left the monisto on the table and it was gone. A very distressed grandmother asked Vanga if she could help find Monisto. "Explain this to me," Vanga said. — Why, when you were wearing this monisto on your wedding day, did your husband tell you to take it off in the evening, put it away and never wear it again?» "I don't know,"said the old woman," but I heard that my father — in — law stole this monisto." "That's right," Vanga confirmed, — and he took it from the great - grandmother of the girl your grandson married. And now it's time for monisto to go back to where it came from. Even if someone else took it, these gold coins do not belong to you, because they were obtained in a dishonest way." "Well, then, I won't look for him again," said the old woman, and went away.

A young visitor's car was stolen. By hook or by crook, he managed to get to Vanga out of turn. "My car was stolen," he said to Vanga, "a new and very good one." Vanga scolded him for crawling out of the queue, where sick children and elderly people who really need her help have been waiting for her for a long time, and then asked him where he got so much money for such an expensive car? "Saved up," the young man replied. Vanga: "Maybe you can show us a place where we could take it and save it. You stole them, man! Robbed a poor old woman. Why did you bring her here?» Indeed, behind the visitor was a woman in her seventies, and the man was not even forty. From the conversations it became clear that the young man found out that the woman was single, but rich, married her and actually robbed her, because he became the owner of all that she had. "I love him," the woman interjected, " that's why I give him everything, and now I'm worried that he's angry." "Poor women —" said Vanga, "if you see what this man is doing behind your back, you won't die for long!" And the old woman is deaf and asks Vanga several times: "What did you say? "A thief is not supposed to find anything, "said Vanga," and therefore he will not find it! " The ashamed husband grabbed the old woman by the hand and both quickly left.

A man in his fifties waits more than ten days to get to Vanga. "Why did you come to me," she said — " I don't see the disease?» "I had five gold coins and they were stolen," the visitor replies.

"But where did you get them from?" interrupted Vanga. "I bought them once for the children —" he replied, " I have four daughters and two sons." "Oh, no, no," Vanga raised her voice, — you didn't buy it!" "Why did you take them away? Vanga asked. "Because he doesn't need them, they'll be lost for nothing." "And you don't need them. That gold would make all your children quarrel. It's even better that they're gone now. Otherwise, you and your wife would have quarreled, because you think that she hid them. Your children will grow up, have their own families, and earn enough money. You don't need that gold."

The guy's car keys clink in his hands, and Vanga asks where his car is. "My license was taken away and I won't be able to drive for a while." "You are not only punished by the traffic police," Vanga tells him. "But also for driving girls of easy virtue in it."

The young woman left a small bag wrapped in white paper on Vanga's desk. The woman was fashionably dressed, with beautiful jewelry. "What did you bring me?" Vanga asked her. The woman replied that she had baked a very delicious cake and brought it to Vanga. "Take it back," Vanga said. — I would never accept food from you." Look at your nails, so long, I disdain to take from such housewives. Woman: "I had a gold piece of jewelry given to me by my mother-in-law, and I lost it. "Where's your mother — in-law?" asked Vanga. Visitor: "Yes, we were very crowded and we sent her to a nursing home."

Vanga was very angry: "So you can't explain why you lost the gold jewelry? You don't deserve such gifts at all. Your mother-in-law has been saving these ornaments for so many years, so that when you appear in the house, she will give them to you. And you sent her to a nursing home in gratitude. Get out of here. You miss the first seven years of your upbringing, your mother missed you. If a person does not learn the virtues in the first seven years of life, he will never become humble and kind. Humility is a great thing."

And Vanga began to tell something like a fairy tale, making us all think:

"A rich and very proud man was sitting in his garden and resting. Beautiful flowers bloomed all around, and the air was cool. Suddenly a snake crawled up to him and quickly wrapped itself around his body. I started choking him. The man tried to free himself, but it was not there. He was sweating all over from the futile effort and fear, but at some point he decided to shrink in size, to shrink in order to slip out. It shrank, shrank, until it shrank to such a small size that it slipped out of the snake's iron grip, and finally took a deep breath."

"Every person has difficult periods," Vanga summarizes. — Even the richest and strongest. Therefore, a person should strive for humility, so as not to die in the arms of evil."

And again: "If you are not able to forgive in your heart, you are simply nothing. You will become like pieces of paper carried by the wind, which will never find their place on earth."

An elderly man complains that his house has already been robbed seven times and asks Vanga to tell him who the thief is. "These people are not strangers, no outsider knows what is in your house. Even if they were strangers, it was only from your family that they could learn the details. "True," the man replied. — My son is a terrible talker. As soon as he gets together with his friends for a drink, he will blurt everything out." "Well, what can I advise you? Don't keep anything of value in the house, and the thieves will leave you alone."

There are also many who come to Vanga to tell her what numbers will fall out in the lotto and lottery of the next draw, in order to buy the right ticket and win. They send cards even from abroad. The treasure hunters also come, bringing bundles of earth, so that Vanga can determine where the treasure is buried. Some even promise that if they find the treasure, they will give her half of it. Vanga is terribly outraged by such people: "Oh, how stupid they are. If I needed money, I would buy a lottery ticket myself, or fill out a sportsloto card, or find a treasure trove. But I don't need the money, it's of no value to me. And then, why do you think that it is you who should be favored? If you need money, work! Let them be the fruit of your hands and your mind! But you don't need gold! The day will come when the buried treasures will come to the surface of the earth, but the water will disappear. Will we be able to drink gold instead of water? What do you think is more valuable?»

The visitor is eager to find out if there is a treasure buried in his yard under the well. He lived in an old Turkish house, and someone told him that the former owners had buried a lot of money at the well before leaving for Turkey. Even the card was sold to him for 500 levov. "Yes you that, — after she insulted his Wang. — Can you be such a complete fool?" That's how you get tricked. There is no money there and never was. You shouldn't have paid so much for the card. You won't get rich off the hoards. Wealth will come only as the fruit of one's own hands."

"Greed. - says Vanga, - must disappear from the face of the earth. This is a very terrible quality, from which we must protect ourselves at all costs. We should not strive to accumulate wealth, there is enough sun and goods for every person on earth."

The old woman, digging in the garden, found a clay pot with gold coins. She covered it again with earth and, without telling anyone, came to Vanga to ask what she should do with the treasure. "Don't tell anyone," Vanga said. "Especially someone you live with." He's a terrible miser, too greedy, and he'll kill you first."

Once I asked my sister, " says Lubka. "to see a friend of mine who I thought was very ill." "No, she's not sick, she's a bad person! She wants everything in this world to belong only to her and her children. Let her tell you what kind of shack she grew up in and now lives beautifully, but her excessive passion for cars, apartments, cottages — greed will ruin her. And this is a disease for which there is no cure."

A very plump woman came to ask Vanga if she would get an apartment, because she has been living in a small room with her children for many years. And Vanga stamped her foot and said very angrily: "Why do you need another place to live? You're wearing two houses on your back. Or not so?! I see it! You sold and ate your two husbands ' houses, so what kind of housing are you lamenting now? If I had my way, I wouldn't give you any apartment, because you have no right to anything else."

And now another interesting case.

An elderly couple from a certain village came to Vanga to ask her about their illnesses. Suddenly Vanga turns to the old man and asks him:

"Grandpa, why is there always a rope trailing behind you wherever you go?" - The old man could not remember anything intelligible, but the old woman remembered and told…

When they were still young, they had melons and they had a lot of money from watermelons sold in the bazaar. Once my grandfather was driving a cart with watermelons to the market and a child clung to the cart and stole a watermelon. Grandfather (then still young) he was so angry that he grabbed the first rope he saw and beat the boy severely. His wife barely managed to pull the guy out of his arms.

"You will pay for this crime, Grandfather," Vanga said. — How much would you get for this watermelon?

The woman brought some herb wrapped in paper and tells Vanga that this herb was given to her by her friend, who claims that this herb is healing. "If that's the case," says Vanga, " why don't you offer it to some institute for research. If it is curative, it will be used to treat the sick. But I can see that there is nothing healing in it, you just want me to tell you whether it cures or not, so that you can give it to the sick later.

And you're not afraid to offer it to patients without even knowing exactly what you have in your hands? What if you hurt a lot of people? Drop this grass and go. Not everyone can become a healer! "

"And the violent runs away from the drunk!" — says the Bulgarian proverb, and Vanga joins her, because alcohol abuse brings people no less trouble than any other misfortune.

A young man, a former doctor who has abandoned his profession, with a big belly and so drunk that he can hardly find the door handle, enters Vanga's room. "Why did you come? - says Vanga, - Look at what you look like! "And he answered her:" Tell my wife that I am unique! "" Yes, unique, - confirms Vanga. — I've lost my human form, and what's the use of studying so long, reading so many books?" There's nothing left of your knowledge. You still don't understand. But nothing! The bottles won't let you grow old!»

The girl anxiously turns to Vanga and tells her that her father is very depressed, he is ill, and the doctors can not determine the cause. And Vanga asks her: "Why do you smoke so much? What is your job?» "I'm a journalist," the girl replies. "Why do you smoke? If we had to smoke, the Lord would put a pipe on our heads. You'll smoke for two more years, and then you'll bitterly regret this habit. Even the very word "tobacco" will be disgusting to remember. And your father's illness comes only from jealousy. He has no right to treat your mother so badly, because it's not her fault. He will realize this and overcome the crisis. But think about yourself. Your illness is worse."

There are hardly any everyday problems that would not touch the threshold of Vanga. In this regard, I really like the statement of one of her fans: "Even if she does not predict anything in particular, it is enough just to come to her for advice, because Vanga reads from the Book of Life."

If you ask Vanga which people she likes to talk to the most, she will answer:

- For me, all people are the same.

She often backs up her prophecies with parables: "The time came when the Lord ordered all the graves on earth to be opened, and sent an angel to see what was in them. The angel returned to heaven, and God asked him what he had seen there, whether he had seen who was the defendant and who was the judge." "No, God," replied the angel, " I have only seen white bones under the earth!»

Vanga is often asked, " Don't you get bored with the people who come to see you every day?" "No," she replies, " I just don't like it when deaf old women come. I tell them, I tell them, and they make me repeat it several times, all shouting: "Well, say it again!»

And most of all, walking women are annoying. "No," I reply, " stay at home and put up with your husband. "Well, I can't stand it anymore, I also have the right to be happy!" I can't understand what they mean by this word… Probably, by happiness, people understand that everything is in order for them, so that there are no problems. But it doesn't happen that way. There is no person who was born only for happiness. Here, for example, one is a great worker, but there is no happiness in the family. And the other has both, but no health. And the third is healthy, but the children are sick, and so on. In every person there is both good and evil. That's how the world works. For me, the root of happiness is in a person's patience.

They ask me: "Why does it have to be bad? Is it really impossible to avoid it?» How why? Because the earth demands a gift for coming and living on it. We pay taxes to the land as payment for the apartment… Here even for departmental housing, which is provided by the state, and then take a fee. That's it! We all pay... for as long as the world has existed.

But the best people are those who live in the mountains. A woman takes a spinning wheel and spins, takes the sheep to the pasture — and sings. Find a husband — so much for love. They raise their children and live for themselves…

And there is something terrible in the cities. People pass in front of me, and each of them has a sign around his neck that says: "I'm a hypocrite"," I'm a thief", on the other: "I'm a liar", on the third, fourth: "I'm a villain", "I am a scoundrel" and things like that. Therefore, many people are now returning to the villages, and this process will increase.

"But is man so insignificant?" I once exclaimed.

"Yes," answered Vanga. — From the height of the vast universe, man is nothing. A tiny speck of dust, lost in the infinite, a vain being who constantly explores something, searches for something, and still does not find it. But man is charged with a "divine spark" that allows him to surpass his own growth, to seek, to take risks, to unravel the mysteries of the universe, to make stunning discoveries. He resolutely looks even at the sky and is not afraid of its challenge.

Remember! In two hundred years, man will make contact with his brothers in mind from other worlds. Hungarian equipment will be the first to pick up a reasonable signal from space... and the truth about this space should be found in the old holy books! (I had this conversation with Vanga in 1979-author's note.)

MAN AND THE CURRENT TROUBLED TIME

Vanga persistently predicts the establishment of intelligent contacts with beings from other planets. But that time is still very far away. What will happen to people before that?

"Before that, humanity will experience many natural and social disasters and violent events. Gradually, the human consciousness will change. Hard times will come, people will be divided on the basis of faith. The most ancient teaching will come to the world. I am asked: "How soon will this time come?» No, not soon. Syria has not yet fallen! " (This statement was recorded by me in 1980)

Indeed, we have witnessed incredible events. Rapid changes in all areas of life are shaking the earth. Doctrines and dictators are crushed, old myths are debunked, people's concepts are changed, conservative thinking is liberated, every day is saturated with new things to the limit. Is it accidental, is this almost universal social upheaval arbitrary, where does this sudden change come from? "Nothing is accidental, nothing is accidental," says Vanga. — That's why I tell all people that our consciousness should be transformed into kindness. And this is not just a wish. The earth is entering a new period of time, which can be described as the time of virtues. This new state of the planet does not depend on us, it comes regardless of whether we want it or not. The new time requires new thinking, a different consciousness, qualitatively new people, so that the harmony in the Universe is not disturbed. Many people try to adapt to the current changes, but this will not help them to enter the future. They were needed by the time that passes, and they fulfilled the mission assigned to them by heaven. Others, good people, will serve the future: the preservation and development of life.

What does not the current person worry about? Along with the anxieties and hopes that he places on the future, the restless human spirit is looking for answers to many other questions. Vanga calms the curious: "The time will come for "miracles", many mysteries will be solved! "At the beginning of 1968, Vanga often fell into a trance and exclaimed:" Remember Prague! Remember Prague! Large forces are circling over the city and shouting: "War! War! " Prague will turn into an aquarium where people will fish!»...

Despite the fact that we did not understand the meaning of what we heard, it was scary to listen. There are many people who have heard these words of hers, because she has repeated them many times. Then we really witnessed the events in Czechoslovakia, but what Vanga wanted to say, that Prague would turn into an aquarium, we still did not understand. She usually does not explain and rarely interprets anything said, especially when it comes to major, fateful events, while saying that she herself does not understand.

Usually Vanga avoids talking about politics, and for this she has good reason, because her words can be interpreted as you like. But still, sometimes, though very little, he speaks on such topics.

Here, for example, is an interesting conversation she had in 1982 with the Lebanese journalist Abdel Amir Abdallah. He shared his impressions of this meeting in the political weekly Al Kitah al Arabi, published in Beirut. His story has come down to us in translation from Italian and was published in the magazine "Bulgaria d'oggi". No. 2 of 1982. The journalist was a guest of "Sofia Press". Here is his story with abbreviations:

"At Vanga's.

A room like so many others. In the Middle — an electric fireplace. Vanga was sitting on a sofa covered with a carpet with blue and orange stripes. I tried to concentrate all my mental strength so as not to fall under her influence. He took off his glasses and peered into the faces of the other three women sitting in the corner of the room. Everything was imprinted in my mind.

There was silence. It came from Vanga's face. Then she raised her head and said in a strong and confident voice that expressed unwavering will,

- Lebanese journalist, come and sit here! Let the driver come out!

"That was the first signal that revealed Vanga's power to me. How did she know that the driver was in the room —

- Give me sugar, Lebanese journalist!

I took a lump of sugar out of my pocket and put it on the table to watch Vanga take it. Without any effort, she reached out and took the sugar. She began to feel him, her hand was firm.

She turned to me. It seemed to me that she was watching me from the inside, and she said:

— You wear glasses, which you wear primarily for important meetings and other circumstances. Why did you take them off now?

This was the second blow that Vanga dealt to my disbelief.

"Look," she said, " your father and your mother are alive and they're in Lebanon. At this moment, my mother is at home, but my father is not, maybe on the street, in the field. You've lived in the city and been a journalist for about twelve years. You write about the service sector, but you can also write about politics. Although your contribution in this area is small: you rarely write about politics. In 1982-1983, you will have a great success in your work... You will have seven children, and when you turn 42, you will witness a great war, but I will not tell you who will unleash it.

There were unintelligible words, mixed in tones of command and admiration.

— You are a Muslim and observe the holidays of the Muslim calendar. You have an important holy text — the Koran. You need to read it in full and in more detail chapters 9, 10, 11, and 12.

Vanga continued:

— In 1984, Syria will fight a big war, the situation will be very complicated. Have you ever been to Jerusalem? I can see Baghdad now. What is this, Baghdad? You're going there.

She kept talking, not giving me a chance to ask questions.

Lebanon will have problems from the north and south, from the west and east.

I see the Nile. What is the Nile? You're going there. There are many roads in front of you.

Listen, journalist, you should have a deep respect for your mother. You have to remember that she wants something from you.

Lebanon is surrounded by flames. There's a lot of red fruit and a lot of water. But there is no oil in your country and there will be no oil.

Then Vanga asked me:

— Who told you about me?"

— Editor-in-chief Walid Al-Husseini, he wanted to talk to you.

Vanga was silent for a moment and then began to twist the sugar cube in her hands again and said:

— There are a lot of armed vehicles in Lebanon right now. In May 1982, your sky will turn black. Then she continued:

- There are many committees in Lebanon, but they are not able to do anything. The trenches will remain open and the barricades will not be destroyed.

Who was your prophet? The one who preaches and looks at the three planets? I see his soul enter my room.

Who is Elias Sarkis? Your president, a Christian, a bachelor of Arab descent. He's a good politician. But now there are a lot of troops in Lebanon.

Your relations with Syria should always remain very good. In the future, this relationship will be even better.

Vanga paused for a moment, then added —

" There's a war in Beirut right now. After that, he said:

This fire is dying out, but then it will flare up again.

By contacting me:
— Do you approve of this war?"
I answered:
"No, I don't approve.
Mrs. Vanga told me this on December 2, 1981, at 8: 45 a.m.
When I returned to Lebanon, I rummaged through the archives and found materials that said that on this day there was an armed clash between two groups in the western part of Beirut. Vanga doesn't usually talk about politics. Everyone warned me about this. But why did she talk to me about politics? Perhaps because I was concerned about the political situation and the fate of my country. I thought about it the night before and my secrets were imprinted on a piece of sugar, and Vanga translated these secrets through the chemistry of sensations into words.

Returning to Sofia, I thought a lot about this woman, whose gift is recognized by the state. When I returned to the hotel, I decided not to publish any material that related to me personally, as well as the one that concerned all of us, primarily what concerned my homeland — Lebanon.

Why? Yes, because if everything that Vanga said is confirmed, it's terrible! I wanted to believe that it was all just words."

Vanga spoke about the political situation and the future of Nicaragua with a high-ranking representative of this state in 1978. The guest expressed hope for at least a partial normalization of the situation there in the near future, and Vanga told him:

"No, there will be more blood spilled there. Rivers of blood will flow. What awaits you, you can not even imagine!»

I want to tell you about one of the evenings I spent with Vanga. It was Christmas Eve, the eve of Christmas in 1981, and we have a holy family holiday, and on this day we all get together no matter where we are. Vanga is very punctual, with great respect for religious rituals. And from each of us requires serious preparation for the holiday.

We gather in a large room in Rulit, where a hot, cheerful fire burns in the fireplace. The street is dark, the surroundings are covered with darkness and so quiet, as if there is a meter of snow in the yard. But there is no snow. He goes here very rarely, to the great regret of the children, but this does not spoil our mood at all. We set the festive table. According to tradition, there should be thirteen lenten dishes on it, and in the middle of the table a round warm pie with a coin baked in it. A little later, Vanga will break the pie and whoever gets a piece with the money will be lucky for the whole next year. We are all adults, but to this day, as once, we are waiting for this moment with great excitement. Just a little more patience. Before dinner, the children come out into the courtyard with a lit candle, a Christmas cake and a censer with incense and invite the Lord to a festive dinner. Then we go around the meal with the censer, say a prayer, and only after that we start eating. The fire in the fireplace gradually burns down, and the logs flare up with beautiful red embers. There is another belief in our area. By the way the firewood burns and what the heat in the fireplace will be, they determine what the next year will be like. To prophesy on such a responsible occasion is entrusted to the oldest person in the family. Our" elder " and undisputed authority, of course, is Vanga, so when this moment comes, we all listen to her with bated breath. She does not see the dying fire, but "calculates" the signs with the help of her incredible gift.

"In 1981, our planet was under very bad stars, but next year it will be inhabited by new "spirits". They will bring goodness and hope. 1981 did not give people anything good, but it took a lot from each of us."

1981 will be an anxious and difficult year. Many cities and villages will be destroyed as a result of earthquakes and floods, natural disasters will tear the earth apart, bad people will take over, and thieves, drunkards, squabblers and harlots will not be numbered.

Between people, fragile, dubious connections will be created, which will break up at the very beginning. Feelings will be greatly devalued and only false passions, or rather ambitions and egoism, will become incentives in human relations.

The year 1982 will shine in a new good light. New souls will populate the earth and some of them will manifest. A brighter light will shine in Jerusalem. People will come not from culture, but from knowledge. The word "Volga" will come and it will magnify the planet.

1981 brought misfortune to many people, took away many leaders. The year 1982 will be good for the culture, but the day will come when many people working in this field will be sorted, separated like wheat from beans. The year 1982 will bring a lot of kindness and a lot of new things. The year will take effect on March 22. This will be a year of new fasts, kingdom and power, and it will begin in the spring, when the first flowers will appear and birds will fly in from the south.

There will be many changes, new people will come, many old people will be dismissed, women will take high positions, but this is not their vocation. Many will retire out of fear, and others will be swept with a filthy broom. Wait for a change for the better."

VANGA - CLOSE - UP PORTRAIT

Know that you can't see everything with your eyes. Only the heart is sighted.

A. Saint-Exupery

I want to describe to you the daily life of Vanga, because despite her phenomenal abilities, she is the same person as the rest of us, and there is nothing unusual in her everyday life.

The house of Vanga in Petrich on St. Opechenskiy, 10 is unlikely to impress you. It is modest, two-storeyed, covered with white lime outside, and on the second floor there is a small balcony facing the street. Sandwiched between tall and modern buildings, the house would not have attracted attention if not for the huge flower garden beside it, carefully tended and lavishing fragrance far around. Vanga's love for flowers, trees, and nature in general has become literally proverbial. In the distance behind the house rise the gently sloping foothills of the mountain Bjelasica.

A spiral staircase connects the two floors of the house, with two rooms on each floor on the left and right along the corridor. What really makes an impression is the perfect cleanliness that reigns everywhere and the mistress's predilection for white color. You might even think that the desire for cleanliness has become almost a mania, but Vanga has another explanation for this: "Every day I am visited by different people. I help them, but they leave me with their illnesses, their sometimes impure thoughts. This burden is heavy for me, so I start to put things in order and it brings relief. "Everything is white - the crisp white curtains, the bedspreads, and the tablecloths. Vanga's house has almost no furniture — especially expensive. Only the most necessary things. The only luxury is the numerous souvenirs given by long — time friends and visitors of Vanga, and they are everywhere in the house. A lot of toys and objects made of wood and metal, all kinds of candlesticks, horses, dolls, boats and everything else. For us, these things are not of great value, but Vanga is very careful about them, as they remind her of a particular person, and she evaluates objects not by their value, but by their beauty and the work spent on them. When we were little, this toy kingdom was the most attractive place in the world for us. But Vanga did not allow us to play with them, but only allowed us to look at them and admire them. So sometimes I wanted to play secretly with some doll, but the respect for Vanga was so great that we never dared to break her ban.

In the garden, we played to our heart's content, although Vanga always tried to combine the pleasant with the useful. She considered it a great crime not to teach children to work from a young age, but only to indulge their desires. In her opinion, this is the biggest mistake that cripples the

child, making him lazy and irresponsible. Our games were always combined with sweeping paths, collecting leaves, weeding herbs and weeds,   watering...
Vanga very strictly ensures that everything is performed as it should be, and does not allow the slightest mistake. An attempt to sweep through the sleeves, an unnoticed lying piece of paper caused her dissatisfaction, and she forced her to finish and redo. Vanga seemed to see better than us, even pointing out where we had missed something. We had plenty of time for children's fun, but there were also responsibilities. Often they had to clean beans, lentils, or rice at the large kitchen table, and then Vanga sorted and poured the food into special ceramic jars so that everything was at hand. We unraveled the yarn, rolled up the balls, which we kept in a beautiful box, from which Vanga knitted our clothes. To buy the products — was entirely our concern. Vanga loved to tell us. "Don't think that when we were little, we were allowed to sleep late, like you, or play without working. No child had ever thought of such a thing. In our neighborhood, all the people grew tobacco, and even early in the morning, by two or three o'clock, they would wake up and go to pick tobacco leaves. They carried lanterns with them, as it was dark. Donkeys were hung on the sides of baskets, where they put the still sleeping children, they also helped with the collection of tobacco. Then the collected leaves were put in these baskets, and the children went on foot. Tobacco was collected until 7-8 o'clock in the morning. The leaves collected later lost the desired qualities.

We didn't grow tobacco (only once in the summer my father planted a small plot), but we helped the neighbors all summer. Around ten o'clock, when we handed over the bundles of leaves strung on a string, the owner gave us a watermelon, which was our breakfast. Approximately the same hours on the street were "urcia" (the seller of curdled milk), and cried: "Yurt, yurt." (curdled milk). Willing to buy gave an egg or two dinars, and "urcia" was cast from a clay vessel one ladle. Then the halva seller would appear. For one egg, he cut off a piece of halva no bigger than a matchbox. Your mother's (sister's — approx.) sometimes, secretly from me, she would take an egg from our chicken and buy halva. But there were four of us, and each of us got a tiny piece of paper, and Lubka licked the paper."

I don't remember that we had any money. On Sundays, however, they received money from Vanga for movies and treats. But the change was returned to every penny. Having money for children is just as harmful as not learning to work, because it is easier to spend other people's money than to earn it. But despite all these strictures, the time I spent at my aunt's was the happiest of my life. She knows how to communicate with children, they become obedient and executive. Besides, Vanga never gets bored. Many people come to her, holidays are arranged, and in the evenings Vanga tells us funny stories from her childhood in Strumice and the stories of long-past years.

In the morning, no later than five o'clock, Vanga is already on his feet. Washed, neatly combed, her braids are arranged in a knitted net, in a clean, ironed skirt, in an apron — she has a toned look, she breathes cleanliness, freshness and cheerfulness. This is how I remember her from my earliest childhood. Usually, Vanga dressed in dark clothes not only because she was already a middle-aged widow. "One day," she says, " I wore a beautiful red blouse, a gift from an American woman. But then the "voice" reproached me: "Do not seduce me with your clothes!» I took it off, put it in a bag, and it's still in the closet."

Vanga's day begins with a ritual that she never changes, even when she is ill. As soon as he comes down from the bedroom on the second floor, he goes straight to his oratory. The room is small, with flowers on the windowsill, and a large painting of The Last Supper hanging on the wall opposite the door. To the left of it is a miraculous icon of the Virgin in a silver frame, a gift from Jerusalem. There are other icons and lamps that burn around the clock. Under a large painting is a bed covered with a beautiful white bedspread. She gets down on her knees and sends the morning prayer to God. I remembered at the beginning of the book that Vanga is a religious person, but I would like to go into more detail about her religious feeling, because it is not just a custom or tradition for her, but a deep belief. Vanga's faith in God is huge and it can be said that she is one of the most diligent Christians. She demands the same attitude to religion from her relatives. When I were young, Vanga and I visited all the churches in the city and in the neighboring villages, and visited many monasteries. Vanga knew all the liturgies by heart and stood all the church services from beginning to end. She said that if you go to church, you must be present at all the rites until the end, otherwise visiting the temple does not make any sense... I remember how often she made remarks to the faithful, who whispered and did not listen to the priest. She said to them: "It would be better if you, little wives, sat at home and cooked dinner and did not interfere with those who want to hear God's word." After returning from church, we read the Bible. While we slept after dinner, my mother read, and Vanga listened with great enthusiasm. And to this day, she still loves most when the revelations of the prophets are read to her, where they talk about the suffering of the world. Then they discussed what they had read for a long time. Vanga said, " Do not grumble against the suffering that falls to you. Suffering is a cleansing agent, like, say, a jacket that will be dirty if it is not cleaned."

Every day for Vanga begins with a prayer to God - she asks for strength and inspiration to help all those who suffer. This touching picture is worthy of the brush of a great artist. I have never seen a person who prayed with such fervor and with all his heart. Her face seems to light up, and her lips whisper some prayers only known to her, which come from the depths of her soul. Sometimes, in these most intimate moments of communion with God, she cries: so strong is her plea for help, inspiration and strength. Sometimes her prayers begin with a question that comes straight from the heart: "What is my fate, God, and who do I serve? For the edification of the world, or for the strengthening of the faith?»

Now many scientists are trying to understand what Vanga owes its prophetic gift, but it has its own explanation. "After the big storm, when I lost my sight and cried around the clock and prayed to God that he would not leave me so defenseless, a burden to my poor family, he heeded my pleas. This gift was given to me by God! He has deprived me of human sight, but He has given me other eyes with which I can survey the whole visible and invisible world. It so happened that I, who was left disabled and myself in need of help, began to help all the suffering and became a support and hope for them."

In reference to this power of the Most High, she says, "If God does not please, not even a hair of the head will fall."

I remember her sharp remark addressed to an intelligent visitor with an incurable disease, whom she soothed with the words: "What can you do, since the Lord has punished me and you — we will endure!» To which he replied: "There is no God!" And Vanga added: "There is a God! And if you are silent forever, then the stones will also speak of God. As the blind know that there is light, as the crippled know that there are healthy people, so the healthy must know that there is God!»

Despite her love for the church, she is not afraid of criticizing its ministers — priests, monks, and clergymen of higher rank. I remember once she kicked out a priest for changing his cassock for secular clothing, which, in her opinion, is blasphemy against the church. One who has devoted himself to it cannot walk like an ordinary citizen. She also made a sharp remark to the monks of the Rila monastery, who started the monastery because there was no cleaner, there was garbage everywhere. Not to maintain, in her opinion, perfect cleanliness in God's abode is a crime. "Do not take care of the decoration of the monastery," says Vanga, " you will be punished. I see in a little while here, in this place, there will be a huge fire burning. This abode will burn down, because the life you lead is unworthy of the God to whom you have dedicated yourself. "You need to try to shake off your sins every day," says Vanga.

After morning prayers, Vanga took up her homework. When we woke up, breakfast was ready and on the table. I watched her cook, and I was always surprised at her dexterity and quickness of hand. She cooked on a wood-burning stove, which was always so clean and shiny that it glowed like a mirror. You could look into it. I was always surprised: she doesn't see how she manages to light the wood with a match without causing a fire, without burning her hands. As she prepared the food, stirring it, she put the lid of the pot under the spoon, so that any drop would not fall on the stove. After cooking, the oven was as clean as if nothing had ever been cooked on it.

For breakfast, we ate various delicious bagels, milk rolls, or something like that. I don't know if it's just a childhood memory, but I thought her food was the best in the world. She usually prepared dishes of the famous Macedonian cuisine, but often came up with her own recipes, combining, in my opinion, incompatible products. However, what she prepared was of unsurpassed taste. For dinner, Vanga would prepare something light, because, in her opinion, a person should take good food, but little by little. Overeating, she claims — is a disease followed by other diseases. Then she washed all the dishes perfectly, and we cleared the table and cleaned the kitchen. "My poor and orphaned life taught me ingenuity and a special perception of the products and taste of the food being prepared," says Vanga. — Our yard was large and there were a lot of nettles growing in it. Almost every day we made something out of it. The children (my sister and her brothers — ed.) got tired of eating the same thing, and I had to somehow get out of it to diversify the food. Meat was a rare guest at our meal. I remember when my father died, we had a little pig that we had to sell. He gave us the ears, the legs, and the tail. That was all our pork. They usually ate like this: soup and cornbread, but it's not every day. You could still eat this bread hot, but as soon as it cooled down, it became so dry that it could not get into your throat. My brothers dipped it in water and ate it. Sometimes they caught small fish in the river, rolled them in flour, and then baked them on a metal lid. Looking at what we eat, our neighbor, Aunt Tina, said: "Oh, poor children, I don't know how you live!»

Now Vanga does not cook, but whoever is engaged in this responsible business, the requirements for it are very high. God forbid you use the wrong or not perfect cleaned the dishes. It feels like she's watching your every move and noticing the slightest mistake.

For us, Vanga was like all the other aunts in the world — both affectionate and loving, but often dissatisfied with our bad behavior. We must pay tribute to her — she brought us up strictly, she had an "iron hand". However, we were incredibly happy when after dinner, especially in the summer, we all went out of town together, or went up to some clearing on Belasitsa, or visited the town of Melnik and the Rozhensky Monastery. Even then, in my early childhood, I realized that our aunt was an extraordinary woman. She would sit down a little apart from us and be silent. The adults did not allow us to disturb her, saying that it was better for her to rest. After the walk, our most interesting experiences began. Vanga told incredible stories and legends about this place, about the life of local people from ancient times, about their life, about the battles that were fought on various occasions. It always shocked me, because I don't remember anyone telling me anything like that at home. These were endlessly fascinating stories, probably born out of the paintings that Vanga observed with her superhuman vision. One day, greatly surprised by what I had heard, I asked her how she knew such details, and was told: "That story was just told to me by that old tree over there, at the edge of the forest." Well, how can you not be stunned!

Lubka recalled the following story: "We were in Sandanski and my sister said to me,' Take me to St. George's Church.' It was not far from our house. We went on a Sunday afternoon, it was deserted. We sat down on a bench in the church garden. Vanga had been in pain for a long time before, especially her knee joints: one knee seemed to have passed, but the other still bothered her. She sat down on the bench with difficulty, and then said that she could not get up at all. Suddenly she asked me: "Bend down and pick some grass under the bench." "Which one?" "It doesn't matter," Vanga said, " give me any one." I handed her an armful of grass and she rubbed her knee. In less than five minutes, she got up cheerfully and said that we could go home, as she was fine."

By nine o'clock, after finishing the housework, Vanga would enter a specially designated room and begin to receive her many visitors. After the sessions, tired, pale, and exhausted, she would return to the bedroom again. A little later I had lunch and then rested. Now Vanga does not receive in her house in Petrich, but goes to the area of Rulite, where people are waiting for her from early morning.

Rulite is a wild, pristine and beautiful area known since ancient times. Long ago, when Vanga fell ill with rheumatism, she discovered the healing power of spring hot water and silence, and since then this place has become very close and dear to her.

At the end of August and the beginning of September, we loaded things on a cart and went there. We drove almost all day, although the distance from Petrich is no more than twenty kilometers. It was an incredible challenge for us. Upon arrival, the adults pulled up awnings and made a hearth on which to cook food. We felt like Indians on the prairie. The next day, each family dug a large hole in the sand — it turned out to be a kind of small pool, surrounded by bushes that gave off a sharp pleasant smell. So every day people took baths, and many of the patients received relief. For us, the most interesting thing began in the evening, when people were going to chat, sing wonderful songs of this region or dance in a round dance. How fun it was back then! Of course, everyone gathered near Vanga's tent, as she was able to tell a very fascinating variety of stories and people listened to her with great pleasure.

I don't know why, perhaps the situation predisposed, but I remember Vanga's story about her hometown of Strumice best of all from those evenings. With what sincere feeling she told the legend…

"The city," Vanga said, " was named after the beautiful daughter of a local ruler who lived in a large palace on top of a hill. And down in the field, in another beautiful palace, lived his daughter Strumica. Once the city was attacked by a large Tatar army, but the brave citizens did not give up and boldly defended the city gates. Strumitsa went up to the roof of the house to watch the battle, and noticed the young leader of the Tatars. I immediately fell in love with him and wanted to take a closer look at him. She left the city by a secret passage and went to the Tatar leader. Up close, she found him even more beautiful, so when they started talking, without thinking twice, she gave him a secret passageway. Then the Tatars poured into the city and took it in a matter of minutes. Many of the people were killed, and the local lord was taken prisoner. When the father realized what his daughter had done and that it was she who had put thousands of innocent people to death, he cursed her. After death, let the earth not accept her body and throw it away seven times, and the soul will never find peace."

Vanga said that at the end of the city on the hill from ancient times there are seven steps, and the locals believe that these are the traces of the coffin of Strumica, which the earth rejected seven times. She told this legend to connect it with the theme of betrayal and the responsibility of the individual, who must sacrifice personal interests if they do not serve for the benefit of people.

"Many years later," Vanga continued — " during the Turkish slavery, people saw in the evening in the sky an angel with huge wings, who told them in a loud voice that they must endure, that they should not despair, because freedom is near. This angel, according to the old people, was the spirit of the father-cursed Strumica, who thus expiated her sins for a terrible crime, but never found peace."

I remember another story about those times. Vanga remembers that the old people said that their grandfathers had seen a huge pillar of fire on the hill. In their opinion, at this place, again, during the Turkish slavery, fifteen martyrs, defenders of the Christian faith, were slaughtered. Then there was a church of St. George the Victorious, but the Turks destroyed it to the ground. Vanga says that in 1941, a huge temple appeared to her, supported by fifteen holy officers. Who are they, and where did they come from? When later excavations were carried out, the columns of the former church of St. George were found at this place. And then the citizens of Strumica built a large church, which they called "The Fifteen

Holy Martyrs of Strumica". But the opening of the Church of St. George is ahead. Vanga herself still lives with the desire to open this temple, because she hears a "voice" that says, " Come and open the gate. They are iron and heavy, but behind them is a bright light" During conversations, time passed imperceptibly, and when it got dark, people lay down and fell asleep, lulled by the sweet songs of grasshoppers.

Now you will not see any awnings in the Rulite. Vanga built herself a small house, many of the regular visitors to these places followed her example, but the wonderful beauty remained untouched.

Vanga's house is visible from afar. A beautiful garden surrounds it on all sides. When the flowers bloom, they give off such a pleasant fragrance that you just don't want to leave. And the quiet and excited people are waiting to be invited to enter Vanga.

These people have always made a great impression on me. They are different, each with its own problem, with its own pain, with its own questions, but there, in front of Vanga's door, they freeze in anticipation of meeting with the extraordinary, with the phenomenal, becoming equal. Every person has a desire to become better, more patient, more responsive, not to pay attention to inconveniences. There are people who wait for a meeting with Vanga for more than twenty days, spend the night in different hotels, apartments, even in a clearing, but no one grumbles, but lives with the feeling that they have come to worship. I am absolutely sure that there is no person who, having visited this place, would not have changed for the better.

It is also visited by well-known personalities — public figures, clergymen, people of art. Thanks to the peculiarities of my work, which is most associated with people of the pen, I know about Vanga's meetings with such writers as John Cheever, William Saroyan, John Columbo, Eddie Brown from Canada, Sergey Mikhalkov, Rasul Gamzatov and many Bulgarian artists. But the most exciting thing was Vanga's meeting with Indira Gandhi. They met after lunch in Sofia. Unfortunately, there was only a translator at this meeting, and Vanga, as you know, does not like to repeat his words. I only remember Vanga's brief comment about Indira: "She is a great woman, and her whole life dedicated to the welfare of the Indian people is worthy of respect and admiration." Unfortunately, I have forgotten his name, but he was a professor and a public figure, a good friend of Indira Gandhi. The meeting was very interesting. Vanga said to him: "Now, here is your spiritual mother, whose portrait you carry in your briefcase. This is the mother of India. She was a very virtuous woman, like a nun in the world. Her nationality was French, but her life was entirely devoted to the spiritual revival of the Indians. She is your spiritual teacher, but she is not happy with you because you did not fulfill her wishes. I promised, but I didn't fulfill it." The professor was so

startled that he got down on his knees and said: "I'm sorry, Mother!»
Before the death of India's mother, he promised to build a school, but he
has not done so until today. "Did you come of your own accord?" asked
Vanga. "I was sent," the professor replied, and Vanga added. "Tell the
one who sent you that she is now in disgrace, but will sit on the throne
again. Only she needs to be very careful and not share everything with
her daughter-in-law-a widow. You should keep your distance.

Soon after, messengers from India arrived again, and Indira, as a sign of
respect and appreciation, sent Vanga an Indian sari, very beautiful in a
transparent green cloth. The Indian women wrapped Vanga in a sari and
were about to put a red dot on her forehead, but she protested. Vanga was
very pleased with the respect and good feelings that Indira Gandhi had
shown her.

Vanga also had interesting meetings with the Soviet writer Leonid
Leonov. Their acquaintance took place more than twenty years ago. Even
at their first meeting, Vanga saw the end of the novel that L. L. had begun
to write, and he was extremely surprised by the power of her talent. After
that, L. L. often wrote to her, and she helped him solve a variety of
problems. The writer is now dead. In recent years, he has been writing
some kind of global novel about humanity. I started it more than thirty
years ago and couldn't finish it. Once upon a time, L. L. he asked me to
ask Wang what the fate of this long-term work would be, and she
answered me as follows: "The book should be finished in three years (the
conversation was in 1989). - author's note), and it will have four images
(four themes-author's note) — - man, the universe, God, demon. He also
writes about ancient people. The soul of his deceased wife, T. M., is
pleased that L. L. has again purchased a philodendron for the house. She
often visits him, helps him, supports him, and then rests on this plant. L.
L. still has life potential. He'll live another day. And let him not leave the
house, only from time to time he needs to breathe the mountain air. But
his vision will remain the same as it is now, without any changes.

The novel is due to appear in three years and will be edited by a woman,
but she must be a very trusted person. The book will be a huge success
and will be well received by all people, even young people. The fate of
this writer in literature is complicated, but happy. Much will be said about
him after his death. Now he is appreciated, but many people envy him
because of his talent and well-chosen topics. The novel will be translated
abroad — in Germany, India, Brazil, America and many other countries
around the world. Does he have any enemies? There were, but they are
already dead, so there is no need to talk about them. Let him not fear the
living. He will release three books (maybe three editions-author's note)
that will go around the whole earth. He was ten years old when God
blessed him and gave him the ability to predict humanity through the

written word. He has a very strong spirit. Unfortunately, no one in his family will inherit either his talent or his intelligence. His talent is blessed by heaven and Maxim Gorky, who believed that L. L. would become a "big man".

Extremely surprised by everything Vanga said, Leonid Leonov wrote: "Vanga's childishly simple and at the same time brilliant, divinatory gift deserves the most profound, thorough and respectful study of all its parameters. This would bring people closer to discovering the mysterious continent on the globe of eternity, which is still ignored by skepticism.

In this case, instead of the usual tools — the old ship's compass, observation devices, natural qualities — will and dedication — computers can also be used, but despite all this, a restructuring of thinking in relation to the research methodology is necessary, and without this it is better not to get down to business.

One who invades this immeasurable world must leave all the treasures of accumulated knowledge behind the door, just as in some countries one leaves shoes before entering a temple. This has happened many times before: despite the pile of library volumes, the scientist was faced with questions of the future and reality, which he was unable to answer, because they do not have a verbal designation in the earthly language.

The prediction of great and fateful events would facilitate the transition of people to a more meaningful stage of existence, which is our present. We bow to the clairvoyant gift of the deeply revered Vanga and wish her, on behalf of all her contemporaries, long life and good health."

However, Vanga's attitude was not so affectionate to all writers. Take, for example, a meeting with the Soviet writer E. E. Even from the door, Vanga told him: "Who are you? ""A writer," the poet replied. "Well, what a writer you are-you smell like a barrel. Stay away from me." A little later: "You know a lot and you can do a lot, but there is no place for you where you are going. Why do you drink so much and why do you smoke so much? Fix your teeth and stomach. Don't write at night. Get up early and then work. Write from three to seven in the morning — then the greatest inspiration comes. "I am writing a book," said the poet. "About a woman?" asked Vanga. "Yes, and about a woman." "About the war?" asked Vanga again. "Yes." "Good. Write, but try to go deeper into the subject. And then you jump like a magpie from branch to branch. "

A. Ya. - a writer from Italy. Vanga: "And you are a lover of women and a bad person. And very greedy. You are looking for a wife again (the writer had several marriages-ed.), but know from me: the devil has taken possession of you! You are going to look for a spouse and you must look for either a very smart one or a very stupid one. But since everyone has both, I'm not sure you'll be lucky this time either."

The famous opera singer E. G. visited Vanga in 1982 and shared with her that he was very scared, because suddenly, while performing an aria, he suddenly became speechless. He considered it a serious symptom. "It's not what you think," Vanga said — " but while you were singing, you deliberately missed a phrase that spoke of God, so your voice broke. However, not only did you feel your voice drop, but you also saw something." "Yes," the singer confirmed, " I saw a wave of the hand that told me to stop. "And now," said Vanga, " you will do the following: the day before your next appearance on the stage, you will put a basket of white flowers in front of the altar of some church. After that, you can sing calmly.

Singer A. T.: "You are very smart and gifted. Give your spouse more attention and respect, because he worked around the clock so that you could learn and succeed. When you are in Italy, go to the Roman Cathedral, buy a toy bird that sings, and leave it there where no one can see, and it will bring you success."

To two singing brothers: "One of you is a very clean person, and the other is very lazy. One man's wife will be a great debauchee, and the other will marry a good girl, and she will love him very much."

I will give an interesting conversation with an actress from the USSR- L. S. Vanga told her: "You have two husbands." "Not one," the actress said. Vanga: "No, there is. It was and still is. Your husband is alive, and you know it very well, but you live as if he is not there. The one you're with right now is not your husband, and he's very ill, his excretory system is not in order. We have a herb - red oregano, brew it and give it to him to drink. And with your husband, the situation is this: when he went to the front, he told you that if he returned crippled, he would follow your life from afar, but he would not appear before you in this form."

"The actress said that before going to see Wang, a friend said to her:" I think I saw your husband. This man has no legs and lives in a home for the Disabled, I don't think you'll see him again."

A famous atomic physicist came to Wang because his son is very low and he does not know what to do with him. The physicist: "I studied for a long time in another country, and when I returned, the guy had already set foot on a slippery slope." Vanga: "Your son will improve when he joins the army. Everything is clear with him. But where you work, you can get people into terrible trouble, do you know that? If you scientists can and know, make people proud of you. Are you aware of the responsibility you have to people?»

My sister studied in Moscow and there met the famous Juna Davitashvili — the largest psychic in the USSR. The mother decided to go to see her sister, but told Vanga that she wanted to meet Juna. Vanga said: "Give her my regards and tell her to always remember her thirteenth, nineteenth, and twenty-first anniversaries." My mother said hi. Juna was overly surprised, because she had never met Vanga, and she said something really incredible: "We were living in the village when my six-year-old brother fell into a well. I was thirteen years old. People ran up, shouted. Without thinking, I stretched out my arms and rushed into the well, grabbed the drowning child, threw it up, and people caught it. I felt some incredible force near me, which allowed me to throw the boy out with my childish hands and held me on the surface of the water. I stayed down there. People were afraid for me. They lowered some iron hooks and they hooked my dress. Meanwhile, I was taking some incredible underwater walks. When they pulled me out of the well, I said I felt fine, and I didn't have a drop of water in my mouth. They started shaking me upside down, but it was completely unnecessary.

When I was sixteen, I was coming home from school and passed a house that said "Be careful, the house is emergency". However, I climbed inside, and heavy beams began to fall on me. But two of them stopped criss-crossing over my head and I was unharmed. The ruins were cleared for more than six hours and they found me under the crosspiece without a scratch.

When I was nineteen years old, walking down the street, I saw a house on fire, and in the burning rooms a man was rushing around and shouting for help. The flames were very strong, and people were afraid to enter. I reached out, smashed the glass, and ran inside, grabbing the burning man and carrying him out into the street. But nothing terrible happened to me. Only his hands were cut by the glass and his hair was burned.

And when I was twenty - one, on my way home from work before Easter, I decided to stop by the church and light a candle. I had long hair back then. When I entered the temple, I corrected them, but I don't know why they suddenly ignited. And I was nine meters away from the candles."

A French woman who has opened courses in France for clairvoyants and has already taught more than twenty-five women, visited Vanga. "Why did you come to me? I don't need teachers. I'm told from above what to tell people. But you tell me, who is this old man who is standing beside you?» "This is my father," the woman said. Vanga: "He told me to tell you that all the money that he left and that you earned went to the wind. What happened?» Woman: "Yes, I had a lover, but he left me after he' ate ' all my money." "So that's why you came," Vanga said. -But you tell me something else: you bought something for me, didn't you bring it?" The woman replied confusedly that she had bought her a white negligee, but left it with a friend in Sofia.

Vanga, as you know, receives many gifts, but keeps only those that remind her of someone. Most of them are given away to churches, monasteries, and poor people. I have heard her often say, " You receive for nothing, give for nothing." And here's what I noticed. As soon as she gives something, the next day she is given twice as much. Vanga has many admirers and friends, but there are also people who seek her closeness out of selfish motives. Some people want to do themselves a favor by using her name or advertising their acquaintance with her. Thus, she says to people: "Do not seek to benefit yourself by using my name, authority and gift, because they are received from human misfortune, and whoever comes to me with an unclean heart and self-interest, human grief will pursue and severely punish. Come to me as true friends for my own sake, and I will answer you with my friendship. You keep asking me, asking me, why don't you ask me how I am, whether the cross I carry is heavy, what my desires are? Where can I get what you want from me? Personally, I have nothing but myself. What can I give you? I can give you advice and teach you something, but you don't understand and you don't learn anything. You have nothing more to give. I only need spiritual food — which few people can give, because you are all poor in spirit. Greed alone guides you, but I disdain it."

— You're strong, honey, and you have the strength to give everyone a little!" (remark of the visitor — author's note)

Wang: "Dam (to give), it would be for what!»

Not only visitors are interested in this power of it. Scientists and journalists come and ask her how she went blind, how she began to predict. Vanga does not like to talk about his misfortune, because there is a coal that smoulders, but never goes out — do not put your finger on this burning wound. I can't talk about it with anyone who's curious. Few people will understand me."

I have saved one interview with journalists about her gift, where she says: "I can't tell you anything more: the voice tells me, the voice tells me, the voice shouts, but to say that I saw Christ or the Virgin - no. I only know prayers… When my husband was very ill, I stood up in front of the icon and said: "Teach me, God, how can I endure this suffering and how to swallow this poison?": "Take the glass, cut your heart open, and you'll still survive." But now he is in the analysis (Vanga does not understand what this word means in this situation-ed.), on Sunday he leaves. (On Sunday, at 12: 20, April 1 (1962 - ed. ed.) Mirko (Vanga's husband — ed.) died).

I cried like any other person, and then I say: "God, what should I do next?» "Don't cry. The time has come when an iron pillar will be placed at your door to guard you. A year or two has passed, a post has been set — here is the watchman at the door for many years."

Question: Do you talk to spirits?

Vanga: They come a lot and all are different. Those who come and are constantly around, I understand. Here comes one, knocks on the door and says: "This door is bad, change it!»

Question: Do you remember when you go into a trance?

Vanga: No. I don't remember much. After the trance, I feel really bad all day.

Question: Do they try to deceive you?

Vanga: Very rarely, most people are afraid.

Q: Are you taking medication?

Vanga: No.

Question: Never?

Vanga: No. Once the doctor prescribed me pills for blood pressure, but as soon as I started taking them, my mouth started to dry, I just couldn't move my tongue. And the drowsiness is terrible. I drink water-it's tasteless, so I gave up the pills.

Question: How are you treated?

Vanga: As I can. I really want to be silent after the sessions.

Question: How do you rest?

Vanga: I'm not saying anything. I lock myself in a room and retire. I lie down on my back and say nothing. It's the only thing that saves me.

About the rest I want to add more. I have already said that Vanga sleeps very little and recovers quickly. I asked her more than once why she didn't get enough sleep, and she told me: "But how can I sleep? I lie down to rest, and all the human tragedies that I heard about during the day pass through my mind again. A lot of grief in the world! But there is another reason. In the quiet, especially in the evening, I hear all the heavenly sounds. I hear the heavenly bells that ring every hour, and all living things respond to this rhythm. Therefore, the flower knows when to bloom, and the rooster will never make a mistake when to crow. How to sleep? If I could tell you everything I see, it would be a miracle. The secrets of the world that I know about, but can't tell you about, are almost at the edge of the airlock. Just a teeny little bit, so they opened up and then God will come to our aid!"

Platanthera sister Wang recalls that in the first years of its existence clairvoyance, Wang was forgotten and for hours remained silent with a blank expression. Then She is told her that her consciousness was carried away to prison, to a concentration camp, to unfamiliar villages, she was present at bloodshed, at various natural disasters.

By the way, this mental movement in space continues even now. This explains to myself Vanga's prolonged silence, when it seems that she is watching something with close attention. Her sister Lyubka tells of the following event: Before the big earthquake in Skopje we went with Wang to visit Strumica to our old friend the Panda Askanova. He seemed very excited, because his house in Scople was almost completely destroyed by water, and he asked his sister for advice — to repair his junk or to raise money for the construction of a new house. And Vanga said to him: "What a new home for you, man! Run from Skopje, because there will soon be a terrible tragedy. Stay here in Strumice! " Soon after, a strong earthquake actually occurred in Skopje, with destruction and loss of life.

I know of other cases told to me by Vanga herself. I must have been a little girl when the waters of the Struma River overflowed in the spring and flooded huge areas, even the bridges over the river, on which trains ran. Vanga was traveling with her family from Sandanski to Petrich. When the train was approaching the bridge, behind the station General Todorov, she heard excited voices nearby passengers, who watched floods and said scared that the bridge might collapse from the weight of the train and water pressure. "At this time," says Vanga, "the women and children began to cry, and I heard a man's voice from the next car:" Vanga is in the next car, let's go to her, only she can save us!» I was scared myself. People began to run into our car, distraught with fear. How can I help them? If they drown, I will drown. I gathered my strength and prayed: "God save the lives of these people!" And then she shouted to them:"Don't be afraid, nothing bad will happen to you." I told them this just to give them courage, without knowing what would happen. But truly a miracle happened. Slowly and steadily the train passed over the bridge, and we reached Petrich safely."

Little house of Vanga in the Rulite i remembers a lot of tears and human suffering. But the biggest tragedy is that of its owner, the prophetess Vanga, who passes through her heart human grief, giving everyone hope and healing. The room where Vanga receives visitors is still full of the tension and anxiety of the people who have passed through it. The ashes are cooling in the fireplace, and the snow-white curtains on the small window flutter like the wings of a tired bird. In the middle of the room is a large table, littered with gifts for the clairvoyant and countless pieces of sugar wrapped in paper. Sugar is also one of the secrets of Wang's gift, as it requires everyone who visits it to bring a piece of sugar that has been in his house for at least a few days. When a visitor enters, she takes this piece, holds it in her hands, feels it, and begins to guess. Why sugar? What is imprinted in the sugar crystals, by which Vanga accurately guesses the fate of the visitor? So far, no one has been able to answer this question. Can't answer myself Wang. She told me that in the early years, when she began to predict, a candle was lit in front of her. "But since I am blind and can't see, some misfortune may have happened, and the voice told me to replace the candle with a piece of sugar, because it is clean."

Vanga is sitting at a cluttered table. Pale and so tired that she can barely breathe. I can't even speak. I've heard her whisper something sometimes, and if you listen carefully, it's like, " My God, am I the biggest sinner, since you've put this heavy cross on me? You have given me much, but You also demand much from me." Then she slowly gets up from the chair where she has been sitting for more than three hours, takes off her outer clothes and slowly goes to the room where she is resting. The cool whiteness and the smell of freshness and cleanliness of the room gently takes her for a short rest. But, as we already know, she does not sleep. He lies there for a while, is silent, and often begins to knit something. She loves this activity very much — the spokes quickly knock, the loops are strung one on top of the other, fatigue quickly passes. Vanga is a great craftswoman. She knits quickly and tightly, and all her inspiration is reflected in the knitted things. She has beautiful models that she comes up with herself. Countless knitted vests, sweatshirts, skirts, blouses. Happy with her creations, she gives many of the things and is happy if you like the gifts.

On Vanga's passion for knitting Lyubka says the following:

"Vanga sent me to buy 2 kg of yarn, which was then dyed blue. That was about twenty years ago, before Easter. All through the fast until Good Friday, Vanga knitted a large and beautiful shawl. Then she called the priests from Sandanski and said to them, " I have been knitting this shawl for forty days and nights. On each loop, I said a prayer for all the people. Prayers were born in my heart and in my tormented soul, which dictated them to me. I have a big request for you. I ask you to consecrate this shawl at Easter and let it remain in the church. Cover those suffering from insomnia and headaches with it. May all the people who touch it find peace."

Vangin's rest in the afternoon is brief. By five o'clock, the silence is broken by the newly assembled people. After lunch, Vanga does not accept, but there are some visitors who, having visited her in the morning, did not understand something or did not remember it. These people she can rarely help, because she is not able to reproduce what has already been said.

What she said should be remembered immediately — even the most ordinary words at first glance, because they were not uttered by chance and they need to be interpreted...

I was under the impression that during Vanga sessions, human memory is not very helpful and the visitor remembers little of what is said. This applies not only to her visitors (this is understandable: contact with the" supernatural " breaks people and blocks their memory), but the same applies to us, her relatives, who are always hanging around and are used to her talent. When we attend a session, it turns out that one of us has memorized one thing, the other another, but even the information gathered together is very scarce.

I would like to tell you two cases about this.

The writer Leonid Leonov, at one of his meetings with Vanga, decided to record on a tape recorder what she had done, so that later he could translate it into Russian. He wanted to have such a record so that he could listen to it in a quiet environment. The writer brought his own cassetophone from Moscow, personally put it on record and asked that no one walk past him, fearing that something would spoil. Vanga then had an inspiration and she spoke about the fateful events for his country. She made contact with a long — dead clairvoyant of Russian origin-Elena Blavatsky. We really heard some amazing things. Extremely pleased with the meeting and the fact that he had acquired a truly unique record, Leonid Leonov went to Sofia very excited. But when we entered the hotel, it seemed to me that the writer would have a heart attack. There was absolutely no recording on the tape, not a single sound, not a single word said by Vanga. Hoping this cessation, and we are accompanying him, not especially tried to remember what he said clairvoyant. Despite great efforts, we were able to reconstruct very little of what we heard. Leonov was in a terrible state. Wang was asked if it was possible to return to her again, but she said that she could not repeat what she had said. The moment was lost.

A similar case occurred with other friends of ours-P. C. and L. G., who, during one of their visits to Vanga, also made recordings on a tape recorder. Vanga also spoke about big, significant events this time. But when they got home and turned on the tape recorder, they were both amazed to hear only folk songs, although there was no radio, transistor radio, or tape recorder anywhere around them...

Of course, there are records of Wang's predictions, in 1974 they even made a film about Wang. The film is a documentary, and we think it is very interesting, but Vanga does not approve of either the film or the recordings, because she considers what is recorded insignificant, even the sensitive equipment has escaped the main thing that can reveal her gift.

However, the film was not accepted by many viewers. For many years, until 1989, it was actually banned and was shown only in private and only to a select few. As the official science is completely denied the gift of Vanga, this objective, in my opinion, the document was also prohibited. And there was nothing incriminating about it. The film titled "Phenomenon" is divided conditionally into two parts. In the first part, Vanga's sessions with various people are filmed, her successful and less successful prophecies are shown. The second half presents the discussions of our scientists and specialists about the Vanga phenomenon.

The behavior of our specialists caused a wave of indignation and disagreement of ordinary people.

A group of viewers from Blagoevgrad writes: "The film is indeed made accurately, but we can not approve of such trivial truths, which were easily presented to us by the intelligent and intelligent-looking specialists involved in the film-psychologists, sociologists, doctors. During their comments, we had the feeling that they really wanted the audience to believe in a truly disinterested interpretation of the collected facts, but their words leaked doubt, as if they did not believe themselves. Their position is clear to us in so far as their skepticism is not contagious. It is clear to us what kind of people they are, but we do not approve of their purely standard thinking on the issue. What kind of subjectivity in relation to the phenomenon of Vanga? It is impossible to offer such an orthodox interpretation of the facts, namely, if one truth is objective, then it is almost impossible to prove it-so it does not exist. Many truths in life do not really exist, they can not be felt with your hands, but they were deduced logically, and then manifested and confirmed by reality.

Why don't we assume that this phenomenon also has some explanation. Why should we deny the unknown and the inexplicable? Who needs this rather biased negative attitude?

Let's leave this useless argument and go back to Vanga's daily life. Usually after five o'clock in the evening, Vanga goes around his "possessions". Cheerful, rested, fit, first of all suitable for flowers. It has flowers that bloom all year round. Either because the soil here is fertile — the houses are located in the old bed of the Struma River and there are fertile sediments for hundreds of years - or because Vanga is very diligent in caring for them, but there are plants above it. Vanga is short in stature, has grown slightly stout with age and is often lost among the overgrown vegetation. These are the happiest moments for her. In this contact with the beauty of nature, she feels like in paradise, touches all the pots, all the leaves, knows which flower to water, which to pour fertilizer or change the soil.

Often I was surprised by Wang's incredible awareness and knowledge of floriculture. She says that the plants themselves whisper to her what they need. I remember one woman asking her what she should do — there was a bushy plant in her house that was wasting away because someone accidentally cut the stem and a big hole was formed. "Take some oil paint," Vanga said — " and cover up the hole. The stem will grow and your flower will not die." "Can oil paint be a cure?»"What is it?" the woman asked. "I don't know," Vanga replied, " but the flower itself told me what medicine it needed."

Vanga really lives very close to nature and her way of life makes us nostalgic for the past time and the forgotten feelings of patriarchal life. In addition to flowers, it is surrounded by animals - dogs, cats, goats, chickens. In this area live eagles, foxes, hares, there are also snakes. Not to mention the birds. Since this place is blessed for hunters, often during the hunting season there are men with guns, ready to kill. But they always meet with fierce resistance from Vanga. With all its authority, it forbids anyone to destroy plants and animals. Perhaps, thanks to her, this corner has been preserved almost in its original form, despite the proximity to the cities of Sandanski, Petrich and villages. Vanga always checks everything: whether the plot is cleaned, whether the animals are fed, whether everything is in its place, the people who now help her around the house — a woman from a neighboring village and a caretaker appointed by the council-know that Vanga is very demanding and try not to provoke her anger, because she is merciless to the sloppy and lazy. Behind the houses there are plowed fields belonging to the collective farm of the neighboring village, where various crops are sown, and they give a good harvest. Here the climate is warm and peanuts, sesame, cotton grow very well, sometimes wheat is grown. It is especially beautiful in the spring, when the green stalks sway in a light breeze, and the fields look like beautiful green carpets. People often ask Vanga how best to plant and how to alternate crops. She enjoys talking to them on agricultural topics and talks about the problems of the land as if they were her own personal problems. Shows a keen interest in everything that is being done not only in Rulit, but also in the entire region.

It's good that people ask her for advice and listen to her, because she helps them make the right decision. And here we are not only talking about agricultural work. Vanga is also very active in the social life of this region. He gives advice on the construction of houses, bridges, posts, the appointment of people to work, the opening and closing of production, and landscaping. Let it not look like an exaggeration, but I think that today's Petrich owes his beautiful appearance to a large extent to Wangin's active intervention. She talks with great excitement about the specialists and bosses from Sofia who visited her, and she asked them to get street lamps for the city, or some construction materials, or even equipment for various enterprises in the city. The fruit of these numerous business meetings is her acquaintance with many architects and specialists of the country. With what pleasure Vanga listens to the guests of the city, who notice that the city has changed and has become extremely beautiful. She loves her city, because her life was spent in it and the most precious memories are connected with it. This is mutual love — the people of this city give her honor and respect, and she gives them friendship and help. Therefore, it does not seem strange to me that our old friend from Belgrade addresses Vanga's letters in this way:"Bulgaria, Vangingrad". Apparently, she understood this mutual connection very well.

This region is rich. The Mediterranean influence-near the border with Yugoslavia and Greece - gave it a blessed, wonderful climate and hardworking people. But people, according to Vanga, make up the greatest wealth. She knows many of them, her acquaintance with entire families goes back to 1942. She knows the fate of these people, follows their future with interest, the lives of their children. Often her evening hours are devoted to them. Their meetings are difficult to describe — they must be attended.

In Rulite, behind a high ridge of mountains Koguh from the sun. Silence gently envelops the sleeping nature. Vanga sits on a bench among her favorite flowers and rests like a hardworking housewife who has finished all the housework. Vanga eats very little, but she knows that there will be expensive guests at the meal this evening and she will treat them with pleasure. These guests are her big family and an integral part of her life. I don't remember a single evening, even in winter, even in bad weather, when Vanga was left alone. People come from everywhere — from nearby villages, from nearby cities, even from more distant places. They come just to see Vanga, to talk about today's problems and about the past. There is something sweet and touching about these meetings. Most interesting in winter. It's cold outside, and in the room where Vang's guests gather, a fire burns brightly in the lit fireplace. The warmth in the room is not only from the wood burning in the fireplace, but also from the good mood that reigns at these evenings. One of the guests-a good singer and encouraged by the pleasant atmosphere in the company of Vanga, sings a song. It seems to me that it was here, in the modest room of Vanga, that I heard the best songs of this region, born of the soul of the people.

But this usually happens towards the end of the evening. And before that, there is a heart-to-heart conversation. People talk about their families, their loved ones. They share their impressions of what they have heard or read with Vanga. She's interested in everything. She is a very good listener, but also a great conversationalist. He likes to ask women: "Well, tell me if you have prepared for Easter, like in the yard, what you have planted in the garden, what you are cooking. I remember a woman saying that they had slaughtered a lamb and didn't know what to do with the offal. "How to go where," said Vanga — " I'll tell you. You will make a kukurech (I do not know what this food is called in other places — ed.). Take the lamb's stomach, intestines, green onions, mint. Fill your stomach and intestines with warm water and hold them until they turn white. Then you cut the intestines into strips of 20 cm. in length. Try to cut evenly so that the food is beautiful, appetizing — beauty is judged by whether a woman is a good hostess. Cut the stomach into pieces in the palm of your hand. Finely chop the green onion and mint and add salt to taste. Then you put half a tablespoon of the green mixture in the pieces of the stomach-like in cabbage rolls, and tie it tightly with the intestine. Cabbage rolls are stacked tightly one to the other until the entire pan is filled. Top with sunflower oil and sprinkle with red pepper. Bake in the oven for about an hour at a moderate temperature until the liquid evaporates and the surface is covered with a red crust. Then, "Vanga laughs, ""kick the kids out" and eat. I know a few more types of kukurech, from my father's recipes. He was a shepherd and knew how to cook very tasty dishes from lamb meat. But, as a rule, "Vanga continues —" I cook according to my own recipes, and those who try my food say that it is very tasty."

And this is absolutely true. I remember to this day the taste of the lenten cabbage rolls, stuffed peppers, zucchini, eggplant, and various desserts prepared by her. Unfortunately, I have no passion for the culinary arts and now I regret that I did not write down these recipes. Because every time Vanga cooked in a new way.

According to Vanga, every meal should be prepared in perfectly clean dishes, in a clean room and from carefully washed products. Vanga, as I have already written — is a great neatness in all respects. "This great love of cleanliness," she says, " I probably inherited from my grandmother Katya, who was known in Strumica as a real hostess and an incredible neatness. For example, when she began to weave a cloth, she tied a white towel as an apron, so as not to accidentally stain the fabric. All the houses were embroidered, starched, whitewashed, and gleaming clean. Once he and his grandfather had a room for growing silkworm cocoons. Many people in the city were engaged in this trade, as many mulberries grew in Strumica. From silk threads, my grandmother wove such beautiful, thin sheets that all the women envied her."

One evening in Rulite, a woman from a nearby village brought Vanga a knitted tank top to show off her beautiful knitting. Vanga took it in her hands, felt it from all sides, and said, " Not a good job. If you were a knitter, you wouldn't be able to earn your bread. The knitting may be interesting, but with such rough knots on the underside and uneven loops that you can only wear it for menial work. You are young and should know that any thing, regardless of what it is intended for, should be done with love and attention. Only then does work bring benefits and joy. Here, for example, it is easy to make a sheet from the purchased canvas - cut and hemmed. But I don't like them. They're too simple. It costs nothing for the hostess to sew lace to them. They start to look very different. It's nice to sleep on a sheet like this. Or take the windows. They should be washed every week — the work will be richly rewarded, because the sun looks in them, and more light enters the house. But the curtains should be washed every month. It's beautiful and useful."

My aunt's house was constantly being washed, sheathed, shaken out, and tidied up. However, this has remained until now.

People read in the newspaper that a woman had given birth to five twins. They comment that the mother must be very happy: such an event doesn't happen often. Vanga listened, and then said to them, " You haven't thought about why so many twins have been born lately. As if in groups, these children appear in groups. This is no accident. These are the souls of the "heavenly host" who arrive en masse on earth, because there is a great spiritual struggle ahead. They are the harbingers of a new time that requires new people. Aren't you impressed by how intelligent children are now from birth? Even when they are very young, they talk about technology, about cars and planes, about computers and devices, and many other things. So compared to the previous generation, they are born just geniuses. There are very interesting events ahead, but we need to be patient to wait for them."

One evening Vanga was talking to our friend from Sofia, the writer P. M., about the meaning of the names of the villages. The guest was an intelligent person, engaged in art and the topic was extremely interesting to him. "You know,' said Wang, which means the name of the village Slepce? [2] (a village in Macedonia-ed.) There lived blinded soldiers from Samuel's army and the whole village took care of them. From there and Slepce (Blind), from the blind.

And Badoca? Do you know where this name comes from? From "poke out the eyes" (vadya ochi — "poke out the eyes" / bolg./ - approx. near this village, Samuel's soldiers were blinded. Maybe you don't know what Ohrid means (a city in Macedonia — ed.)? Once upon a time there was a deep moat at the edge of the city, where women went and wept when they were in trouble. Their sobs began: "Oh, the moat! Oh, Reed! Oh, Reed! " and that's where the name Ohrid came from."

I was no less interested than the guest. How good was Vanga's story, but how could she know all these things? From these evening visits in 1988, I remember a conversation between Vanga and a Bulgarian woman, M. D., who lives in Switzerland. I find it interesting, so I want to offer some of it to the reader.

MD: I've heard so much about you, Vanga, and now I'm happy that I can finally see you.

V: Why are there three men following you? Are you married?

MD: I divorced my husband and now live with another.

V: And why did you leave him, he was right for you. Did you work as an engineer?

MG: Yes, he was a chemical engineer.

(2) A famous battle in 1114 between the troops of the Bulgarian tsar Samuel and the Byzantine Emperor Basil II, who defeats Samuel's soldiers and blinds them. For every hundred, he leaves one soldier with one eye to guide the rest.

V: Where is he now?

MG: In Iran. A representative of the company. Very rich.

V: You also have two children. Are they from the first marriage?

MG: Yes. They're already big. I don't have a problem with them.

V: But now he has another woman.

MG: Yes. But I do not know if they are married or not.

V: And why did you leave him? It suited you.

MG: We had a big age difference. Frequent separations — he regularly left, and I sat alone in another city.

V: No matter what you do, you will have a third husband until you are forty, and then you will be alone for the rest of your life. Here they are! You'd walk into a room and they'd follow you. What does the man who is with you now do? Writes, sometimes draws something.

M. G.: Yes, he likes to draw and has collected a lot of pictures. He is engaged in journalism. But we have a problem with him. There are no spiritual contacts, and he seems to love me.

V: He's sick, so he's avoiding you. If he is cured, there will be a slight improvement, but he will not be able to recover completely.

MG: Can I help him?

V: You can't help. But after 2-3 years, you will leave him, no matter how dear you are, because you are young. It's us, the old ones, who don't light up. This man may be a good one, but your first husband was more suitable for you. I'm sorry you left him. And this guy you're living with right now has a kid ?.

M. G.: Yes, he was divorced a long time ago, and the child does not live with him. But this man's mother really wants us to be together.

V: why don't you adopt a child?

M. G.: I haven't decided yet.

V: You had surgery?

M. G.: Yes.

V.: Erosion of the uterus.

M. G.: Yes, but I was very afraid.

V: It's not cancer.

M. G.: Yes, and the doctors confirmed.

V: what do you do? And you draw? You draw on a canvas.

M. G.: I design models for clothes in a fashion magazine, take photos, consult.

V.: Why don't you live in your own house?

M. G.: I live in the groom's house.

V: But there is a young woman living in your house now. Who is she?

MG: This is the niece of her ex-husband. She had nowhere to live.

V: What did you do to the house? It looked like an inn.

MG: I took down one wall and got a big room.

V: Just like an inn.... But nothing. Whatever happens, do not give your house to anyone and save money for a "rainy day". But you will leave this man.

M. G.: In different ways, sometimes a lot, sometimes less. Now I work under a contract.

V: You smoke a lot.

MG: No, not a lot.

V: Not true! Many. I should quit. And then there will be big problems with the throat and lungs. Don't wear high heels! You have salt deposits in your feet.

M. G.: Yes, in both cases.

V.: But the left leg is more affected.

M. G.: That's right.

V: Should I do the operation? Where are your parents? Why is your mother lying like this?

MG: She's dead.

V: And your father is lying. Here it is!

M. G.: And he died.

V: Who Is Maria? mother? What did she die of? Purulent nephritis.

M. G.: Yes.

V.: The father asks about the younger one. Is that you?

M. G.: Yes, I am.

V: Who raised you?

M. G.: my Father and I loved him very much.

V: And another child?

M. G.: She's my sister at the mother from his first marriage.

V: You and she communicate?

M. G.: Not really.

V: Why?

MG: I think she's being too selfish.

V: She's not being selfish. Her life is also not easy and has turned her in the wrong direction.

MG: I would also like to ask if I will be lucky in the work for which I came to Bulgaria?

V: Very difficult. You need to attract high-ranking people.

MG: I would like to start working together with one of the fashion magazines. I brought the relevant materials with me.

V: And you think that if you do a job for a Bulgarian, he will then say "thank you" to you. Never! But you take care of your house, save a little money, and don't leave Switzerland. Do you want to go to America and Italy?

M. G.: Yes, I do.

V.: But why? on excursion or work?

M. G.: Rather for work.

V.: And again I repeat: do what you want, but do not leave the country, this is your destiny — to live with your third husband.

But the most interesting thing is to come to Vanga on a holiday. For example, on the Annunciation, March 25. On this day, Vanga's name day, the name Vangelia means "bearer of the good news", and this holiday is very dear to her. Guests gather from everywhere to congratulate her. The glade in Rulit is filled with festively dressed people and everyone is having a lot of fun. Songs are sung. Until recently, Vanga loved to sing a duet with her sister Lubka. Both are very musical, they have good voices,and they performed folk songs perfectly. People listened to them with great pleasure. After that, again, all together in several rows danced the Bulgarian "horo" (dance).

Another holiday, also revered by Vanga, is Maslenitsa. This is a great holiday for all Bulgarians, as on the last day of Maslenitsa - the Forgiven Sunday - they forgive each other all the insults and sorrows that were voluntarily or involuntarily delivered to each other during the past year. This is the day of universal forgiveness. Then, in addition to relatives and guests, many parents flock to Vanga, whose children were born thanks to Vanga's help. She baptized many children and became " the spiritual mother of more than five thousand newborns. What mother can boast of such wealth!

Interestingly, Vanga remembers many children and their parents. She remembers the first time they came to see her. When and how the children were baptized — in the church or here in Rulit, who was the priest, etc. I've always been amazed by her incredible memory. She continues to be interested in these children, asks how they study, live, what problems they have. These children already have their own children, who also come to the holiday. They kiss her hand with the same respect and reverence, and address her as " Godmother." These meetings are very touching, hundreds of people gather at them, united by Vanga's humanity, love and respect for her. How nice it would be if there were more such holidays.

Traditionally, a pie, white halva and tahini halva are served on the table. One of the men hooks an egg on a rope tied to a rolling pin, then a piece of white halva, and carries it around the table. If you catch an egg or halva with your mouth-without the help of your hands-then it will be a happy year. Then they bring a coal to each of the people present, so that all the bad things burn up.

And the most interesting thing happens on the street, where a big bonfire is burning, and everyone jumps over the fire to burn all the evil forces and increase their health.

Vanga loves Easter and Palm Sunday very much. [3]Palm Sunday in Bulgarian - Cvetnica (the flowers bloom)

Maybe because they are related to colors. Now these holidays are not celebrated here as before, but Vanga remembers how in Strumice the girls gathered nettle, cock's comb and baked a lenten layer cake-banitsa for Palm Sunday. And in the evening, the girls filled their baskets with Strumica tulips, wove wreaths of flowers — decorated their heads and put on beautiful folk costumes. And then we went home and sang:

"The virgin sweeps the level courtyards with two wreaths from the white basilica. A wild fellow looked into the courtyard to her, beckoned and told her: "Come here, give me a tulip, maiden, scarlet-scarlet — I will adorn myself, I will become dear to you»…

Vanga was so inspired that she began to quote the first words, and then got carried away and sang. Her sister Lubka adds: "On Palm Sunday, the whole city and all the schoolchildren went out of town, carrying willow branches in their hands. The priest, riding on a donkey, sang: "Communion, Sunday." We schoolboys were given a small bell on a ribbon with a bow, which we hung around our necks, and they rang pleasantly with every movement. Was in the area of Sofular. And then they made wreaths from palm branches and put them on the iconostasis."

I always admired Vanga's ability to tell stories and organize holidays. I have very vivid memories of how we celebrated Christmas, Easter, Epiphany, and the Exaltation of the Cross. Her attitude to the holidays is respectful and childlike. Its full dedication to religious rituals is not accidental. This is her way of life and a way of unloading from the hard everyday life. These are the days when Vanga gives herself completely to God, and everything she does is a deep tribute to Him.

But let's not get distracted and return to the evening conversations at Vanga's. One of the guests says, " Aunt Wang, I've already paid off my family. I earned a lot of money and gave it away. The children graduated from the institute, they have a job, cars, apartments, so I have no problems." "Wait," said Vanga, " now you want to sell the house, and where will you go?" She answered him: "Poor man, Kocherinovo is waiting for you! "(a village outside Blagoevgrad, where there is a nursing home-ed.). And so it happened. A man died in a nursing home, away from everyone. And he believed that he had secured a quiet old age among the household. And it turned out that he worked all his life to die in a nursing home.

"Some people think that having money can buy love, but this is in vain. Money can't buy love. Or thinks: When I get rich, I'll have everything in order, but even that's nothing. A person works, works, saves money and things, and then he will just die and leave everything to others. Those who have accumulated a lot are unlikely to use what they have accumulated. Others will get it. Therefore, it is more reasonable not to save, but to spend money — this is a means, not the goal of life."

Says another guest who came from the wake of a close friend and shared how much food was prepared by her saddened relatives, and Vanga said: "I do not approve of such waste. Such a show-off is not dictated by great love or grief for the deceased, but rather a demonstration of his ostentatious kindness in front of people. This grief is not real, because the depth of feelings cannot be measured by the amount of food. My family knows how much I loved my husband, but for the rest of his soul, I only give out a plate of millet, a little olives and a glass of wine. The dead are more important to honor and remember them alive, not food: they don't need it. Take, for example, Melnik. In the city there is a memorial plaque to our national heroes who were killed by the Turks in 1912. Their descendants erected a monument and calmed down, believing that in this way they paid tribute to them. What else? The dead have already left — we need to take care of the living, but this is also not quite true, because the dead continue to live. They are among us, they love us, and they help us to see the eternal truths of life. Therefore, we must give them the memory of our hearts."

Speaking about the football team, about the fans 'dissatisfaction with the poor work of the coaches and players, Vanga sums up:" This will continue until football specialists learn how to attract children no older than six years, as, for example, in art schools. And now they take big guys who are already looking at girls. You can't revive football like that."

It's already late. They touched upon the topic of radiation and its danger to humans and nature. Vanga ends the conversation by saying, " Eat more nettles, because no radiation takes them." The modest meal was over, the dishes were thoroughly washed, the table was cleared, and the floor was swept so that everything would be clean by tomorrow.

The car assigned to her by the Council pulls up to take her home to Petrich. They accompany her only to the gate, Vanga is not afraid of anything, and calmly turns the key. Then he walks confidently into the house. Of course, there are no light bulbs anywhere, since she does not need them. Someone might think that she would go straight to bed to sleep and rest, but I know that this is not the case.

Speaking of Vanga's daily life, I want to present another story of her sister Lubka:

"Vanga is not afraid of anything. I don't know how a snake crawled from the garden to her house in Petrich and curled up on the plush path. Vanga stepped on it, but was not afraid, and the snake did not bite her, but quickly crawled away. We searched for her for a long time, but we didn't find her anywhere, and she didn't appear again.

Although she lives alone and is blind, Vanga comes down from the second floor in the middle of the night, walks around the garden and waters the flowers. It has a healthy nervous system and is very hardy. I wonder how she has the strength to meet, listen to, instruct, expose, and advise thousands of people for so many years without showing almost any fatigue.

A few years ago, she had a cashier boy, and one day she told him to write out receipts to people without restrictions — she would accept everyone as long as she could stand it.

The crowd of people - one going in, one going out - is endless. The boy is drenched in sweat, he just doesn't have time to write out the receipts. At one point, he said: "Aunt Wang, do you want more? I'm writing the hundredth receipt." It wasn't until she was sure there wasn't a single person left outside the door that she told him enough was enough. Everyone was terribly tired — so many people, so much tension, and she at least had something-cheerful, in a good mood, she was ready to start doing something else… Yes, she had an inexhaustible energy: just three years ago, she was very strong, she could move a wardrobe from one end of the room to the other.

Vanga bought a transistor "Falcon" and, wherever we went, I plugged it in. We were the only ones listening, and she was lost in her thoughts. This transistor was always in her bag.

Somehow, I don't know why, or by whose order, some officials broke into the house and made an inventory of all her belongings, down to the last gift from grateful visitors. Because of this dirty act, Vanga fell ill and spent more than a month in the Sofia hospital. All this time the house remained open, and unscrupulous employees, in addition to the described, took away what they liked.

When she returned from the hospital, she did not want to enter her house, but stayed in Rulit, saying: "I do not want to follow the footsteps of thieves!»

Everything had been repainted, re-washed, swept, and put back in its original place, but she still harbored a pain in her soul that still lingered.

Then she asked me if I could see a transistor somewhere. I searched, but I couldn't find it anywhere, and she answered: "Never mind, he'll bring it himself."

She worked as a cashier an elderly man who was seriously ill. One day, very ill, he came to her and confessed 15 years later that he had taken the transistor and something else, thinking that she was so seriously ill that she was unlikely to return from the hospital. He handed over the transistor and asked for forgiveness. She did not touch the object, but only said to him, " Well, you have already paid the tax for stealing this thing. And you will have to suffer a lot more because of this act."

Soon this man died in terrible agony.

I don't know if she forgave him or not, we never talked about this case again, but I'm surprised at her behavior — all these 15 years she knew where her favorite transistor was, but she didn't even hint who the thief was, and didn't offend him in any way. In the end, all the guilty ones came to her doorstep to ask for forgiveness, but what she was hiding in her heart was known only to herself.

Often we sit, talk, think about life, and Vanga suddenly says:

— We live in difficult times. People have nothing in common with each other. Mothers give birth to children, but they do not have milk to feed. Justified: neurosis, they say. No. It's just that children have nothing to do with their mothers, they just came into the world through them. Children get nothing from their mothers, neither milk nor warmth. Very young children are sent to kindergarten, they are put to bed separately in the evening, they rarely see a smile on their mother's face. Mothers are unhappy that their husbands do not value them enough. Husbands, for their part, believe that they got married, because it seems to be the way it is supposed to be. Adults are also dissatisfied with their children — there is no respect from them. No one is friends with anyone. People are only interested in money. They think that if they have money, then everything is fine. They do not know that the day will come when this money will not serve them in any way.

There is a very old fairy tale: there was a time when one camel cost 10 pennies and was considered very expensive. Then there came a time when there were a lot of camels and any of them was worth a penny, but there were no buyers.

Think about this fairy tale, because the day will come when people will have everything, but they will not be able to buy anything that really has value and constitutes priceless wealth — friendship, love, participation.

One day we received a letter from a distant Spain. It was written by the woman to whom Vanga's fame had reached. Apparently, she had been interested in her for a long time, since she knew many details about her life. I recall the following passage from her letter: "I am surprised at your gift, Vanga. There is no mysticism in you. But I understand you, and I know how difficult it is for you. Seeing everything in plain sight, you must (and I believe you do!) inspire courage in everyone who stands in front of you, waiting for help, even if you see its tragic end»...

This statement of an unknown Spaniard is symptomatic, because it very accurately characterizes one of the main features of Vanga's character — her nobility and indestructible humanism.

Everyone knows (and I know better than anyone else) that Vanga can't see at all. But one morning, when she was about to leave for Rulit, it turned out that her black hair net was missing. There were four women in the room and they all began to search diligently. They even lit a lamp. Her net seemed to have fallen through the ground.

Suddenly, Vanga stretched out her right leg and pointed with her fingers to where her net was:

"Look with four pairs of eyes, but you can't see anything.

My friend, Z. B., from Sofia, tells with great pleasure the following adventure:

"It was winter when I came to Vanga. She received me in a tasteful room with a large fire burning in the grate. Vanga was sitting on the couch opposite him, knitting something. Her hands moved quickly and deftly, like those of an experienced knitter. I was surprised how she knits so fast and tight, without confusing the loops, because she can't see anything! While I was looking on in wonder and admiration, she suddenly turned to me and said:

— Go tell the woman who cooks in the kitchen to prepare the fish pan.

I went willingly to the kitchen, but as I wanted to do something for her myself, I asked if I could clean the fish.

She laughed:

"You can't, because there's no fish yet, it's just coming towards us. After some time it will bring people from the village of Pripiceni.

I was speechless. The fact that Wang said, was just incredible. I decided to wait at all costs and see if what I had said would be confirmed. About two hours later, a guy came by and the first thing he said after saying hello to her was. "Aunt Vanga, I caught some fresh fish and brought some for you to try!»

I want to note that Wang's clairvoyance covers all aspects and problems of human life. But let's get back to the main question: What kind of person is Vanga? I have lived with her all my life, and I can answer with conviction: she lives like all people, and there is nothing special about her being. But it lives in complete harmony and harmony with nature, it is truly "part of it" — in the full sense of the word. That is why all nature sounds so clearly in her, speaks to her, and she picks up her signals with her perfect sense organs. It can receive signals from everything that surrounds it: from grasses and trees, from stones and flowers, from objects and from space, from the past and the future. Mountains and ridges reveal thousands of years of secrets, and rivers-the legends of long-defunct cities and people. According to her, "everything lives", there is no "inanimate nature", everything is subject to a higher organization and reason.

There are times when she does not want to talk to anyone, and if someone shouts from the courtyard, she gets angry and asks that they do not disturb her peace, because she has to listen for hours to news about a variety of events and people from the past and future:

— It's not good when I go deep and you come to me, it bothers me, even though you can't see who I'm talking to... Sometimes I am surrounded by higher - ups, sometimes by their subordinates, but they are all from outer space, and when they speak, they put something like headphones on my ears, their voices come to me from somewhere far away and sound like an echo. So I need peace and quiet.

Sometimes I get very nervous, and people think I'm bad. I see a ring that gradually tightens around the Earth, I experience the torment of all people and I can not, and I do not dare to explain it, because one very strict voice constantly warns me not to try to explain anything, because people deserve the life they lead. How to help these people who do not respect anyone, rush to the distillery for money and things... As if a person has no other goal than the desire to trample all that is bright and holy, which he has achieved at the cost of such expensive sacrifices...

On that day, May 30, 1988, Vanga said that a very beautiful woman dressed in white was walking around her and she had already stood in front of people who were about to enter her. She watched her for a long time with pleasure, as the woman's clothes shone like silver.

Naturally, no one saw this woman.

When the manager began to let people to Vanga, the "silver" woman rose about two meters above the ground. She was extremely beautiful. "When I was sighted and could see like you, I didn't see so much beauty gathered in one 'human figure, '" Vanga said.

It's almost twelve o'clock. The city is already asleep, and Vanga is still awake. Washed, clean and cheerful, just at midnight, she will kneel before the miraculous icon for the night prayer and will pray for the health, life and success of all mankind.

HEAVENLY MESSENGERS

We are entering upon a very delicate part of our narrative, which may very loosely be called "The Messengers." Some of our intimate conversations with Vanga were described in the first chapter. Let's continue.

One of the summer days of 1979. Vanga is in a great mood, she is more talkative than ever. I write it down hurriedly:

— I've been seeing them for about a year. They are transparent. They look like a reflection of a person in the water. Their hair is as soft as duck down, and forms a sort of halo around their heads. Behind me I see something that looks like wings. Very often, when I get home, I find them in my room. I talk to them before I reach the gate, and I hear long and slow, very melodious sounds, like a choir singing psalms. They say they come from the planet Vamphim - the third planet from Earth, or so I hear. I don't know why they come here. Sometimes one of them takes me by the hand and leads me to his planet. I am following him. I walk on the earth (but this is not the earth!), dotted with stars. It's like I'm trampling on them. The ones that drive me move very fast, in leaps and bounds. They leave and come back. On their planet, everything is very beautiful, I just can't describe it. For some reason, I don't see any dwellings anywhere. These creatures are very strict. When they speak, their voices are carried like an echo. Sometimes they put something like headphones on my ears. What for? Don't know.

They work hard, clearly and in an organized manner, they say that there are very few people through whom they make direct connections with the Earth. They control us. They won't let me talk about what I hear and see from them.

Here is what I heard recently: "We come for a moment — we must quickly return. Do not expect much from us, do not ask questions: we are forbidden to speak."

One day they set up two sculptures on the Ground, apparently of their most prominent fellow citizens. I know the exact location, but I can't show you. One sculpture is like this: a man sitting on a flat stone, thinking, his head propped on his hand. Another: a man stands and looks into the distance, holding in his right hand an object that looks vaguely like a gun.

When they were setting up the sculpture, one of them said, "Maybe we should move the figures a little to one side so that people can't see?" The other said,"Don't be afraid, don't you see, because they are blind."

A few years later…

One day, as I was about to return home from Rulite, my mother was telling me something, standing at the gate, and accidentally slammed the gate hard. Vanga immediately said:

"Don't talk so loud and don't make any noise, there are a lot of people in the house.

Of course, my mother didn't see anyone: the house was dark, quiet, and deserted. My mother says that it's always like this in the house when Vanga is not there.

And here's what Vanga herself tells you:

— That time I went into the house and sat on a chair in the middle of the room, and they sat around me. They were elderly men, rather old men, in dazzling clothes, and the room seemed to be lit up by the sun. One of them said to me, " Get up and listen, and we will tell you something about the future. Don't be afraid of anything, because there is a guard at your door. So: the world is waiting for a lot of changes, it will be reborn and destroyed again. The balance will come when we start talking to people! "

Or another of her statements, no less interesting, in my opinion:

— You can't see it, but there are a lot of strange flying machines in the sky right now. I see three "people" inside each one (of course, the word "person" is in quotation marks). I hear the words: "A big event is being prepared!" Lubka:

- May 1989. We sit with Vanga and talk. Suddenly the radio went silent. Vanga: "Here they are. They came, and the radio went silent."

He accepts people, talks, talks, and suddenly stops. Explains: "I'm tired, and then the one who tells me to go away suddenly, and I can't say anything to the visitor. I say, I say, I say, and he just disappeared. Everything I pass on from his prompt never changes. Even after 20 years, it remains in force."

Vanga:

- Dolphins also come to me, talk to me, and I understand them. Complaining: "It's getting too hot under us. We can't stand it anymore."

"Forces" told me once that Gagarin did not burn in the plane, and did not die, but was "taken". By whom, why, where - do not explain.

Vanga's definition of time: there is a "big time", just "time" and "times".

— I watched the astronauts from Earth with great interest, — she says, — when they landed on the moon. But they didn't see even a thousandth of what I saw there…

So what are the creatures that communicate with Vanga and visit her home? In her opinion, they have a strict hierarchy, there are their "superiors", who are less frequent and usually only when it is necessary to report exceptional events, or when serious natural disasters are expected.

When my poor aunt learns of the impending disaster, she turns pale, faints, incoherent words come out of her mouth, and her voice at such times has nothing in common with her usual voice. It is very strong, and has nothing to do with Vanga's everyday vocabulary. These words seem incoherent to me. It's as if some alien mind is taking possession of her to inform her of fateful events. She calls it "big power" or "big spirit". I see skeptical smiles on the faces of readers and I want to clarify that all definitions of Vanga should be taken conditionally. In fact, we do not even have the terms to define the pictures and the phenomena that are revealed to her. Let's imagine how you or your friends would behave in Vanga's place... It is clear that she has found the words that she understands, they are the closest to her understanding and perception.

The "voice" that tells her something should also be taken conditionally, because it sounds in her, "in my head," as Vanga says. However, she hears him, understands him, responds to him mentally. How this happens, she can not explain, but the communication is easy and natural, without any effort on her part. She is not very keen on this kind of communication and can avoid it if she wants.

Vanga explains that it is "forces" (again using her term, it is difficult to think of a more expressive one) that have risen from the ground into the air, because the Earth is now unclean." It is not difficult to assume that a scientist-if he understood what is happening and what is so clearly visible to Vanga — would find completely different terms and give different explanations, but it is enough for Vanga that she knows.

Once again, I want to emphasize that the reader should not accept as" the ultimate truth "Vanga's statements about" the indwelling of the spirit in her body", about "forces" circling in the air, or about "voices" that she hears and understands. But we should also not assume that we are dealing with a manifestation of mysticism, much less disease. The fact that she, a poorly educated, already elderly woman, tries to fit her undoubtedly grandiose feelings into some generally accepted framework, to put them into words known to her, does not in any way belittle her, does not simplify the task, the condition of which we may never be able to understand, let alone talk about the solution yet. This is my opinion — scientists probably think otherwise.

The newspaper "Narodna Mladezh" in the issue of August 11, 1988 published an article about a woman from Plovdiv, who, like the Muscovite Juna Davitashvili, has the ability to "hear her hands". The first half of the publication talks about the woman herself, her feelings, that she was once visited by "extraterrestrial beings" who hypnotized her, did something to her brain. I found it interesting, so I asked my mother to read Vange's article. Mom did just that. Vanga listened to what she read, and then said briefly: "Why be surprised? They are already walking among us."

Under the title "Where is Planet X?" in the issue of September 23, 1988, the newspaper "Rabodnichevo Delo" published the following message from its Moscow correspondent: "A well-known scientist from Turkmenistan, Odek Odekov, has proposed interrelated hypotheses that can explain some natural phenomena occurring on Earth, the influence of extraterrestrial civilizations.

According to the scientist, approximately once in 3600 years, our earth is located favorably in relation to Planet X. Drawings and notes of astronomers of the Sumerian civilization tell about this mysterious planet. According to the ancients, the Solar system consists of 12 celestial bodies — the Sun, the Moon and 10 planets. The 9 planets we know. Scientists continue to search for this planet X, which may be moving in an inclined orbit, making it very difficult to detect.

If it is known that at the third cosmic speed it is possible to go beyond the Solar System, then it is not difficult to assume the possibility of visiting the Earth by representatives of extraterrestrial civilizations. The legends about atmospheric anomalies in ancient times, which have come down to us in the form of hieroglyphs, legends and biblical myths, coincide with the approximate time of possible extraterrestrial visits: 7600 and 3600 years ago."

Let's imagine for a moment that this planet was already "discovered" by Vanga in 1979, that its name is really Vamphim and that it is the third from Earth, and the extraterrestrial aliens with whom it communicates and to whom it owes its prophetic gift are the inhabitants of this particular planet. Is this possible? Apparently, we can only wait until we get a convincing signal from other intelligent beings. It is also possible that the future achievements of science will explain our misconceptions, and we will finally accept the idea that there are no intelligent beings in the Solar system, except for us. I think if I told Vanga all this, she would just chuckle, saying, nonsense, I know that they are there. And indeed, how can I otherwise appreciate one amazing event that I happened to experience eight years ago and that will forever remain in my memory.

People turn to Vanga with the most incredible questions, problems, and requests. It's funny, but fans of "Sportloto" (lottery) come to her»... to consult what numbers to specify in order to hit a solid jackpot. The treasure hunters come. Some of them bring old documents and maps, thinking that if Vanga holds them in her hands, she will easily orient herself and show them the exact place where the treasures are hidden. Such people Vanga indignantly expels, as she does not recognize "easy" money and can not stand fans of easy money. So, once to my mom in Rupite, a man came: asked to persuade Wang to accept it. He showed my mother a crumpled piece of paper with ten rows of characters written, or rather very clumsily copied, like hieroglyphs. There were scribbles on the top of the sheet, as if a child had scribbled them. The man said they were old maps.

I listened to their conversation with half an ear, with increasing annoyance, since we had to go to Petrich urgently.

And the guest explained at length to my mother that he had already shown the map to scientists in Sofia, but no one had been able to decipher it. He was even told that it was a hoax-just a row of ridiculous icons, not like written signs, neither modern nor ancient. Our uninvited guest decided that only Vanga would be able to decipher the map and indicate where the huge treasure was buried.

My mother knew that Vanga did not like to receive such people, and advised the guest to refuse the meeting. He insisted, and she suddenly felt sorry for him: to my great surprise, I heard my mother explain to the guest that her daughter, that is, I, studied hieroglyphs, and maybe she could decipher the mysterious writing. Like any mother, she clearly overestimated my modest abilities.

The persistent treasure hunter came up to me — I was sitting on a bench near Vanga's house — and again told me all the details of his story.

I didn't listen to him much, just glanced at the crumpled piece of paper he handed me. Where there! How can I decipher the text, if my knowledge of Arabic and Old Turkish hieroglyphic writing is rather poor, no, this gibberish is not for me. Although the experts from Sofia are probably right, many of the signs were similar to Arabic hieroglyphs, but among them there were also completely incomprehensible, resembling small geometric shapes.

Yes, I immediately realized that there was nothing I could do to help, and yet I decided to rewrite the text so that I could once again show it to serious specialists in Sofia, who might be able to solve the mysterious letter.

The treasure hunter was very happy, and we agreed that after a while he would come for the result.

I must admit that I forgot about him and our conversation at once, because I was convinced from the very beginning that I was dealing with some nonsense. I remember that we went to Petrich with my mother, did our shopping, finished our business, and returned to Rulit again after lunch. That's when Vanga called me to the room where she usually rests: she said that she had heard what we were talking about with the treasure hunter. She was silent for a while, lost in thought, and then she spoke confidently and loudly.:

— This isn't stupid. We are talking about an important document, but not for Senka cap — not for the teeth of this text, no one will be able to read it today. Both the text and the map have been copied many times: from generation to generation, people are trying to discover the secret of the text. But no one can decipher it. And this document is not about hidden treasures, but about ancient writing, still unknown to the world. The same hieroglyphics are inscribed on the inside of a stone coffin, hidden deep in the ground, many thousands of years ago. And even if people accidentally find the sarcophagus, they won't be able to read the writing. There are so many interesting things there-it tells the story of the world as it was two thousand years ago and as it will be in another two thousand years.

This sarcophagus is hidden in our Land by people who came from Egypt. It was like this: there was a caravan of camels, it was accompanied by soldiers and their highest commanders, in addition, they were accompanied by many slaves. When they came to our land, they stopped for a long rest, and one night the slaves began to dig a deep hole. A mysterious cargo — a sarcophagus - was lowered into the pit, and the pit was quickly covered with earth. Those who did the work were killed, every one of them. This mystery has been sprinkled with streams of innocent blood, the mystery is waiting to be revealed, solved by people, the message of a thousand years ago is priceless, it belongs to humanity.

I listened to Vanga and couldn't believe my ears. Is such a miracle possible-the existence of a hitherto unknown written language addressed to future generations for two millennia to come? Knowing Vanga, I can't help but believe her, but this story seemed more than incredible to me.

When I happened to go to Sofia, I gave my colleagues a copy of the letter to look at, and they all confirmed that the text is impossible to read, the ends do not meet. I stopped thinking about it, and one day I tore it up and threw it away.

After a while, Vanga and I started talking again about the map and the hidden "treasure". It was felt that Vanga was interested in talking about this topic. I got the impression that she was surprised by the words she said.

"Today, the most learned of scientists, the most learned of professors, will not decipher the map and find the sarcophagus. The time has not come.

— Maybe we should look for it." I asked. — If I only knew where to go, my friends and I would go to the end of the world." Do you know where to look?

Vanga did not answer. Then other people came to her, she talked to them, but I noticed that she often turned her face in my direction, it seemed to me that she was listening to something that we could not hear, peering into something invisible to us.

When we were alone again, Vanga, concentrating, spoke slowly and clearly, as if reading from a book.

— I see mountains, this place is in the mountains, in the mountains…

I had a feeling that Vanga herself was now somewhere in the mountains and was telling me in amazing detail about what she saw: small hard grass, pebbles, paths. And then-sharp as the tooth of a predatory animal, the rock.

"You will go to this rock," said my aunt. — You will go on May 5. I asked, why on this particular day?

"Because of the location of the celestial bodies," she said. — The most important thing can be seen in the moonlight, as well as at sunrise. Then she made it clear that she didn't want to talk about it anymore.

Actually, I wasn't sure what that last sentence meant. However, we, her family, are used to not asking too many questions. My friends enthusiastically welcomed my idea, and on the morning of May 4, we were ready for the"journey". In the afternoon we set off.

Wandering through the hills was more depressing than enjoyable. There were times when, doubting the success of our enterprise, I offered to return to the city, but my friends did not agree. To our great surprise, we were there in the afternoon. Vanga described it so accurately and in detail that it was simply impossible to make a mistake. We also saw a rock as sharp as the tooth of a predatory animal, which closed the northern edge of a small clearing, saw small stones under our feet and hard grass made of wire. The sun-warmed land was very peaceful to look at, butterflies flickered in the clear mountain air, the leaves of large spreading trees shimmered in the sunlight.

In the late afternoon, the sky suddenly darkened, and it rained so hard that in an hour we were soaked to the skin. The tarpaulin tent didn't help either, the water even got inside the bags of food and spare clothes. The rain fell for about two hours, then also suddenly stopped, only the sky remained cloudy and gloomy. It was dark. We built a big fire to keep warm and dry. And they were so relaxed by the fire that they decided to spend the whole night here.

So the five of us sat around the fire, the darkness swallowed up the surrounding area, the extraordinary silence rang in my ears, and it seemed that there were no people left in the world except us, I was haunted by the thought that we had come here in vain, that with such a cloud cover, neither the Moon nor the Sun could not be seen. My heart was scratching, I didn't want to think about anything, my eyes just closed. Both I and my companions were dozing by the dying fire.

And in the morning the sky cleared, we settled down at the foot of the cliff and waited impatiently for the first rays of the sun.

I do not know why we stood there, but it was probably the "discovery" made the day before that played a role: on the surface of the rock, at the level of our faces, there were three depressions the size of a saucer and the same shape. They formed an isosceles triangle, the top of which pointed to the ground.

Half an hour passed, but nothing interesting happened. The sun was slowly rising. And suddenly the sunbeam shone on the sharp tooth of the rock, descended, reached the triangle, and slowly crept from left to right, as if following the depressions in the rock. We observed this phenomenon for about twenty minutes, and then the whole rock was suddenly illuminated with bright sunlight. I do not know whether this play of rays on the rock was accidental or whether we witnessed some interesting phenomenon, but the fact remains: on May 5, a sunbeam drew a triangle on the rock, noticed (and marked!) someone before us. We were given a sign.

All day we discussed what had happened, looked at the rock, the circles forming a triangle, and waited impatiently for the night to see what the Sun's "sister" — the Moon-would show. And by nightfall it was raining. Rain again. Once again, we were soaked to the skin and dried by the fire, looking hopelessly at the gloomy, inhospitable sky. Still, it was easier than the day before. We trusted Vanga and hoped for a miracle. Towards midnight we took up our post at the rock. So what? The clouds gradually dispersed, and after half an hour the stars appeared in the sky, and soon the moon came out.

Suddenly, one moonbeam — we didn't even know where it came from-repeated the light play of the sunbeam. He touched the top of the rock, then, repeatedly touching the rock depressions, for fifteen minutes described a triangle from left to right with the top pointing to the ground, and then disappeared, we stood motionless two or three meters from the dark rock, and no one dared to utter a word. I assume that we all thought about one thing: is this play of light on the rock random, or is there some kind of pattern in the two cases?

But the most incredible thing was yet to come.

A few minutes later, the southern smooth side of the cliff we were standing on flickered with a light gray light, like a TV screen. And a moment later, two figures appeared on the "screen". They were huge and took up all the light space. The smooth part of the rock had a height of about 5 meters and a width of 3-4 meters. The figures were so clearly visible, and stood out in such relief, that at any moment they seemed ready to detach themselves from the rock and step towards us. It was amazing, we were literally petrified from what we saw and ... what a sin to hide, from fear....

I remember these figures so well that I will not forget them as long as I live. To the left, on a rock in the foreground, we saw an elderly man, rather an old man, standing at full height. He had shoulder-length hair and wore a long robe. His left hand was lowered, and in his right, stretched out, he held an object — a round, ball-like object, but it was not a ball, but rather some unknown apparatus.

In the background, above and to the right, was another figure. I don't know why, but she reminded me of Pharaoh. A young man, sitting in a chair with his legs pressed tightly together, his hands resting on the arms of the chair. On his head was a high cap, on both sides of which were something like antennas.

The "screen" glowed for quite a long time, so we got a good look at the shapes and memorized them. Then the rock "went out", and everything was plunged into darkness. There was not the slightest hint of any light anywhere around, so there was simply nowhere for the light effects to come from.

When we came to our senses and shone a flashlight, looked at the clock, we found that we had observed a strange picture for about twenty minutes.

In silence we went to the tents, as if on command, hurriedly began to collect our luggage, and in the pitch darkness, lighting the path with a lantern, bumping into roots and stones, we quickly and silently went home. Two hours later we saw the first lights of the city.

Feeling relieved by the proximity of the people, we suddenly spoke at once. It turned out that all five of them saw the same thing... maybe it was a mass psychosis? But we did not know why we were standing near the rock, and we could not have imagined what we would see there. I remembered Vanga's remark: "You should watch the first rays of the sun and moon."

Since Vanga and I are related, someone might think that I was mentally prepared for some event, without even knowing what it was. Well, what about the others? We were different in age, education, and beliefs. And I didn't remember about Vanga's" visions " connected with the installation of two sculptures by some aliens. I wouldn't have thought about it today if I hadn't found my notes left in the library back in 1979. So suggestion is out of the question. So what was it? And why did Vanga send us to that particular place?

The very next day I went to Vanga and told her everything in detail. She found all this interesting, but refrained from commenting.

What we saw still haunts us. We went there a few more times, morning and evening, but we didn't see anything else. We decided not to tell anyone about this extraordinary, almost fantastic case. I remember Vanga's words: "The time of miracles will come, science will make major discoveries in the field of the immaterial. In 1990, we will witness amazing archaeological discoveries that will radically change our understanding of the ancient worlds. All the hidden gold will come to the surface of the earth, but the water will be hidden. It is so ordained."

I deeply believe in what Vanga said about the future discoveries of modern science. I also hope that one day she will give me and my friends the key to the strange mystery that marked our lives with a touch of the supernatural, and that so completely changed our understanding of the real world. What is real in the world and what is unreal? And where is the border between them, if there is one at all? I don't know if I can find an answer to these questions. I don't know if I can understand what the Vanga phenomenon is.

But, without hurrying to look into the future, let's go back to the present and listen to what else my wise Vanga could tell us about our land, about our time. My mother remembers:

— That was in 1948. Vanga said to me, " Mark my words, there is unrest in the Balkans right now, but the day will come when all the Balkan capitals will give each other a hand — a hand of help and friendship. Major leaders from Sofia and Bucharest, Athens and Ankara will come together, and will have a leisurely and dignified conversation in order to find a way to mutual understanding."

The forecast made by Vanga 40 years ago, I think, is interesting. After all, it is beginning to come true. When I sat down to write this book, a meeting of the foreign ministers of the Balkan countries began in Belgrade. There was a discussion about ways to achieve good-neighborly relations and lasting peace.

Vanga repeats:

- It is not necessary to fight for peace with weapons in your hands. If you breathe good thoughts into people — you will take a serious step towards achieving peace. Many leaders of various countries have directed their efforts in this direction. There is no other way out. We need to treat each other with kindness and love in order to be saved. All save themselves. Together. If we do not understand the simple truth with our minds, we will be forced to understand it by the indefatigable laws of the cosmos. But then it will be too late, and the epiphany will cost us too much.

My 1987 recording, recorded from the words of Vanga:

- People come up with new laws-sew clothes of a new style. But it will still be a long time before we create a strong fabric. We don't need artificial clothing, but natural clothing that radiates warmth. Yes, it will be years before a tall man, an alien, arrives, and he will be a good cutter and a good tailor…

And another entry, dated January 1988:

— We are witnessing fateful events. Two of the world's greatest leaders shook hands to prove that it is possible and necessary to take the first step towards achieving universal peace. But it will take a long time, a lot of water will flow, until the Eighth comes - he will sign the final peace on the planet.

If we exclude now those phrases whose meaning is not quite clear to us ("the Eighth will come" — who is it, from what country or from what planet?), we can only admire Vanga's ability to express himself in such a beautiful poetic language.

Let us imagine for a moment how amazing and in what exquisite form she could tell us, if she received a timely education and education worthy of her sensitive soul and beautiful heart. But everything happens as it should.

...I've come a long way before I've reached these pages. Guided by pure, sincere love, I tried to look together with you into the mysterious world, whose name is Vanga, to show Vanga herself as she really is, to tell about the wide range of her interests, her worthy moral image, her high human morality, as well as about her difficult mission to show us the way to good, love and brotherhood.

Again I quote her words: "I am placed here and strictly measure a certain time of my stay on earth. I give my hand to the desperate and show them where to go."

"Isn't this the only way that leads us to a brighter future? Is it not our earthly destiny to give a hand to the desperate?» And again: "We must be kind and love each other to be saved! The future belongs to good people, they will live in one beautiful world, which is now even difficult for us to imagine."

How much hope and confidence Vanga gives us! In these troubled days, it is especially gratifying to hear that life on Earth will not perish, because " the time will come for inspired work, love and brotherhood among all people on the planet." She, the beautiful and only life, has been served by Vanga for a long half - century. We can trust her, because every day she convinces us of the accuracy of her predictions. Guided by her incredible gift, Vanga overcomes all our skepticism, distrust and rejection in the most categorical way. We would be poorer without Wang, it is the gift we need, despite our lack of understanding. After all, it is necessary that we have someone to share your deepest secrets, to know that we will listen and understand, to believe that we love with all our heart only because we are in this world, and that someone sympathizes with our pain, to be sure that the eternal and wise mother nature sends us through a blind priestess Wang his most important message — life on earth will not die, it is necessary to the future!

THE MEMORIES OF WITNESSES

Says Sergey Mikhalkov

Unforgettable meetings

On August 22, 1979, I recorded: "For several days now, I have been under the impression of visiting Vanga, a clairvoyant from the city of Petrich. Her name is known throughout Bulgaria and beyond. The amazing, difficult-to-explain ability to look into a person's past, to see his present and future — a unique phenomenon! This ability was manifested in Vanga in 1941, when she was once, during a thunderstorm, lifted off the ground by a whirlwind and blinded by lightning. Currently, Vanga is on state support, receiving a salary of a researcher. The reception of visitors is regulated and is on a special account. Law enforcement agencies resort to its help, because it can not only indicate the location of a particular person, but even predict that on a certain day and at a certain hour in a certain place a border crossing will be carried out. A number of prominent foreign writers, Americans John Cheever, William Saroyan, Italian Alberti and our Russian classic Leonid Leonov were accepted by Vanga. They were shocked by her providence.

After a conversation with Todor Zhivkov and the Bulgarian writer Lubomir Levchev, I set a goal to visit Vanga without fail. Before that, I recommended my son Andrey to see Vanga, which he did on the way from Moscow to Paris. My son told me briefly about this meeting. It is unlikely that Vanga could know my son's personal life, as well as his plans and intentions.

Nevertheless, she told him that he was going to America, that he would be a "star" if he engaged in art and in no case in politics. She mentioned me and my wife, saying that Andrey has good parents."

All her predictions to date have come true. Andrey went to America, made several interesting feature films, and became a world-famous film director. He is engaged in art and does not engage in politics.

I arrived in the town of Petric, on the border with Yugoslavia, at 11 o'clock in the morning, accompanied by an interpreter, Maria. Vanga was warned of my arrival, waiting for me in a small reception room, sitting on a couch covered with a carpet. The house where she lives is surrounded by flowers, which Vanga loves very much, as well as children's toys and scented soap. Her niece also came with us. Her mother, Vanga's own sister, is always present at the reception of visitors. I must remind you that Vanga is completely blind. And at the same time — sees what is inaccessible to human vision:

"Oh, this Russian will live a long time!" exclaimed Wang, when I crossed the threshold of the room. This exclamation alone relieved me of the tension I had been under on my way to meet her on such an unusual date.

Vanga speaks in small speech blocks, sometimes raising her voice sharply.

I have heard that when receiving visitors and entering a trance, Vanga sees with his inner vision the souls of people close to him who have appeared next to the interlocutor.

"I see your mother," Vanga said. — She stands behind you, she's angry at you for stopping celebrating your birthday. You should definitely celebrate your birthday. That's your lucky number. (I really haven't celebrated my birthday for two years in a row.) You have a son, Andrey. I spoke to him, " Vanga continued. — He wants to leave Russia for America. Tell him not to get involved in politics.

— He doesn't want to leave Russia, " I said.

- "People who are stronger than him now want it," Vanga said.

— Who is it?" I asked.

"Andrey's wife," Vanga said decisively. "Peter has appeared, — she continued. "Tall, handsome, with big eyes. He died a long time ago. Who do you think he is?

- "It must be my uncle…

— Did you know your grandfather?" Vanga asked. — He's here, too. He was a military man. Lieutenant Colonel ... crazy ... now he's healthy and salutes you. (My grandfather, my father's father, a retired staff captain, died in 1916, being mentally ill. He suffered from black melancholy after the death of his beloved wife). You have two brothers and a sister, "Vanga continued," one brother has suffered a lot, had four surgeries, and your sister is here now...

— I don't have a sister…
- "I can see her," Vanga repeated.

— Then who is this little girl?" Vanga exclaimed irritably. "It's your sister!"

And I remembered that I did have a sister who died at the age of five.

"Here comes another Peter, with his brother by his side. Who are they to you?

I couldn't have guessed at that moment that they were talking about two brothers: Pyotr Petrovich and Maxim Petrovich Konchalovsky...

He came here, too.

— I didn't have a friend like that…

- "But I can see him, too," Vanga said.

And again I remembered that I had a close friend named Bayan.

— How do you tell the living from the dead?" I asked.

- The living stand on the ground, and the dead are transparent… And they wobble in the air — " Vanga explained. "You were in America recently," she continued, " in New York and other cities. You live by reason, you have nothing to fear. You don't like money, you live clean. Keep living the way you live, don't change anything cool, everything will go by itself… You talked to Brezhnev, talk to him again.

- "It's hard, — I said.

— It doesn't matter. He'll talk to you if you want to. Talk to him… Your father died early. Has he ever traded? (Admittedly, for the first time during the revolution, my father was engaged in commercial affairs). Our earth is visited by aliens, changed the subject Wang — from the planet Vamfim. The equipment installed on the spacecraft will be the first to catch their signals. But it will take them two hundred years to come into direct contact with humans. Honor the memory of Gagarin. He's right there, directing your astronauts in space. And you live according to reason and do good to people…

Vanga spoke openly and unflatteringly to me, touching also on the personal, intimate aspects of my life. Everything she said was true. It is amazing how this blind Bulgarian woman could so accurately penetrate into the life of another person…

Subsequently, I saw Vanga three more times. She accepted me willingly, gave me worldly advice. I was told afterwards that she had hardly spoken to anyone for so long... all that she had. I predicted, came true or is coming true…

The Russian classic Leonid Maksimovich Leonov, who visited Vanga, repeatedly recalled her in conversations with me. And Vanga, in turn, always asked about him. As Leonid Leonov himself told me, she talked to him about his novel, which he had been working on for forty years.

"You will live as long as you write and don't put an end to your book," Vanga predicted.

Perhaps that is why Leonid Maksimovich constantly said that the work on the "Pyramid" is not yet complete and therefore he does not give it to the press. In the end, he was persuaded... the Pyramid was printed. A very short time passed — and Leonov was gone…

And there was no Vanga from the city of Petrich. A church has been opened in her memory. People remember this blind clairvoyant with gratitude…

Andrey Sergeyevich Konchalovsky (Mikhalkov) - son of Sergey Mikhalkov, known in the world as Andrey Konchalovsky. In 1980, he went to the United States, to Hollywood. He made several films there, among which stands out the blockbuster "Tango and Cash" (1989) with Sylvester Stallone and Kurt Russell in the main roles. The last film in 2020, "Dear Comrades" , was nominated by Russia for the "Oscar" for best international feature film.

Sergey Mikhalkov - Russian writer, poet, playwright and publicist, war correspondent, screenwriter, fabulist, public figure

Kirsan Ilyumzhinov
Predictions for the young President

The young president of Kalmykia (Kirsan Ilyumzhinov) was part of a narrow circle of people who had the happy opportunity to constantly visit the famous fortune teller. Here is his story:

"Vanga really had a premonition of her imminent demise. But I tried to turn all such conversations into a joke. When men in the prime of life came to Vanga's reception, she also found an excuse to make fun of them. One day a friend and his wife came with me. And suddenly, during the conversation, my grandmother abruptly changed the subject and began to list the mistresses of my friend, and by name and with episodes from life: they met Valya at the hotel, went to the Canaries with Maria, and the connection with Tanya was short... A friend almost had a heart attack. He started actively shoving me under the table with his foot. Vanga immediately caught the friend's condition and found an opportunity to turn everything into a joke, so that he remained faithful in the eyes of his wife.

A grandmother's (Vanga) house in Petrich stood among the mountains with healing hot springs. People, waiting for their turn at the reception, treated their sores in these natural springs. There were flowers everywhere on the property, and a lot of them were in pots on the veranda (the entrance hall in the houses of rural residents, often attached to the house) where she held receptions. Sometimes a grandmother would walk around the plot and talk to each flower. And she could talk to animals, too. The dog stands, looks at her with faithful eyes and listens attentively.

Vanga loved to eat in the open air. For dinner, I liked to sip a glass of whiskey, 150 grams. I drank to the very bottom, but I strictly followed the norm. By the way, the most favorite gift for her was just a bottle of whiskey.

So I always brought the best varieties I could get with me.

My grandmother's working day started every day at eight in the morning, regardless of anything, even her health. At some points I asked: "Maybe you can rest, take a day off?". "I can't," Vanga said. "People have come to me from so far away." During the day, from two to four o'clock, she always took a break for sleep, and then again until the evening received visitors.

With my grandmother, we communicated in a peculiar way. She didn't speak Russian. But as soon as I opened my mouth to ask a question, she was already answering. All I needed was a translation of her words for me. I remember attending the reception of a rich Arab sheikh. The visitor told about his wife's illness, the translator translated the first sentence, and Vanga is already beginning to explain in detail the nature of the disease and why it appeared... There was no language barrier for her.

Wang did not come to Kalmykia. And I certainly haven't read any books on the history of the Kalmyks. And then one day she says: "Your people have endured many trials, three migrations, but the time of prosperity will still come to the Kalmyks"... In 94, for special services to the republic, Vanga was awarded the title of honorary citizen of Kalmykia. She wasn't wrong in any of her predictions. For example, she accurately indicated an oil field in the Chernozemelsky district, which is not far from the Caspian Sea. Now we are going to build a large oil refining plant there.

By the way, Vanga has this only honorary title, although she has been visited by many presidents of the former republics of the USSR and other states. I remember bringing her a special ribbon and a Kalmyk folk costume. She put it on, went to the mirror, prettied up, and said, " We can go to the dance now." And she stands there, dancing.

I can tell you about one more prediction a grandmother. Last summer, she told me: "I see two presidents of Kirsanov." I was terribly surprised. Everything was clarified in November, when I was elected president of the International Chess Federation. Soon I arrived in Petrich. And she chuckles: "I told you so»..... Sometimes I would sit there, not knowing what to decide on some very important issue. And suddenly a phone call-a relative of my grandmother calls: "Vanga told me to tell you to do this and go there."

By the way, here is another legend that has already appeared in our press. Allegedly, Wang's grandmother was in a coma for the last two months and moved only with the help of assistants. It's not true, she never showed her weakness, tried not to let anyone notice her. She never took any money, except in the form of donations, which she directed to the construction of the church of St. Vanga.

Surprisingly, my grandmother personally supervised the construction of the church. I witnessed her reprimand the foreman for an incorrectly positioned beam. And the design of the church Vanga completely came up with herself...

To give the reader an idea of Vanga's manner of communication, I will almost verbatim describe our first conversation.

"You're as healthy as a dogwood tree... Like a wolf, "the seer began," Why did you come to me?"

I explained that I would like to ask a few questions about my family.

— You must take care of your mother, " she continued. — You don't think about your father...

"Yes, he's dead," I said.

"I know I'm dead. Now I see him next to you, he thinks about you — " and Vanga pointed to the place where, in her opinion, my father's soul was at that moment (the famous Bulgarian poet Lubomir Levchev told me that he once asked Vanga how she could so accurately distinguish the names of living people from the names of the dead; her answer: "I see the dead floating above the ground"). After naming my late father's profession fairly accurately, she continued:

— Why do you go to him without candles and flowers?"

I shrugged, not understanding what she meant. And a few days later I remembered that when I was on vacation in Moscow, I was late for the cemetery, and I really didn't have time to buy flowers, and I never carried candles to the grave.

— Your mother's name is Maria?

- No, Larisa.

"Strange," Vanga said. When I returned to Sofia later, I called Moscow and told my mother about the trip to Petrich, and mentioned the confusion with her name. My mother did not say anything about this, but a few days later she called and said that she had spoken to my grandmother and that she had first discovered that my mother was first named Maria in the maternity hospital, and only two months later they changed her name.

And Vanga continued about her mother: "She has to go to surgery before the end of the year, everything will be fine»... And so it turned out: the operation was successful, and in the time frame named by Vanga. Quite accurately, she diagnosed my grandfather, told him how long he had to live, under what circumstances he would die. Then, after asking about her son, she said: "I see that you will have another child. If there is a daughter, you should call her Anya or Elenushka. But here "(she pointed to the table) "it says' Anya.'"

Eleven years later, after I managed to get a divorce and start a new family,I actually had a daughter. They called her, as Vanga wanted, Anya. But the most striking thing is that when I came to the registry office to write out a birth certificate, there were Svyatcy (For believers (Orthodox Christians): list of saints and feasts in calendar order) on the table, as if specially for me. I decided to check what name we should call our daughter in accordance with this holy book. It turned out that Anya!

...at the end of the conversation, it was my turn. I asked how much longer I would work in Bulgaria.

"You'll live here for another five years. But you can leave this year if you have to. I see that at the age of 38 you will be studying. And don't put a cigarette in your mouth...

To tell you the truth, I was skeptical. Well, first of all, by that time I had been living in Sofia for two and a half years, and I could not live for another five years due to the terms of my official business trip. Secondly, I reasoned that many people can predict like Wang, "either you will stay for five years, or you will leave this year." And finally, the warning about the cigarette looked ridiculous: I had never smoked in my life and had no intention of smoking.

However, life made me believe Vanga... I have worked in Bulgaria for seven years - longer than any of my colleagues... When I turned 38, I was offered to continue my education at the Academy of Social Sciences. And after a while, life made me smoke..."

Recorded by Albert Minnullin and Andrey Smirnov

Kirsan Nikolaevich Ilyumzhinov (Kalm. Kirsan Ulmжln (born April 5, 1962, Elista, Kalmyk ASSR, RSFSR, USSR) is a Russian statesman and politician, entrepreneur.

President of the Republic of Kalmykia from April 23, 1993 to October 24, 2005. Head of the Republic of Kalmykia from October 24, 2005 to October 24, 2010. President of the International Chess Federation (1995-2018).

VANGA'S SISTER CONTINUES THE STORY

"Vanga and I are blood sisters-the children of one father and two mothers. Vanga was left an orphan like me when she was two years old. Her mother Paraskeva died in terrible agony at the birth of her second child and is buried with him. My mother also died during the birth of my second child, who was to be born after me. However, we both survived and, thank God, lived to an old age. We were together in joy and in trouble.

From a young age, I remember secretly watching my sister Vanga. When she cried, large tears flowed from her permanently extinguished eyes. She didn't say anything, just cried, but in spite of everything, we believed that our life of poverty would come to an end.

I will not forget one unfortunate moment. Vanga was walking around the yard and accidentally came across a large cauldron. From a severe bruise on the leg, a deep wound was formed. It took more than a week, and the wound did not heal. Vanga did nothing — no drugs, no bandages. The neighbors looked on and pitied her, but no one offered any treatment. One morning, she woke me up very early — apparently, she hadn't slept a wink all night because of the pain. She said: "Go to Maria's neighbor and ask her for some copper vitriol." I went. After hearing what I needed, the neighbor decided that Vanga wanted to poison herself, so she personally came to us. Vanga said: "Go out on the stairs, rub the copper vitriol into a powder, collect it in a piece of paper and bring it! Then sprinkle the wound." Aunt Maria was frightened and said that it was dangerous, that the copper vitriol was poisonous, but Vanga insisted. After I sprinkled the wound, she picked up her knitting needles and started knitting. She knitted very quickly, apparently, she wanted to drown out the pain. She must have been in a lot of pain, but she didn't say a word. Only the needles clicked faster and faster. At some point, the wound boiled. It boiled for a while, then the liquid flowed out of it, and then everything stopped. Vanga asked me what I saw, and I said that nothing was leaking, but the wound was white. Vanga seemed to calm down. The next morning, the neighbor came running at the crack of dawn to find out how Vanga was doing. She was afraid that something would happen, but her sister said that she slept like a log last night. In a few days, the wound healed and Vanga quickly recovered. We were very happy, because we had lived together for many years and could not imagine how we would exist without each other.

In a similar strange way, she treated her father. The Turks beat him terribly in Yedikule prison, and his whole body was covered with scars. Even with a slight bruise, the skin became inflamed and infection began. Once he hurt himself, and the wound did not heal for a long time. Then

Vanga made him an ointment of ground hemp and melted lard. None of the neighbors had heard of such an ointment, but it helped — after twenty days, my father completely recovered.

We were very poor and had almost nothing — no clothes, no shoes, so Vanga was given the clothes of dead women. I remember my neighbor Veselina - she died of tuberculosis, and the clothes were given to my sister. People were afraid to come to us, knowing that the disease is contagious. But we did not think about it - as they say, infection does not stick to infection.

When we arrived in Bulgaria, it didn't get any easier. My son-in-law, Vanga's husband, was again taken to military training in Belomorie. The official authorities in Petrich regarded Vanga as a sorceress and a charlatan.

The authorities of the Council forced her to serve her labor service — to work for 15 days a month. And if you can't, you know - pay a fine. The money that people gave Wang was small change. Every day I took them to the tax office. There, officials swore that I did not exchange for paper bills, and they do not "shine" to count this trifle all day.

With Vanga took a lot of taxes. We kept track of how many people visited it and how much they paid, so the taxes were different every day.

After returning from training camp, the son — in-law slowly began to build a new house in Petrich, but died very young - he was only 42 years old. Vanga completed the house and brought it to its current state. But then she left him, moved to the marshes in Rulit. Why she did it, I still don't understand.

Wang was visited by many prominent personalities. She was obliged to receive them at any time. No one counted on her - whether she was tired, sleeping, or eating lunch, it didn't matter. The "big shot" shouldn't and couldn't wait. They need everything at once. And one more detail: many of the local "majesties" had a direct benefit from Wang's services. If someone had problems - to get a scarce product or building materials, or someone's child to get into the institute-they found out who could help and took this person to Vanga, and she was out of turn guessing and predicting his future. Then, of course, the person thanked the person who had arranged the meeting with Vanga in a proper way. However, the same thing is happening now, despite the poor health of the sister. Some of the people in power, if they were interested in her health and problems, were only interested enough for as long as they were with her. Then the promises were forgotten.

The only people who felt sorry for her and stood up for her were Dr. Georgy Lozanov, and then Venko Markovsky and Ivan Argentinsky (may the earth be their down). Until Vanga became a "civil servant", the local authorities constantly bothered her and bothered her with all sorts of denunciations. She became the object of bullying. One day a policeman was sent to arrest her and take her to the police station. Vanga was alone in the house and asked to wait until her husband returned from the market to see her off. But the policeman replied: "I can't wait! Listen to my footsteps and you won't get lost." Vanga cried for a long time after this incident.

Vanga is an attractive center for many people. They visit it for various reasons. And despite countless acquaintances, my sister has long repeated: "I am lonely, lonely, and one day I will be left alone on the planet." She is well aware that almost everyone who calls themselves her friend or close friend comes to her out of self - interest, not out of love for her.

Now she is lying sick in a small house in the Rupite, almost never speaks and, probably, constantly leafing through the pages of his tragic life. Sometimes, sitting next to her by the bed, I remember aloud various incidents from our distant childhood. We sometimes feel funny, and most often - sad. But I try to remember or tell her more fun moments, to distract her attention. She revives from the memories and keeps asking me to tell her something else that we went through together. However, our memories are more bitter.

I remember the time when Serbian power came to Strumica. The old people did not understand their language. My teacher was from somewhere in old Serbia. Every day, after the end of classes, he repeated: One day my father crumbled some dried tobacco and went outside, he was a heavy smoker, but he didn't have the money to buy cigarettes. On the street, he was met by officials of the financial service and asked in Serbian what kind of cigarettes he smokes. My father did not understand, but stood still, not saying a word. Then they searched his pockets and found crumbled tobacco and cut from the newspaper a piece of paper for cigarettes. My father did not read the newspapers, because he did not know the language, they served him only as paper for cigarettes. While they were standing there, the officials found something else wrapped in a handkerchief and explained to him that he should go to the mayor's office and pay a fine, since smoking unprocessed tobacco is prohibited. My father, of course, had no money and then for this "terrible" crime he was arrested and spent 15 days crushing stones on the highway to the village of Dobilya. They didn't give them a crumb in the morning, but I don't know how he stood it. Perhaps the workers at the construction site fed them.

Our brothers also went ragged, in patched clothes, so that it was difficult to tell where the patch was and where the foundation was. But they were very beautiful boys, rosy - cheeked, as if they had a life like people.

Saturday was a market day in Strumice. Our neighbors regularly went to the market, we rarely did. From time to time, my sister sent me to buy some salt, which was already used to salt the meat. When the meat was salted, the housewives shook off the excess salt, collected it, and sold it mainly to poor people like us, but for double the price, since the salt had absorbed the smell of meat. And when the beans were cooked, they poured this salt, so that the water at least smelled of meat.

A man was walking along our street with an earthenware jug on his shoulder and a ladle. He sold milk half - diluted with water. For two dinars, he poured one ladle. At home, we still diluted the milk with water, crumbled dry corn bread in bowls and poured milk, the food smelled very good.

We had one chicken and one rooster. The hen was laid every day, and for a few eggs we sometimes bought pepper, and if there were more eggs, we bought a little sugar, but this was very rare.

When Vanga started guessing on sugar, I was very happy, because I loved sweets very much. Although Vanga did not approve of my ideas, I still managed to make something similar to dessert. But in 1942, Vanga got married in Petrich and that was the end of our "culinary idyll".

Brother Vasil went as a soldier to Dupnitsa, he was enlisted in the 7th quartermaster brigade. Tom's younger brother went to Germany, or rather he was forcibly taken away along with many other guys. He was only 17 years old. When he returned two years later, he was unrecognizable. He had lost so much weight that his clothes could barely hold on to him. But we were glad to have him back alive. Then he went as a soldier to Sukhodol, near Sofia. After returning from the army to Strumica, he married and lived with his family in Serbia. He died in 1981.

In 1947, I also got married. All three of my children were very attached to their Aunt Vanga, because they grew up next to her. And this attachment continues to this day. But in recent years, our family has begun to be infiltrated by strangers, morally not too clean people who are trying to quarrel with Vanga and me. We can say that we have become a victim of intrigue and slander. My children are very worried about such an abnormal situation. Is it possible to cross out so many years lived together with Vanga? And for what? I am very sad, but the children reproach me and do not allow the slightest criticism of Vanga. And this is natural: after all, their best memories-as children - are associated with Vanga.

"You'll see what happens soon," Vanga says. It will probably be so that everything will fall into place and it will become clear what role each of her surroundings plays in her life.

Books are written about it, but few people try to get to its essence. Most of all, the author tries to show how intelligent he is, how well he understands everything and how close he is with Vanga. But in reality, no one knows her — not about her inner world, nor about her real life. How long she will live, God only knows, but her mystery will remain.

Some try to find a path to her talent, leaf through the books of her life, but find only white pages. Scientists and pseudo - scientists, psychics, fortune tellers have come and come, but they do not understand anything of what Vanga is talking about. She is angry: "If you knew what you were trampling on with your feet and what you couldn't hear with your ears, you wouldn't be standing here for a minute." A scientist came to see her and brought a tape recorder with him. He is asked Vanga questions, made notes. He wanted her to open the sky for him, and he would look there and describe everything in his book. And well, the book is out, but there is nothing significant in it.

Often there was a woman who thought that everything was clear to her with Vanga and that she would be able to explain what was what. But Vanga told her that not everyone has the right to know the secrets of heaven, and who is not given from above, no matter what he does, no matter what he listens to and writes down, will remain down there, where he was.

However, such sensationalists and pseudo-scientists come now, but Vanga can no longer, can not, and does not want to accept them. The deteriorating state of her health forces her to lie down, delving into herself, she is silent and is carried away in her thoughts far away from us.

Vanga had been seriously ill before. Some time later, after moving to Petrich, Vanga became seriously ill (a complication on her legs). I couldn't take a step. We went to the mineral baths in Marikostinovo. But the procedures did not help. Vanga became even worse. Then she asked me to take her to an apiary nearer to the bees. She sat down next to the hive, and the bees clung to her legs. They started to sting. I guess she was in a lot of pain, but she didn't even gasp. Either from this therapy, or the time has come, but after a week, the legs recovered.

In Strumica, she had another illness. People call it "rubella," and the doctor said it was herpes. About once every fifteen days, her face would swell and burn, and Vanga would become unrecognizable. There was a healer in Strumica, and Vanga turned to him for help. He began to treat her, cutting her face with a straight razor, then sprinkled something on it and sealed it with thin tissue paper. This procedure was repeated twice a month. When they left for Petrich, the herpes disappeared and did not recur.

Vanga really has very close contacts with nature. In early spring, when gugutka (wild doves) begin to show, we are already in the yard. Vanga listens to them and says: "Here comes the cold weather again." I ask her how she knows this, and she says that gugutka just told her. And indeed, in just a few hours, the weather changes.

There were three dogs in Rulit. Each of them played a different role. The doggie from afar met the car on which Vanga went from Petrich. Every day he waited at a certain place, far from her house, and as soon as he saw the car, he ran in front of it until the car stopped in the yard. There he waited for the mistress to get out of the car and, as soon as she entered the house, ran back to the clearing. In the evening, when we left back to Petrich, the dog again ran in front of the car and accompanied us to the place where he met in the morning.

Once the dog accompanied us to the highway, but did not return as always back in Rulite, and continued to bark and run after us. I told the driver to stop, because the dog clearly wants something. They opened the door to see what had happened, and at that time the dog jumped into Vanga's arms. He barks again and doesn't come out. The dog jumped out of the car, but did not return to the house, and remained lying on the side of the road. It turned out that Vanga had left the keys to the house in Petrich in Rulit. We got out of the car, and the driver drove back alone to collect the keys. Seeing the car, the dog returned to the Rulite and stayed there to guard the house.

Now all sorts of impostors are swirling around her sister, who call themselves her "sons" and "daughters". It's very dishonest. Her real children are my children, because she raised them. My brothers and I were the real children, because when we were sick, she stood by the bed, watching at night, easing our pain and suffering with her great love, which only a mother can show. Then she helped me when my children were sick. My son was seriously ill with bronchitis as a child. He was constantly wrapped up, he took medications, syrups, but the disease did not go away. One day, my children and I went to visit my sister in Petrich (at that time we lived in Sandanski). I remember a theater company came to town on tour. They played "Iron Lamp". My brother-in-law bought tickets for my sister and me. But the child had a seizure, and I didn't dare leave him alone, without supervision. The nurse said: "Lubka, let him eat a spoonful of mustard mixed with honey." I gave the child what Vanga had told me to do, put the children to bed, and we went to the theater. And when they returned, opening the door, Vanga began to listen to something. She has exceptionally sharp hearing. She asked. "Do you hear something knocking?» I said I couldn't hear anything, but when we went into the room where the children were sleeping, I was scared. The boy was asleep, and his heart was beating so hard that you could hear it in the distance. I almost lost my mind. And my sister says. "Don't be afraid, it's nothing. Dissolve a spoonful of sugar in a glass of water and give the child a drink." In a short time, the heartbeat returned to normal and the child fell asleep peacefully. Thank God, the bronchitis has not recurred since then.

The eldest daughter was two years old when she grabbed a burning frying pan with her little hand. My hand was swollen. I was terribly scared and immediately ran to the post office to inform Vanga. Next to her house in Petrich, there was a postal worker who had a telephone. If necessary, I called him, and he called his sister to the phone. When I confusedly explained to Vanga what was the matter, she told me to immediately take a fresh yolk, a tablespoon of butter and beat a kind of cream well, then anoint a clean gauze with this cream and bandage my hand. When the bandage was applied, the child stopped crying, calmed down and fell asleep.

In the morning, I untied the bandage and was surprised: there were no blisters, no burns, and the handle was white and healthy.

There is no mother who could not tell a hundred stories about the diseases of their children, and I am no exception, but now I tell them, because it is connected with the therapeutic activities of Vanga. My daughter was only 20 days old when an abscess the size of a plum appeared on the left side of her chest. At that time, we were at my sister's house in Petrich — there was no water in Sandanski due to a major water supply accident. We wake up in the morning, and the baby is crying. The nurse says we should go to the clinic. When we showed the child to the pediatrician, she said that an urgent operation was needed and asked to bring the girl the next day, when the surgeon would be there. Vanga was indignant: "Well, that's it - just a surgeon? The doctor said that the only effective way to eliminate the abscess is surgery. Vanga signaled to leave, and at home said: "Take a deep bowl and spread some rye flour. Add fresh milk, butter and cook porridge. Apply it to a piece of clean linen or gauze and make a bandage for the child so that it covers the entire abscess." I did everything very carefully, and we had dinner and went to bed. Somewhere around midnight, the child began to cry loudly. We both jumped up, unwrapped the girl, and I was amazed. From the breast to the tummy, everything was smeared with blood and pus. I wiped the baby, and Vanga told me to put it back in its swaddling clothes. I was upset — there was a hole in the place of the abscess, but Vanga insisted on her own. After repeating the procedure, we lay down again. In the morning, the girl slept for a long time. By lunchtime, they had unwrapped her and found that there was no sign of the hole.

Vanga's recipes are infallible, but nevertheless, one day Professor Atanas Maleev came to us and forbade Vanga to practice healing under threat of trial. In Bulgaria, they say, there are enough doctors and specialists who study so much that they can cure any disease.

So, yes, not so. A year ago, my five-year-old son had smallpox, and suddenly something like barley appeared in the corner of his left eye. The doctor could not make a diagnosis and advised to take the child to the district hospital of Blagoevgrad, where more experienced specialists work. I called Vanga in Petrich, and she said, " Okay, we'll go tomorrow, but pick me up today. I will spend the night with you, and in the morning we will go to Blagoevgrad." In the evening she told me: "Melt some wax, make a cake out of it, and when it cools down, apply it to the sore spot. Secure the top with a Band - aid." In the morning we got up very early, the train to Blagoevgrad left at 6 o'clock. When I woke the baby, I took off the Band - Aid and saw the barley stuck to the wax, along with a root half the length of a match. And there's a tiny hole in the sore spot. Vanga said that there was no need to go to the doctor, since the child is healthy, we were very happy, I prepared an impromptu meal - what God sent, and we celebrated the recovery of the child. My father-in-law said: "This is the treatment-help immediately and for sure."

When my father-in-law, already an old man, fell ill and fell ill, Vanga came to visit him. I told him a funny story, and he cheered up. When we left the room, Vanga turned to my mother-in-law: "Aunt Mara, get ready! All his deceased loved ones are near him and waiting for him. You don't have time." The mother-in-law, although religious, was frightened and began to cry, and the father-in-law really died three days later.

Vanga was indeed given the right to contemplate and look into the future. She never tired of saying, " If people knew what was coming, they wouldn't want to stay on earth for a moment." I wonder what these words mean, but she says that it's not time to decipher them yet, and when it comes, everyone will understand everything for themselves.

I don't know why, but some people are trying to change Vanga's birthday — instead of January 31 — October 3. I wasn't present at her birth because she is 15 years older, but who knows better than me when Vanga was born? October 3, 1967 — the day when she was declared a civil servant and enrolled in the staff of the Institute of Suggestology. If there is a different date of birth, then we can only talk about" birth " in a figurative sense, Vanga's birthday is January 31, 1911.

I remember 1967 very well. Vanga was already an officially recognized phenomenon. People began to flock to her from everywhere. The hotels are crowded, and some of the visitors spend the night at the market. Then she was visited by the (now deceased) Professor Yankov. He spoke alone with Vanga. Outside, the crowd grew, and as time passed, they talked and talked. The professor came out and, to my surprise, addressed the people. He said that Vanga was really a miracle and that her gift was a grace sent by nature to this house. It is here, in this modest house, to ordinary people, and not to the palace of kings. And the most amazing thing is that a blind woman gives advice and insight to people, although she has never learned it anywhere. The professor noted that such a gift can only be given from above, and raised a finger to the sky. He did not hesitate to make such a gesture, even though he was a scientist.

I remember another case of those years. Our relatives from Pervomay, Petrich region, who had Vanga as their godmother, invited us to visit and sent a car for us. We arrived, there were a lot of people there. On the same day, the Petrich Library hosted a concert by Stefka Berova and Jordan Marinkov. We were kindly invited and we responded to the offer with pleasure. After the concert, Stefka and Dancho gave us a record with their songs, and Vanga invited them to go with us to May Day. Everyone was very happy. Vanga likes the song. In the past, when we were younger, we used to sing both singly and as a duet. Vanga's favorite song is "Darker, Grove, darker, sister". Among the singers was the sister of Julieta Shishmanova — Veska. She was an actress. As we sat at the table, music began to play. People got up and went dancing. Meanwhile the nurse asked: "Who's sitting next to me?» I said: "Veska". Vanga says to her: "Come on, Veska, and you" ... And she, poor thing, (let the earth be down to her) sits drooping and with a tremor in her voice asks: "Aunt Vanga, just tell me yes or no? I believe you very much and I will understand everything." Vanga said very loudly, " Yes." We all heard the word, but no one understood what it was about. Vanga did not explain anything and did the right thing. Veska asked about the innermost, and the sister does not give away other people's secrets. It wasn't until many years later that I learned from Vanga herself that Veska wanted to know if her sister was still alive. We are talking about Julieta Shishmanova. Everyone knew about the plane crash that occurred in 1978, when the national rhythmic gymnastics team, led by a coach, was killed on the way to Poland. Veska did not believe that her sister was dead, because there were rumors about some major crime, about some fraud, and that the gymnasts were supposedly alive and were being sheltered somewhere. These rumors haunted her for the rest of her life, and she was constantly trying to find out the truth. In fact, the truth is still unknown. What really happened, God only knows. I have not figured out that meant "Yes" that said Vanga. Veska took the answer with her, and Vanga didn't say anything more about it.

When we were younger and stronger, we went for a walk to the restaurant "White Maple" in Petrich. Our old friends, Yorda, Vera,and Marika, were already waiting on the bench. We saw a lot of each other until my sister moved to Rulite. Everything we talked about. Vanga really rested, as no one pestered her with requests.

Ever since I was a child, I have had the habit of getting up in the morning at the crack of dawn. My sister did not allow me to meet the sun in bed. She always said, " As soon as the sun comes up, get to work. The day is for work, the night for sleep and rest." She also said that you can't go to bed without shaking out the covers. "You don't want to leave your nightmares in the unbroken covers," she said.

After returning from Rupite in the evening, Vanga immediately went to the bathroom, bathed, and then washed everything until it shone. And only then did she go up to the bedroom. No matter how late we returned, she never changed her routine. She had an exemplary order in both cooking and eating. Whatever she was doing, at exactly 12 o'clock, the food was ready and on the table — different dishes every day. She felt sorry for modern men, because their wives do not cook for fear of getting fat, and their strong halves in the morning have breakfast with cold rolls, lunch with sandwiches with coffee, and in the evening - all the same.

And how we prepared for the holidays... Before Easter, on Maundy Thursday, we got up before sunrise, painted eggs, baked bread from ground Turkish pea flour for the Assumption of the Virgin, and baklava for Christmas. Veneta, whom Vanga raised as her daughter, came up with different toys for decorating the house and it was very fun and festive.

The citizens of Petrich to celebrate the day of St. George as patron Saint's day. On the eve of the holiday, they kneaded the dough and baked delicious bagels and other delicacies, prepared various meals. The next day, they climbed high up the mountain Belasitsa, spread clean tablecloths and laid out food. Vanga told the children countless stories, never missing an opportunity to teach them a lesson, giving examples of how retribution is given for both good and evil deeds.

During our walks in the mountains, we were joined by a well - known journalist from Belgrade. She asked about the problems of her country and the possibility of solving them. And Vanga told her that the godlessness of the Serbs has already led and will lead to even more serious problems. The meeting took place before the war in the former Yugoslavia. "Do you have any idea why this is going to happen? Vanga asked the reporter. — And because you instead of" good morning "or" good day " swear on every word and even came up with obscene language for God. What mercy, what good can you expect from Him? A person makes his own choice, and then he is responsible for everything."

When our father was still alive and we were living in Strumica, he took us both to the village of Pogolevo. There was the Church of the Most Holy Theotokos, built in an open field, quite far from the house of Velika's grandmother-a woman who was the caretaker of the temple. She received this privilege after she found a small white stone in the shape of the Most Holy Mother of God with a baby at a great depth in the ground at the same place. This stone was lying in a prominent place in the church in a silver bowl. The father brought us here: - The Mother of God stone was considered miraculous. My father's biggest dream was for Vanga to see the light again. So we decided to stay in the church for the night and pray together for her recovery. When it got dark, Grandma Velika locked us outside and went home. Vanga and I lay down on the matting, huddled together. We probably fell asleep quickly, but at midnight we were both awakened by a vague noise. I looked around - I was afraid of the unusual situation. I didn't see anyone, but a bright dot circled over our heads for about twenty minutes, like a small ember. The light flickered across the walls, then disappeared. Vanga and I didn't sleep a wink until morning. When Grandma Velika came and opened the door, we were on our feet. Vanga whispered to me that this light was nothing but the holy Virgin. A grandmother Velika surprised me no less. Opening the door, she said: "You see, the Mother of God visited you last night. You should be very happy." Of course, we were very excited and waited for Vanga to regain her sight. And it has returned, not to look at our sinful world, but to see the vast villages of God.

While we were living in Petrich, Vanga received letters from all over the world. However, we rarely responded. I experienced what was written in the letters, the suffering of those people as my own, I read the letters aloud, but Vanga rarely answered. I don't know why. Perhaps personal contact was more important to her.

Early one morning, two people knocked on the door — a family from the Czech Republic. Their eight-year-old boy suddenly stopped talking. Several times they wrote to Vanga, but there was no response, and they decided to come. The mother told Vanga that a boy had slapped their son in the face at school, and probably because of the fright, he stopped talking. If he wants something, he writes it on a piece of paper. Vanga told them that the child would speak unexpectedly. While we were talking to the parents, the boy was standing in the yard. About 200 people gathered near the reception area. Everyone wanted to go first. People jostled each other as they pushed their way forward. Someone, trying to contain the pressure of the crowd and restore at least some order, inadvertently pinched the boy's hand with the gate. When we heard the cry, we ran out into the street together with the Czechs. Incredibly, it was their son who was screaming. I ran, grabbed his hand and put his finger pinched under a stream of water flowing from the tap in the garden. The parents came running, and the boy easily forgot about his dumbness and began to tell how it happened. A miracle happened, and here, in this very place. That's why the Czechs needed to come here, not wait for letters. It is difficult to describe the joy of these people when they heard the voice of their child again.

Every holiday in Petrich, Vanga and I went to church, and on Fridays, regardless of the weather, we visited the small monastery of Sveta Petka outside the city. My sister was very strong and strong physically. She was walking so fast on the highway that I could hardly keep up with her, leading her by the hand. In 1967, the Council appointed Wang a security guard and he accompanied us everywhere. His name was Atanas, he was a pensioner, a former police officer. He seemed to be a trained man, but it was hard for him to keep up with her. Vanga didn't do it on purpose. She was just very energetic and always walked fast. This monastery was good, where, after praying, we had a wonderful rest in peace and quiet. But then the church officials quarreled, the monastery was struck by lightning, and we stopped going there.

When we decided to move to Rulite, we began to wonder where we could get cold water. The fact is that in these places there are hot mineral springs. Not everyone is healthy to drink this water, and it is not suitable for cooking.

The food took on a very different, not very pleasant taste. One day Vanga said: "Take my hand, I will show you a place where there is cold drinking water." After walking for a while, Vanga stopped and, stamping her foot, said: "There's cold water under here." And indeed. We drilled a well and found water at a depth of 6 meters.

In recent years, a lot of materials about Nostradamus have been published. One day I went to see Vanga and read her a newspaper article about his prophecies. Vanga listened very carefully, and then said very briefly:: "It's really interesting, but not everything Nostradamus wrote is true." Maybe she's right. It's been about five hundred years since he wrote his centurians.

Two years ago, my youngest daughter and her husband were vacationing on the Greek island of Samotraki. When she returned, she came to Sandanski to see me, and that evening she went to visit Vanga. With great excitement, the daughter talked about the amazing beauty of the island and the special atmosphere that captures every visitor. She was constantly aware of someone's presence nearby, and at night she had extraordinary fantastic dreams. Her husband and friends felt the same way. Vanga said: "Indeed, this is a fantastic island, inhabited by souls who lived in this beautiful place thousands of years ago, and they create a special atmosphere. But modern people still do not know much about it. Near the shores of the island, at great depth, there are surprises for archaeologists. I see the remains of marble columns, made with great skill. It is part of the former temples and palaces. They are not yet open, but the day will come when they will be taken out of the sea and they will cause a great sensation. In many years, the island will move from Greece to Italy. Unfortunately, this island has not escaped the negative effects of modern passions and vices. Sometimes I see such a picture — it will not bypass Bulgaria - people will become so depraved that they will start making love on the street. Ah, if they knew the price they would have to pay for their base feelings, they would never commit adultery. But remember, no one will escape retribution."

One day my sister said to me: "People don't understand the meaning of words, so they declare me in the newspapers as a 'living saint', a prophetess, and God knows what else. Are there any dead saints? I think I'm a martyr, but this world is not easy for everyone, I just follow the fate given to me by God. Only He can determine who is who."

A month before her death, Vanga announced the exact date of her death. Of course, this could not fail to attract journalists. Most of the time, Vanga was accompanied by filmmakers making a documentary about her last days. But since August 3, when the soothsayer was transferred to a former government hospital, journalists have not had access to her. Although reports on her health status were received in newspapers and on television regularly…

Vanga could have died four years ago, but she was treated by doctors. She had stomach cancer, and she knew it. In the spring of 1996, she had a severe poisoning. In August, she was poisoned again, and was taken to a government hospital. She immediately said that she would not return to her city again… But then she added: "I'll just lie down for a while and go home."

Vanga refused the operation. She didn't want to be touched. It's very personal. Vanga had a vision. The magnificent white house. Her family is all around her. She felt good. That's when Vanga said: "I will not return to Rupite. I will die tomorrow at 10.10."

Vanga accepted his death with a smile. Exactly at midnight on August 10, the doctors stated a sharp improvement. His pulse steadied, and his breathing became free. According to her niece Anya, the grandmother asked for a glass of water and bread. Vanga then asked to have her bathed. When the process was completed, and the seer's body was pomaded and perfumed. Vanga said something like, " Now I'm all right."

Around 9 o'clock in the morning, Vanga reported that the spirits of her deceased relatives had arrived for her. The soothsayer was talking to them, making movements like she was stroking someone's head. At 10.10 am on August 11, she died…

No one knows if the prophetess has any heirs left. Some time ago, Vanga said that a girl lives in France, to whom she passes on her abilities. When the grandmother dies, the girl, who at that time should be 10 years old, will go blind. However, before her death, Vanga said, " God gave me these abilities, and God will decide who to give them to. Nothing depends on me."

Once we were taught that man is the smith of his own happiness. This is indeed the case. There is no greater gift on earth for man than his will, and there is no greater power than it to make him go against himself.

Freedom of choice and awareness of our own responsibility is the path through which each of us joins the flow of eternal life, striving for universal perfection. One can hardly comprehend this greatest mystery, but one understands that one cannot help but participate in this process. He understands instinctively, as he walks along his earthly path, as he joins the creation of good or evil, as he wanders in different directions and overcomes thousands of obstacles encountered in his limited material world, so that one day he "sees through" and understands that he has belittled his own role as the creator of eternity. Not everyone reaches this epiphany: a dense veil of human vices and passions, major crimes obscures the eyes. It is here that I see the enormous role of the phenomenal gift Vanga, who says, " I am the representative! I help people find the right direction!»

It will take years. Much of Vanga's life history will be forgotten as unimportant. Disputes and passions will be silenced, new "periods of time" will come, new people with new demands, but Vanga's messages will continue to excite the human consciousness, because she serves a life that is indestructible.

Chapters:

Epilogue

The story of Vanga interested me about 15 years ago. But then I did other things. And in 2020, during the Lockdown period around the world, I began to be interested in this theme again.

The fact is that since Vanga's death, many different programs and shows have appeared on Russian television, in which Vanga was often mentioned. In such programs, they often talked about the end of the world - the biblical Apocalypse, praised various politicians, said that Russia would become like developed European countries or the United States, and at the same time referred to Wang, Nostradamus, Edgar Cayce or other prophets of humanity. So I decided to delve into this. I needed to know if there was any truth in all this.

There is enough information about Edgar Cayce on the Internet. Because a lot of what he did was documented. There is not enough information about Nostradamus, his Centurions will remain a mystery to us in many ways. Therefore, the creators of various TV shows can freely use his predictions, which are already understood by very few people. With Vanga, it's a completely different story. Her name is often mentioned when it comes to predictions about politics. And when I found the original source, which tells about the life and work of Vanga, I realized that she did not like to talk about politics at all. If she told anyone, it was very little, and she always tried to avoid talking about it. Therefore, a huge request to all politicians, patriots and showmen: DO NOT LIE!

When I looked for the original source about Wang in English , I didn't find it. Therefore, I wanted to translate from Russian the original text of the description of the life and activities of Vanga in the presentation of her niece - Krasimira Stoyanova.

Thank you Krasimira Stoyanova for this book. From it, you begin to understand a lot about life, learn a lot about Wang and her gift, comparable to the gift of Edgar Cayce. I translated this original story about Wang so that the whole world would know about her and her message to the world. And here are the words of Vanga, which she described herself: "People don't understand the meaning of words, so they declare me in the newspapers as a 'living saint', a prophetess, and God knows what else. Are there any dead saints? I think I'm a martyr, but this world is not easy for everyone, I just follow the fate given to me by God. Only He can determine who is who."

Unfortunately, I did not find any contacts of Krasimira Stoyanova anywhere to get permission for the translation. So I leave my address on Facebook: https://www.facebook.com/iknyazev003

Readers of this book can also will write to me on this account.